KYLE OPPENHUIZEN

A

A Fan's Journey of Love, Heartbreak

PERFECT

and Trusting the Process

STORM

During One Unforgettable Season

For information about special discounts for bulk purchases, or to book the author for an event or speaking engagement, please contact Kyle Oppenhuizen at koppenhuizen@gmail.com.

Cover and inside pages designed by Iowa State Daily Media Group.

First Edition

ISBN 978-0-578-29712-5

ISBN 978-0-578-29713-2 (Ebook)

"There are only a handful of Iowa Staters that could tell the Cyclone football story as well as Kyle Oppenhuizen. With Kyle's lifelong passion for Iowa State, combined with his talent as a storyteller and his dedication to telling the story with a professional approach, this is a book all Cyclones should be excited about. Kyle takes readers on a ride through an unprecedented time in Iowa State football history in a way that will resonate with fans, and he gives a lifelong perspective of why it is special to be a Cyclone. Join Kyle on this ride."

— *BRENT BLUM*

*Contributor for Cyclone Fanatic
and Cyclone Radio Network*

"Cyclone football is about so much more than the game. Thousands of fans like me go for the experience and the connections. Kyle captures the spirit of being a Cyclone fan and the energy of traveling across the country to follow the team while engaging with fans from both sides. Whether you have gone to one game or dozens of games, you will enjoy and be able to relate to the stories Kyle shares in his writing."

— *BARRY PETERSON*

President of the DFW Cyclones

"Kyle does an outstanding job of taking Cyclone fans on a journey not only through the 2021 season but through so many memorable moments that define the essence of what it means to be a fan. Kyle's insightful writing brings each game to life from the storylines throughout the week to the first moments of the tailgate through the final whistle. Diehard fans and casual supporters alike will find something to enjoy in this book."

— *GENE MEYER*

*Iowa State Football season-ticket-holder and
donor and 2015 Cy's Favorite Alum*

"Nobody I know feels the joy and the pains of being a Cyclone as deeply as Kyle. As Kyle's game watch partner for more than a decade, I can assure you his love for the Cyclones is genuine, unwavering and infectious. His journey through the 2021 season not only chronicles the most anticipated season in school history, but also artfully weaves in the highs and lows of many of the biggest moments from the past 25 years in Cyclone football, framing those moments against the backdrop of 2021 in a way few other people could. To Kyle this journey was about much more than a game of football, as he brilliantly and vulnerably lets you deep into the psyche of a sports fan whose fortunes are deeply entwined with the outcome of a game he can't control. Rooting for the Cyclones is not for the faint of heart, but as Kyle eloquently describes, it's a journey that win or lose is worth every memory.

— *CHRIS CONETZKEY*
Group Publisher of Business
Publications Corporation

"Kyle's (both literal and figurative) journey takes us to the places we've all been as Iowa State football fans. Las Vegas and Agony Intersection are both stops on the Cyclone Express in this travel blog detailing the 2021 Cyclone season and many past Cyclone football memories. He's telling our story, and you need to bury yourself in his travelogue."

JAY CHAPMAN
2021 Board President of the
Cyclone Gridiron Club

ACKNOWLEDGEMENTS

I would never have been able to take this journey without the support of my wife, Paige, who immediately gave me confidence in this idea and was my cheerleader along the way.

I am so thankful to have a family that embraces my over-the-top passion of Iowa State sports. My parents, Ken and Kristy, have experienced countless Cyclone memories with me and provide more love and guidance than I could ever thank them enough for. My brother Kent, his wife Renae and their daughter Lauren followed along and gave me encouragement in this project despite being Hawkeye fans! My father- and mother-in-law, Kelly and Jenny, adopted the Cyclones as their team and go out of their way to watch and talk about games with me. My great and uncle, Shirley and Derrill, have done more for me and the entire family than I could ever even try to repay them for.

Thank you to my best friend Chris for experiencing so much of this journey with me, helping me organize my thoughts, providing an editorial eye on my content and pushing me every step of the way to strengthen the final product. Thanks to Kaci for putting up with Chris and my constant existential conversations about the Cyclones. Thank you to Adam and Nicole for welcoming me into your home and introducing me to other Cyclone fans in Waco and Lubbock. Thanks to James for attending many tailgates at Jack Trice Stadium and the game in Las Vegas and introducing me to Derek, who I was grateful to get to know through our mutual connection of Cyclone fandom. Thank you to Charles for attending home and road games with me, including the trip to Lubbock that nobody else raised their hand for. We'll always have the memory of 62 yards…

Thank you to the Iowa State University Alumni Association for being willing to provide a sponsorship for this project and publish my stories in their newsletter and magazine. Iowa Staters are fortunate to have an alumni association that connects Cyclones Everywhere and supports current students and graduates.

Thank you to Jackie Haley with Dream to Author for coaching me through the writing and publishing process. I learned so much that I otherwise wouldn't have known on how to write and publish a book. Your feedback gave me confidence and helped push me in the right direction so often throughout this process.

Thank you to the team at Cyclone Fanatic including Chris Williams, Brent Blum and Jared Stansbury, who published my work throughout the season and gave me encouragement to write about this season.

Thank you the Iowa State Daily for helping me with the cover design and page layout.

I was so grateful to get to know members of the Cyclone Gridiron Club and DFW Cyclones. I had no idea of the networks that existed in these organizations and the tailgates hosted by the DFW Cyclones during road games. The tailgates at Baylor, Texas Tech and Oklahoma added meaningfulness to the season and journey, and so many of these connections carried over to the bowl game and helped me confirm I made the right decision to travel to Orlando. I am looking forward to attending more road games in the future.

My teammates at the Greater Des Moines Partnership supported me every step of the way. Special thanks to Jay, Tiffany, Courtney and Missy, who provided continuous encouragement and empowered me to chase this dream even when it made my work schedule disjointed at times.

Thank you to the many people who I met along the way, friends and family who asked me for updates and vowed to buy a copy of the book, people who supported my work and offered me encouragement on social media and so many more people who I somehow connected with through this journey. You made this project worth it.

Finally, Cyclone Nation, this book is for you. We have the best fanbase in the country, and I hope that comes through in this book. The results weren't always what we wanted, but being part of this fanbase is special during the good and bad days.

FORWARD

2020 BIG 12 CHAMPIONSHIP GAME
SO CLOSE

"They're gonna do it. They're really gonna do it."

I was standing outside, bundled in layers of Cyclone gear in the December weather in Des Moines. Two things that I thought were unthinkable for much of my life were happening at the same time.

One: I was watching the Iowa State Cyclone football team play in a Big 12 Championship Game with a real, true chance to win. Two: I was watching from … a location that was not the stadium.

As a person in my mid-30s, and at this point a superfan of Cyclone football for the past 24 seasons, I always thought if Iowa State ever got to play in a game of this meaning, for a conference championship, I would be there. And then that season happened during a pandemic.

Don't get me wrong. The 2020 season was magical in so many ways. It was the best season in school history with a group of players who were just easy to cheer for. Given the challenges of the rest of the year, Cyclone football was one of the things that helped keep my spirits up.

So, if I couldn't be in Arlington, Texas, at the game, I did the next best thing I could think of during these trying times. I watched the game with my best friend, Chris, a Cyclone fan who was nearly as diehard as me. To be extra cautious, we set up a television outside in his backyard to watch the game. This had worked well for October and November games. It was a little more frigid for this December matchup. No matter. The Cyclones were playing for a championship.

With less than 90 seconds left, Iowa State's Xavier Hutchinson had just caught a two-yard pass that turned into 15 extra yards after enduring a face mask penalty. The penalty gave the Cyclones a first down at the Oklahoma 33-yard line. The Sooners held a six-point lead, but Iowa State was driving with the endzone in its sight. For the first time that day, I really, truly believed. Iowa State was going to score a touchdown and win the Big 12 Championship.

And what a fitting win it would be. It had been well-documented the Cyclones had waited 108 years since their last conference championship, drawing comparisons to another championship drought of the same length — that of the Chicago Cubs — which ended in 2016.

It wasn't just that Iowa State hadn't won since 1912. The program and its fans have suffered a Cubs-like existence. (Maybe worse. At least the Cubs were the lovable losers.) During those 108 years, the Cyclones had a winning team only a handful of times. The few times the program had been close to something special, the rug was pulled out from underneath the team quickly and painfully. Missed field goals in 2004 and 2005 that prevented ISU from reaching the Big 12 title game. The trip to Oklahoma in 2002 on a day that started with championship hopes and ended 49-3 in favor of the Sooners. And the heartburn doesn't just stick to football. Ask any Iowa State fan over the age of 30 about the "blarge" or Hampton or Niang's broken foot or UAB, and they'll likely need a drink.

Perhaps no other series has epitomized the struggles throughout Iowa State's football history as that against the Oklahoma Sooners. Going into the 2020 Big 12 Championship Game, the all-time series favored Oklahoma 75-7 (with two ties). That is even more lopsided historically considering that Iowa State had won two of the last four in the series. And most of the losses in the 20-or-so years leading up to 2017 weren't close.

It was fitting, on the day when Iowa State football had a chance to end over a century of mostly being an afterthought in the national college football landscape, the program had the opportunity to do it by knocking off one of the blue bloods of the sport, who for years had made the Cyclones their punching bag.

The game started off in typical Cyclone fashion. On the second play from scrimmage, Iowa State's Isheem Young, the Co-Defensive Freshman of the Year in the Big 12, went in for a hit on an Oklahoma receiver following a pass reception. As Young went for the hit with his shoulder, the receiver was in the process of falling over backwards. The result was an accidental blow to the head, a 15-yard penalty and an ejection of Young. The announcers and everyone rooting for Iowa State seemed to agree: It was the right call by the letter of the law, but it was horrible luck (or as I think of it, Cyclone luck). There was clearly no intent to injure.

There we were, just 33 seconds into the biggest game in Cyclone history, feeling cheated, just like we always did before. (Cyclone Fans vs. The Refs could be another chapter completely.) Oklahoma jumped out to a 17-0 lead, and then a 24-7 lead, aided by Cyclone turnovers and mistakes.

But these weren't the Cyclones of old, and they fought back slowly, methodically and effectively. A one-yard run by Breece Hall, who finished sixth in Heisman Trophy voting less than a week later, cut the lead to 24-14 heading into the fourth quarter. Another three-yard run by Hall cut the lead to 24-21 with 5:15 left. After an Oklahoma field goal extended the lead to 27-21, Iowa State's offense took the field with 1:55 left and a chance at a game-winning drive.

Thirty-seven yards and just 27 seconds in game time later, Iowa State moved into scoring range. This was the stuff storybook endings were made of. David vs. Goliath. A comeback for the ages. A game-winning drive in the final two minutes that would finally deliver me and Cyclone Nation the feelings of victory we had never experienced.

And then, disaster.

Iowa State found itself in third-and-11, with the play clock winding down. In what felt like a blink of an eye, quarterback Brock Purdy took the snap, rolled to his right and took a hit as he let go of the ball ... right into the hands of Oklahoma's Tre Brown. Game over.

109 years.

It was heartbreaking, but not devastating. For one thing, the Cyclones were still poised to receive their first ever New Year's Six Bowl invitation to the Fiesta Bowl (a game they would eventually win). For another, the overwhelming feeling among the Cyclone faithful was that this run wasn't just some flash in the pan. Iowa State, under the direction of process-oriented fifth-year coach Matt Campbell, had built a program that could last. Throw in the fact Purdy was widely considered the best quarterback in school history and set to be a senior the following season, that Hall would return as a junior and likely Heisman contender, and that gave us every reason to believe Iowa State would be right back in the championship game in 2021. Maybe, just maybe, the Cyclones could also compete for a spot in the College Football Playoff.

Perhaps instead of the storybook ending, it was the first chapter of the next season's storybook ending.

Here begins my journey.

I've been an Iowa State football fan since sometime around 1997. Never did I truly believe Iowa State could win a Big 12 title or something more until Campbell arrived on the scene.

On Dec. 31, 2020, I was seeing social media photos of the Iowa State football team arriving in Arizona for the Fiesta Bowl set to take place on Jan. 2. I couldn't help but think about how much I wanted to be there. I had always dreamed of going to the Fiesta Bowl to watch the Cyclones play football, if only they could ever be good enough to make it. Now they were. Some 30,000-plus fans should have been following them. Instead, the game was closed to fans due to the global pandemic. It was bittersweet that we couldn't be there for the biggest bowl game in school history. I thought about how much watching the team had helped my mental health state during the days of social distancing. I felt a little disappointed the season would be over in just a few days.

And perhaps more than anything, I felt a sense of excitement and optimism. The team was set up to be even better in 2021, and all signs pointed to full stadiums by fall.

Next year, I thought to myself, *I will be able to be there, in person, wherever they go.*

Over the course of the next few minutes, my thought process went something like this: *I can't wait to get back to Jack Trice Stadium to see this team. I should go to a road game next year. Hey, maybe I should go to a couple road games next year, just because I can. Wait … why not go to all the road games? I've always wanted to do that. This would be the season to do it.*

Oh! If I do that, I should definitely journal about it. I could even start a blog. If I'm going to write a blog, I should just publish a book. This is a great idea!

I went into the other room to talk to my wife, Paige.

"I have a crazy idea," I said, and explained all the thoughts I had just had in succession.

It speaks to our relationship that she didn't blink. I had never written a book before. I had a full-time career that kept me plenty busy. She knew how much I loved the Cyclones and could hear the conviction in my voice.

"I think you should do it," she said.

Over the course of the next several months, I began to plan the journey more purposefully. I told everyone I could think of that I was going to go to all the games and write a book about the season. Almost everyone had a similar reaction: "This is the season to do it."

It felt like it was going to be a charmed season. It was going to be the season Iowa State won its first Big 12 Championship in 100-plus years. It was going to be a historic season, and I was going to be there for all of it. Every big play. Every road trip. Every special moment. Every time the team celebrated with its fans after the game, whether it be in Jack Trice Stadium or in any other stadium it played in, I wanted to be one of those fans.

I knew, of course, there was a chance Iowa State wouldn't have as good of a season as I hoped. But I decided from the get-go that I was going to do this and let the chips fall where they may, no matter what. I was locked in.

But in my mind, I was going to write a book about a championship team. I was going to document it in a way that nobody else was.

As a fan, I knew seasons with this much hype didn't come around very often (and no season in Iowa State history was this hyped). Whether or not I was writing a book, I would have felt strong disappointment if Iowa State didn't win the Big 12. The fact that I was writing a book tied the team's success to my success in a way that I had never felt before. I felt like every bad moment didn't just have the potential to ruin my day, but the potential to ruin my book. Every fourth-and-one play, every game-winning drive opportunity, every crucial field goal attempt made my heart beat what felt like 10 times faster than it would have in a normal season. Let's be honest for a minute: It was going to be easier to sell a book about the Big 12 Champion Cyclones.

I imagined the moment sitting in AT&T Stadium in Dallas when Iowa State would beat Oklahoma and be crowned champion. I imagined the sense of satisfaction I would feel about having chosen to write a book about this season.

And then the season began.

If you followed the 2021 season at all, you know how it went. If you didn't, you likely have at least some idea of the outcome. Spoiler: Iowa State didn't make the College Football Playoff, or win a Big 12 Championship, or even get to a Big 12 Championship.

I found myself at times questioning why I chose to do this — even in the very first game of the season against a lower division rival. I joined in with other Iowa State fans in feelings of disappointment as the things we so badly wanted to happen, even expected to happen, became less and less likely.

At times it was almost embarrassing to tell people I was writing a book as the season's success hung in the balance and our dreams slipped away. I specifically remember the moments walking out of the stadium in Lubbock, Texas, with Iowa State having just lost on one of the most improbable plays I'd ever seen: a 62-yard walk-off field goal. In that moment, the Big 12 Championship dream died. Friends sent me text messages wondering if I was OK and apologizing that I had to experience it. That morning I had done an interview on a local Central Iowa radio station about my project. That evening I thought about scrapping it altogether, embarrassed that I had somehow jinxed Iowa State during what was supposed to be the best season ever. (Who knows, maybe I did.) The next week, family members heard my book project mentioned on a local sports talk show, where the host jokingly blamed me for the disappointing season. I knew it was all in good fun; still, I couldn't bring myself to listen to the segment.

It's only a game but, in those moments, it was so much more than a game to me.

I stuck with it, and what I gained was something even more important than cheering for a Big 12 champion. I learned, more than ever, to enjoy the journey.

I had experiences I used to only dream about. I made lifelong friends. I remembered why it was so much fun to be a fan in the first place.

I picked this season for what it could be, not what I knew it was going to be. I went on the journey with the team. My fortunes, and my emotions, tied to theirs. I documented my experiences in the moment. This book epitomizes the experience of being a fan. You never know what's going to happen in a given season. You hope, you have expectations, but you don't know. You just jump on for the ride, and you go where it takes you, knowing the vast majority of the time it is going to fall short of what you've built it up to be in your mind. The unpredictability and the blind loyalty are all part of the magic, along with the hope that maybe *this* is the year.

I documented my journey and published chapters on my blog throughout the season. What you are about to read is true to the thoughts and emotions I had at the time it was written. I did not go back after the season and spin or finesse my feelings. You will read what I felt in the moment, making for a genuine experience that I suspect most fans can relate to. The game previews are more or less a collection of stories and experiences from my 25 years of being a Cyclone fan, meant to set the meaning of each individual game into a larger context. The game recaps document my journey through 2021 in real-time.

When I began writing before the season, I decided to make my working title "A Perfect Storm." This had double meaning. For one, it was the right time in my life to do this. For another, 2021 had a chance to be the perfect season in my mind, or even record-wise if everything went according to plan. As the season went on, "A Perfect Storm" took on a different meaning. Being a fan of Iowa State football is a perfect storm. There is a murky history without much success in the win/loss column, and it often seems like we are always one moment in a game, or one game in a season, from the power going out, from everything just falling apart. But unlike a literal storm, if you become part of *this* storm and learn to appreciate the little moments of beauty, the excitement, the us against the world mentality, it can take you on the ride of your life and bring you in contact with some of the greatest people you will ever meet. It will make you part of something bigger than yourself, and sometimes lightning strikes just right to give you memories to cherish.

It's not always easy or pretty, but it is worth it.

The 2021 season ended up being a perfect storm in its own way to encapsulate what it means to be an Iowa State fan. There was hope, doubt, disappointment, excitement, big wins, heartbreaking losses, bizarre plays and plenty of moments that we'll remember for a long time. The record from the season is going to feel less important in time; yet I believe the memories of the season will gain importance as life marches on. This season featured players that will be remembered fondly for generations and more moments — good and bad — that made me say "Did that really just happen??" than I can remember in any other year.

This isn't a book about a Big 12 Championship football team. Instead, it's about the love I have for my favorite team — the anticipation, the ups and downs along the way, and the irrationality of it all. It is about making new friends, strengthening relationships with old friends and gaining a greater perspective about what it means to be a fan. It is told through the lens of a single season in time, a season that seemed to have it all, and a season that ultimately taught me to trust the process.

Join me on this journey into the storm.

CHAPTER ONE

WHY IOWA STATE

My decision to be an Iowa State fan really makes no sense.

In the fall of 1997, I was 10 years old. Iowa State was preparing to host Iowa in the annual CyHawk game. The Cyclones were, to put it mildly, a poor football team. Heading into the game, they were 0-3 and had been outscored by a combined 130-53.

The Hawkeyes, meanwhile, under the direction of legendary coach Hayden Fry, were 2-0 and had outscored their opponents 120-16. They were led by human highlight reel Tim Dwight and star running back Tavian Banks, who just a week prior had rushed for a school-record 314 yards against Tulsa. Iowa entered the game ranked No. 13 in the country.

The seasons so far had been a microcosm of everything I knew in my young life about Iowa State and Iowa football. It was cool to be a Hawkeye fan. My brother and dad were Hawkeye fans. Most people I knew who followed sports were Hawkeye fans. The Hawkeyes went to bowl games and 70,000 people attended their home games.

Suffice to say it was not cool to be an Iowa State fan, and I didn't even know that many Iowa State fans. Looking back years later, I would put money on the fact that I was the biggest Iowa State fan in my class in school from middle school on (as if you could measure such a thing). There just weren't that many of us. What my 10-year-old self knew is that Iowa State was largely irrelevant. The Cyclones didn't win much. They didn't go to bowl games. The one good thing they had going for them was Heisman contender Troy Davis, who rushed for 2,000 yards in back-to-back seasons in 1995 and 1996. Even still, Iowa State was 3-8 and 2-9 those two years, and Davis was snubbed for the award that he likely deserved to win.

I could go on, but you get the point. Being an Iowa fan was cool. Being an Iowa State fan was uncool.

I didn't watch much football before that season, but for some reason I was into it when that season began. Just one week prior to the 1997 Iowa vs. Iowa State game, I had gone to my first ever major sporting event — the aforementioned Iowa vs. Tulsa game. My dad surprised me the day before the game. I was shocked by the amount of people jammed into Kinnick Stadium and the roar of the crowd for a big play. I'll never forget just how loud it sounded the first time the entire crowd cheered. It reminded young me of a jet engine. It's an experience you can almost never replicate again.

Any logical thinking would lead you to the conclusion that I was set to be a Hawkeye fan for life. And yet, just hours before that 1997 CyHawk game, something stirred inside of me. Just two weeks before the Iowa vs. Tulsa game I attended, I had sat down and watched Iowa State for the first time in my life. The Cyclones played Oklahoma State. They lost 21-14 and there's really nothing remarkable about the game. All I remember is that it was back-and-forth, and I could feel through the television how badly the Jack Trice Stadium crowd wanted that game. I remember late in the game an OSU player missed a field goal while the game was still tied. I remember seeing a few Iowa State fans in the background, on a lift or platform or something up near the scoreboard, jumping up and down, the roar of the crowd in the background. That prompted me to jump up and down myself in our living room. The passion resonated with me.

And so, as the CyHawk game came on the air on ABC — a big deal in those days — I found myself inexplicably pulling for Iowa State. I'm pretty sure I even used magic marker to draw a makeshift tattoo on my hand, to mimic the children they sometimes show at the beginning of a broadcast wearing a temporary tattoo of the logo or mascot on their cheek.

It didn't hurt that my brother, seven years older than me, was actually at the game. Had he been home I'm almost sure he would have talked me out of it. "Knock it off. You don't want to cheer for Iowa State," he would have said. But there I was, cheering for the Cyclones. And there was Iowa's Tavian

Banks, running for an 82-yard touchdown on the opening drive for Iowa. And Tim Dwight scoring three touchdowns. Iowa won easily 63-20.

Still, I was now an Iowa State fan and an Iowa fan. But an Iowa State fan first.

As I began looking at colleges during my senior year at Pella High School, the choice became obvious. I wanted to go to a big school and I wanted to go to a school that had major college football. A tuba player in the band all through high school, I once had the opportunity to see the Iowa State marching band play to cap off a band competition at Ankeny High School. I thought they were awesome, and so rarely did I get the chance to show off in front of my high school classmates, but this was my moment. As the band marched off the field and played the fight song, I sang along. Every word. I felt like I belonged, like I was part of something bigger, somehow linked to the handful of other Cyclone fans in the audience that were clapping and singing along. That experience stuck in my mind as I was making my final college decision. I wanted to play in a college marching band. I wanted to go to the school I had grown up cheering for.

I played in the Iowa State Cyclone Football "Varsity" Marching Band (also known as the ISUCF'V'MB or Cyclone Marching Band) for four years. Every home game was a marathon of a day. We were always among the last people out of the stadium, win or lose, rain or shine. After a year of living out-of-state post-graduation, I moved back to Iowa in 2010, and I have had season tickets ever since. I only missed four home games between 2010 and 2019. Which, now that I type it, I'm a little embarrassed the number is even that high.

It's one thing to say I'm an Iowa State fan and I go to the games. I think that's underselling it a little bit. I am a superfan. I can often remember specific details from specific games dating back 10 years, 20 years in some cases. I can remember where I watched the game, and even piece together life events based on when a game happened. For example, I can remember the first time I hung out with my now-wife one-on-one was the night before the Iowa State at Texas Tech game in 2015.

Simply put, being a Cyclone is part of my identity.

It's not just football. I have season tickets to men's basketball. I follow the women's basketball team closely. I have long been involved in the Iowa State Daily. The ISUCF'V'MB will always be in my heart. I always find a connection with fellow Greenlee School of Journalism graduates.

But Iowa State football is probably the most obvious flashpoint of where my Cyclone spirit shines. Sure, I enjoy the sport, but it's about so much more than that.

My Cyclone football fandom involves pulling into the tailgate lots when they open six hours before the game. Yes, that is 5 a.m. for an 11 a.m. kickoff. I tailgate with a group of fellow diehards, many of whom I knew from marching band in college. There is a group of at least 15 of us who are there nearly every week, and more who join for big games, homecoming, etc. Some of them are among my closest and most trusted friends in the world. Some of them I really only see during the season. I love all of them. Cyclone football brings us together, and there's something beautiful about that.

Usually around an hour before the game, I start getting antsy. This is a critical period to make sure we enjoy one last drink, finish up grilling our breakfast/lunch/dinner, pack up our coolers and begin the walk across the street to the stadium. Long ago, it was my goal to be in my seat before the marching band took the field for its pregame show. I have since learned that trying to get others in their seats by that time can be a challenge when there is more tailgating to be done.

Still, for the big games, everyone goes in a little early. As the stadium fills up, the marching band comes on. The first time they play the fight song, everyone stands and claps in unison as the band marches down the field, except this time instead of hundreds of people in a high school stadium it is thousands in a major college stadium. Anticipation builds during the national anthem. Then the band leads our now-patented chant: The east side of the stadium yells "CY-CLONE!" in unison. The west side answers, "PO-WER!"

After they play the fight song one more time to a nearly full stadium, the band takes a back seat to the video board. A short pump-up highlight video plays, followed by one of, in my opinion, the most unique introductions in college football: the Cyclone Weather Alert. A National Weather Service-like voice speaks to the crowd. "This is a Cyclone Weather Alert. Ladies and gentlemen, radar has indicated a strong storm approaching MidAmerican Energy Field at Jack Trice Stadium. High winds and low visibility are expected. [Insert away team here] fans in the warned area should seek immediate cover." This is paired with fake tornado sirens.

And then … here comes Matt Campbell and the Cyclones. We see them on the video board coming out of the locker room toward the tunnel to enter the field. Kanye West's "POWER" blares as we clap in unison. (The intro song has changed over time, but for my money this is the best one we've had.)

The moments before kickoff may be the best moments of the day. The pregame anticipation hits a crescendo. The crowd is on its feet. The adrenaline is flowing. Nothing has gone wrong yet in the game. You are one with tens of thousands of people you don't know. You all want the same thing — a Cyclone win. Nothing can ruin this moment.

Then, kickoff happens, and for the next three-plus hours I am a basket case of emotions. The rest of the world stops. I don't think about work emails or the errands I need to run tomorrow. I am totally, completely in the moment.

If we win, my day is made. If we lose, I spend the next 24 hours coming to terms with it. On its face, it makes no sense. I have essentially no control over the game or what happens on the field. And yet, my mood, even my very pride, is affected by it.

The entire gameday is an experience that few things in life match.

I'm sure a lot of fanbases can relate to these experiences, but there's something special about ISU fans. Relatively speaking, the Cyclones have not had a lot of success. The fans, however, come out year after year. They pack Jack Trice Stadium. They love their Cyclones. For many people, it is a connection back to their alma mater (and I suspect this is truer for Iowa State fans than many fanbases). Cyclone football is a bond that connects them more than wins and losses.

In recent years, it has been amazing to watch the fanbase grow. We can all remember years where a small but dedicated group of fans — let's say somewhere in the 25,000 to 35,000 range — showed up almost every week, but the quality of the team, or the weather, or the opponent, dictated whether Jack Trice Stadium was full even into the corners. Not to say that there aren't still games that the stadium isn't full, but since around 2011 there has been an increased interest. Rarely are there less than 50,000 paid fans in the stadium and a 2015 stadium addition pushed the capacity up to 61,500.

In 2011, a Paul Rhoads-led Iowa State team forever changed Jack Trice Stadium. A raucous September crowd watched the Cyclones defeat Iowa in triple overtime during the second game of the season. Then, on an unseasonably warm November Friday night, Iowa State shocked the college football world with an upset over undefeated No. 2 Oklahoma State. It was the first win over a top seven team in school history. Countless thousands of people rushed the field. Before that moment, few fans who ever attended games at

Jack Trice believed Iowa State could win that type of game. Since then, we always have at least a twinge of belief.

The Rhoads era didn't end as anyone would have expected that evening in 2011, but the fan support grew enough to justify the stadium expansion. The Campbell era has increased fan interest to levels previously unseen. Iowa State fans are so grateful to have a winner. There is a sense that, given how amped up the gameday atmosphere already is, imagine how great it could be if Iowa State was a winning program playing for championships. You can't tell me that Alabama or Ohio State or Texas or any traditional big-name program appreciates winning as much as Iowa State fans do.

Being an Iowa State fan is special. So many of us share memories beyond the wins and losses. We have a connection to the school, campus and people we meet along the way. We share a formative part of our lives with Iowa State. When the football team plays, it brings us back together. The players on the field are our peers in the sense that they are walking the same campus we used to walk. When they have success, we feel success by extension. And given Iowa State's lack of success throughout history in football, big wins are sweeter.

If I could go back to 1997 and do it again, I'd make the same decision.

CHAPTER TWO

THE OFFSEASON

WIN IN THE DARK

Jan. 19, 2021

In February of 2017, I had the chance to hear Matt Campbell speak at a luncheon for the Greater Des Moines Committee. At the time, he had been Iowa State's head coach for just over a year and the Cyclones had slogged through a 3-9 season in his first year at the helm. Don't get me wrong: Iowa State fans still had hope he would be a good coach and were largely forgiving of a poor record in year one. At the time though, Campbell had nowhere near the celebrity status locally or nationally that he would four years later.

Campbell said two things that stuck with me that day. One was he loved January, February and March, the months when the start of the season is so far away that you couldn't yet taste it. There was no light at the end of the tunnel yet. That's when teams build their true character as a football team. Early morning workouts in the dead of winter. If you did these things the right way, with the right attitude, you would be ready when the crowd finally shows up for that first game in September. But in the winter months, you had to win in the dark.

I have no doubt Campbell and the coaching staff are preparing to win in the dark throughout this January. Iowa State fans, however, are certainly not winning in the dark heading into the offseason. They are shining the lights brightly.

Two weeks after losing the Big 12 Championship, the Cyclones systematically dismantled Pac-12 Champion Oregon in the Fiesta Bowl. This marked the biggest bowl win in Iowa State history. Thanks to social distancing, no fans were allowed in the stadium. While Iowa State played in the warmth of Arizona, I bundled up to watch the game in my best friend's backyard with some tequila to keep me warm during the Iowa winter. Two hours after the game, when I finally thawed out, I ordered a Fiesta Bowl Champions t-shirt, the same one the players wore on the field. It's safe to say I was pumped up.

The other Campbell-ism that stuck with me from that luncheon in 2017 is one I haven't heard him say as often, but I believe to be true. At the prompting of ISU Director of Athletics Jamie Pollard, Campbell shared a philosophy that was demonstrated by the New England Patriots, who had won the Super Bowl just weeks before in a historic comeback over the Atlanta Falcons. Campbell pointed out that Patriots quarterback Tom Brady led his team by making big play after big play. The lesson: You need your big-time players to make big-time plays to win big games.

There have been plenty of years when Iowa State football fans looked around and wondered who the big-time players actually were. That was not true in 2020. Iowa State had the Offensive and Defensive Players of the Year in the Big 12, the Offensive Newcomer of the Year and the Defensive Co-Freshman of the Year. Overall, nine Cyclones were All-Big 12 First-Teamers, more than any other team in the conference.

Perhaps the best part of the hours and days following the Fiesta Bowl was learning how many of those big-time players were coming back. Within minutes of the Fiesta Bowl win, two of those First-Teamers, quarterback Brock Purdy and linebacker Mike Rose, along with second team tight end Chase Allen, announced they were going to play one more year. In the following week, nearly all the key players from the 2020 team who were in position to graduate or leave early for the NFL instead announced their return. This was punctuated by a highly understated tweet by star tight end Charlie Kolar, whose nonchalant announcement of, "I'm coming back to Iowa state for one more year," was at stark odds with the excitement Iowa State fans felt in hearing the news.

Then the rankings started coming out. First came the final AP poll, where the Cyclones finished No. 9. That was a school record. Then came the way-too-early preseason rankings put out by nearly every sports outlet, in which Iowa State was a consensus top 10 pick. Members of Cyclone Nation Twitter made sure to retweet each new ranking. Cyclone fans everywhere were pinching themselves.

As I write this with the 2021 season still nearly eight months away, excitement is at an all-time high.

THE SCHEDULE COMES OUT
Feb. 12, 2021

As I was trying to make plans to go to every game, the first thing that needed to fall into place was the schedule. I don't want to say I checked the ISU athletic website *every* day starting Jan. 3, but I checked it enough and, in fact, much more than necessary.

Before the Big 12 schedule came out, I already knew a few things. The first three nonconference games were set. The Cyclones would host Northern Iowa on Sept. 4 to open the season, followed by the Iowa game on Sept. 11 and a trip to Las Vegas to play UNLV on Sept. 18.

Another thing I knew is where the conference games would be played. Based on the Big 12's rotating home and away schedule, it was already known that Iowa State would host Kansas, Oklahoma State, Texas and TCU. The team would play road games at Baylor, Kansas State, Oklahoma, Texas Tech and West Virginia.

One of the challenges of the Big 12 since conference realignment in the early 2010s is that road trips are more difficult than they used to be. Up until 2010, any given year could include trips to Columbia, Mo.; Lincoln, Neb.; or Boulder, Colo., in addition to Lawrence and Manhattan, Kan. All are drivable in a weekend (albeit a long weekend for Boulder). That means each season included at least two or three drivable road games.

In today's Big 12, Iowa State is the northern post of the league and stuck on an island of sorts with Kansas and Kansas State. West Virginia is on a separate island. The Oklahoma and Texas schools combine to make up the majority of the conference. It simply takes more time and coordination to travel to most road games. (Editor's Note: This paragraph would, of course, be outdated by the time the season started as the Big 12 lost some schools and added others, but this was the reality of the 2021 season.)

Looking at the 2021 road game schedule, Kansas State would be the only game doable as a two-day trip. Depending on game time, I could drive to Manhattan on Friday night or Saturday morning, and then drive back either after the game or on Sunday. Simple enough. Oklahoma would be the next easiest, at a little over eight hours from my home in West Des Moines. The aforementioned Vegas trip sets up nicely as a mini vacation.

West Virginia, Baylor and Texas Tech would be more challenging. My wife's sister lives just outside of Morgantown, which creates the appealing option of a long weekend to visit family. We always planned on going to a game there someday, so this year would be as good as any.

Waco, Texas, home of Baylor University, appealed to my wife. Paige is a fan of the popular "Fixer Upper" television show hosted by Chip and Joanna Gaines, so she was excited for reasons beyond the football game.

And then there was Texas Tech. I had two impressions of Lubbock. One is that it would be difficult to get to. To drive would take more than 13 hours. Luckily, both Des Moines and Lubbock have airports which would make it more workable, but flight costs were quickly starting to add up when factoring in flights to Vegas, Morgantown and likely Waco. The other impression was that I probably would never go there unless it was for this very specific purpose. Don't get me wrong — I'm sure Lubbock is a nice place and has a good football atmosphere — but it wasn't on my list of go-to destinations before this. I also had a feeling that it would be the most difficult trip to find a road trip partner. Paige was not interested in this one.

Another thing I knew before the schedule release was that there were two weddings on my schedule already. One would be Sept. 25 in Iowa, which I am mostly thankful that it didn't conflict with the trip to Vegas. The other would be Nov. 7 in Colorado, Paige's home state. My best hope was that I would get lucky and only one of the two would end up conflicting with a game. More than likely, I would need to work around two games. My selfish hope was that one of those weddings would fall on the weekend of the Texas Tech game to give me a convenient excuse to cross out that trip.

After what felt like years but was truly just over a month, the schedule came out on Feb. 11. I just happened to be scrolling Twitter when I saw it. I'm pretty sure I stopped breathing for a second; this would tell me so much about my life starting in September.

THE SCHEDULE:

Sept. 4:	*vs. UNI*
Sept. 11:	*vs. Iowa*
Sept. 18:	*at UNLV*
Sept. 25:	*at Baylor*
Oct. 2:	*vs. Kansas*
Oct. 16:	*at Kansas State*
Oct. 23:	*vs. Oklahoma State*
Oct. 30:	*at West Virginia*
Nov. 6:	*vs. Texas*
Nov. 13:	*at Texas Tech*
Nov. 20:	*at Oklahoma*
Nov. 27:	*vs. TCU (later changed to Black Friday on Nov. 26)*

The first two things that stood out to me: Weddings conflicted with the Baylor trip and the Texas home game. I knew Paige would be disappointed not to go to Waco, as was I, but it was convenient enough that it took out one of the longest road trips. Regarding the Texas game, this text message exchange with Paige proved how lucky I am to have her support for my passion.

ME: "The ISU vs. Texas game is Nov. 6."

HER: "Is that the one you wanted an excuse not to go to?" (*Guilty.*)

ME: "No. That was at Texas Tech which is Nov. 13." (*Again, guilty.*)

ME: "Texas is a home game."

HER: "Oh. Maybe you can find a flight for late that night and travel separately from me."

Well, OK then. Sign her up for most supportive wife in the universe.

Looking through the schedule more, the real gauntlet from a travel standpoint starts in late October. West Virginia on Oct. 30 will require air travel. Then the next weekend I will need to find a late night or early morning flight to Colorado following a home game. Then, most likely back on a plane the next weekend for a flight to Lubbock. Finally, the trip to Oklahoma right before Thanksgiving. Four weekends, four trips and at least three that require flying. Have I mentioned I work a full-time job? If I am going to pull this off, I am going to need to want it to work really, *really* badly.

Also worth noting: The game at Oklahoma is scheduled to be the second-to-last week of the season. Chances are this game will have major implications for who makes the Big 12 Championship Game. It might even have (dare-I-dream-it) College Football Playoff implications. It also seems more likely than not that it will be a preview of the Big 12 title game just two weeks later. And it feels like a prime candidate for ESPN's "College GameDay" to choose for its live location. This is a game I do not want to miss.

As I looked at the schedule, it dawned on me: *Now it is real.* There was the schedule, right in front of me, in black and white. As I posted on Facebook and Twitter that evening, "I think this is the most excited I've ever been for any season of any team I cheer for."

Game on.

REV UP THE HYPE TRAIN
April 14, 2021

I woke up on the morning of Monday, April 12, for some reason thinking about Iowa State football. Given that I am writing this in a book about my Cyclone fandom, this may not seem unusual. But it's not like I spend *every* moment thinking about Cyclone football, especially during the offseason. I'm not really sure what prompted me to think about it other than I was having some sort of dream. I can't tell you what the dream was, but I can tell you it prompted me to have this thought: *Has any fanbase ever felt more excited about a season for a team they cheer for than Iowa State football fans are about this upcoming season?*

On its face, that seems like a slightly ridiculous question. And there may be no way to really measure it. But there is plenty of circumstantial evidence to point to the fact that it could be reality, even if I'll never be able to prove it right.

For one thing, in the pandemic-effected world, everyone is more excited to get back to doing the things they love.

Even more than that, Iowa State fans are loyal even in the worst of times. This is easily the most anticipated season in the history of my fandom, and it's difficult for me to imagine there has been a more anticipated season for Iowa State fans before this.

Added to that, it's rare that a championship contender in any sport has gone as long as Iowa State football has without winning its league, something Iowa State hasn't done since 1912. When Alabama football or the New York Yankees enter a season with a chance to win, I have a difficult time believing their fans treasure the feeling as much as an Iowa State fan treasures the opportunity of the 2021 football season.

For all these reasons — post-pandemic excitement, this being the most anticipated season in Iowa State history and Iowa State's unique, if unfortunate, status as having not won big in anyone's lifetime — I think there is a very real possibility that this is indeed the most excited any fanbase has ever been for a team they cheer for going into any given season. This was the thought forming in my mind two days prior.

Everything that happened over the next 36 hours or so helped strengthen this belief.

That evening, I listened to the "Williams and Blum" podcast on Cyclone Fanatic. Toward the end of their podcast, Chris Williams, one of the co-hosts and the publisher of Cyclone Fanatic, talked about the charter flight Cyclone Fanatic is hosting for the Iowa State at UNLV game in Las Vegas, mentioning that he expected it to be sold out by the end of the week. Then, he told co-host Brent Blum about writing his preview for the popular Athlon Sports College Football magazine, and how difficult it was to find any holes in the roster. He couldn't remember another time like this.

The morning of Tuesday, April 13, it was pretty obvious why I was thinking about Cyclone football from the get-go.

I woke up, and for no good reason I checked my personal Gmail account. Williams had sent a message to the Cyclone Fanatic premium subscribers the prior evening, sharing a sneak peak of the first paragraph of his Athlon magazine preview. In it, he made the point that with 20 of 22 starters returning, the 2021 Iowa State football team should be the best in school history and a legitimate contender for the Big 12 Championship and College Football Playoff.

What a nice way to start the day.

Then, throughout the day, things got better.

ESPN released its Football Power Index (FPI). From ESPN.com: "The Football Power Index (FPI) is a measure of team strength that is meant to be the best predictor of a team's performance going forward for the rest of the season."

Iowa State came in at No. 4. Right behind Alabama, Oklahoma and Clemson, and right ahead of Ohio State. Anyone who has not followed college football in the past five years would likely think, *One of these things is not like the other.* But there were the Cyclones, listed as part of the who's who of college football.

ESPN's headline on the homepage of their NCAA Football page the prior evening read: "Preseason FPI Rankings: Can Oklahoma (or Iowa State!) Challenge Alabama?"

In true Iowa State fan fashion, some fans didn't know how to handle this type of hype. My good friend Chris sent this to our text message chain of Cyclone fans during the day:

"It's going to be really hard to live up to these kinds of expectations. As we get closer, and I ask you what the definition of a successful season looks like … It's going to be hard to honestly define success in a way that likely makes this season feel rewarding."

To which my good friend Charles replied: "I have no idea how to handle this. We have never had this with the Cyclones."

I get it. When ESPN was predicting your team to be a national championship contender, even a 9-3 regular season, which would be the best in school history, wouldn't quite feel satisfying. Those are the stakes that come with high expectations.

My take: *Let's embrace it.*

My response: "I think failure as a fan is not enjoying the journey. Enjoy each moment and don't worry about the next one.

"But also, we have been waiting our whole lives for ISU to have a chance at a season like this. The anticipation, excitement, nervousness five months before the season is part of the journey. And if we are really as good as we think, I promise it will live up to the hype. If not, it will hurt. And it should."

It seemed like a very rational way of looking at it. *We'll see if that lasts,* I thought.

Finally, my good friend James summed it up this way.

"Playoff or bust."

BIG 12 MEDIA DAY
July 15, 2021

College football fans spend from January through August looking forward to that first game in late August or early September. It's a long offseason, so when Big 12 Media Day arrived, it felt like the season was getting close even though it is still a month-and-a-half away. None-the-less, my excitement level ticked up a notch for the most anticipated season in school history.

While I am doing everything I can to treat this as the most special season of my lifetime, ISU football coach Matt Campbell seems to be doing just the opposite.

The popular narrative among media members: How will Iowa State handle the expectations of this being the best season ever?

He was asked about it in his news conference. "And what I've always said about our program is we're certainly outcome aware, but that's never what we've talked about in our program. What we've talked about is how do you put your ego aside, how do we understand process, and how do we understand our purpose?"

In an interview with local reporters later, he was asked a similar question. "I think the reality for us is, I've said this a million times, there's no expectation greater than ours. Our expectation has never been about winning. It's always been about, man, how do you become the best version of yourself you can be? And I don't think we've strayed too far from that. You know, I think that's what I'm really proud of this year's team, we came back in January, put our egos aside, how do you grow and get better?"

And then in a spot on ESPN's "SportsCenter," anchor Matt Barrie started off with this question.

"Coach, I don't want to alarm you, but the secret is out. Iowa State football is real and on the Big 12 map. How do you manage now the expectations you've built there in Ames?"

"I think the thing that we've grown and as we've learned is really, we're certainly outcome aware, but we're purpose- and process-driven," he answered. "I think the ability for us to kind of push our ego aside, get better one day at a time, and become the best version of ourselves, that's all we can ask ourselves. Coaches and players have really rallied around that and it's allowed us to have success."

Put your ego aside. Be outcome aware but purpose- and process-driven. Become the best version of yourself. It was like pulling a string on a puppet and getting the same answers over and over. And yet, knowing what I know about Campbell, I don't think these were just cliches or coach-speak. I believe he really believes it to his core.

For a little bit of proof on that, hear what senior defensive back Greg Eisworth told reporters at media days: "That's something people talk about a lot is expectations, and we honestly try to push that off to the side and focus on what we do have inside our walls. It's never really been about the wins and the losses. We've always been about the people and relationships that we formed."

And then: "We have a standard. You either meet or don't meet that standard. To me that keeps us process-driven. We're not worried about wins or losses or what he or she is saying. We're focused on our standard."

I have to believe on some level Campbell and his players know what everyone else is saying about them, and that they can feel how much this fanbase want success. That's not how they operate, though. The rest of the world can talk about how they are a top 10 team, a Big 12 title contender and a team worthy of writing a book about.

They will just choose to focus on the process, thank you very much.

As a fan, weirdly, this makes me more excited. There are plenty of distractions even outside the expectations of the program. Earlier in the summer, the NCAA adopted a policy allowing student athletes for the first time to profit from their name, image and likeness (something Campbell said he felt would have no impact on his team's focus). The COVID-19 Delta variant continues to make headlines and was even a topic of conversation at media day. (Campbell also seemed unconcerned about this being a distraction for his team.) Campbell himself had the potential to be a topic of distraction, as national media members couldn't help but ask multiple times why he would stay at Iowa State despite his success and offers from bigger football schools and NFL teams. (He put those rumors to bed, at least for the moment, with possibly the line of the day: "I didn't get into this profession to be somebody. I got into this profession to do something.")

I have a feeling at this moment, if I were to tell Matt Campbell I am writing a book about the Iowa State Cyclones 2021 football season, he would shrug.

It is an interesting dichotomy. Here you have fans that are spending, in some cases, thousands of dollars to see this team play in a nonconference game in Las Vegas. You have people already making plans for a trip to Dallas in December. You have people planning their lives around Cyclone football. For me, this is the season I have been waiting for, a feeling I know I will never quite get again.

The culture of this program is all about tuning that stuff out.

It may be one of their biggest challenges of the season, but if they take after their head coach and senior leader, they should be OK, I thought as I reflected on the media day comments. *Maybe even championship-worthy.*

But that's how I measure success, not how they seem to measure it.

THE NIGHT BEFORE THE SEASON
Sept. 3, 2021

When I began down the road toward this journey in January, I had a sense that this was the season to do it. It would be the most anticipated season in school history, likely the best roster in school history and the first time we could pack 61,500 people into Jack Trice Stadium since 2019. I had no idea at the time that the landscape of college football as we know it was about to change.

Over the summer, the first big domino to drop was the NCAA made it legal for college athletes to benefit from their name, image and likeness. This meant that players could take sponsorship deals, sign autographs for money, appear in commercials and anything else that could earn them money. The impact of this change will likely take years to play out. While I agreed it was time — the fact that fans like me pay hundreds of dollars to be in stadiums to watch these players play is an indication that they should be able to receive some benefit — it did finally, officially change the romantic idea that these were amateurs playing for the love of the game. In reality, in major college sports, that hadn't really been true for a long time. I think we can safely assume that some athletes at some schools had already received substantial payments in a much shadier way than the new rules allow. And even if that's not true, many players were using the college system strictly as a way to get to the pros. It was truly their only avenue, as a player can't choose to go pro without first playing in college. So, while I agreed with name, image and likeness rules, I still recognize it as a shift that could ultimately change the way I view games.

The other, in my opinion much larger, domino to drop was when the University of Texas and University of Oklahoma decided to leave the Big 12 for the SEC. This had the effect of putting the remaining eight schools on life support in terms of their major conference status. This led to heartburn over the status of Iowa State's future, heartbreak over watching national media members and rival fans talk about how my school had no value in the conference realignment discussion, and just general uncertainty. One thing that was certain was the Big 12 as we knew it would no longer be the same. (Editor's note: In later weeks the Big 12 added Cincinnati, BYU, Houston and Central Florida to the conference.) It adds just a little extra juice to our desire to see Iowa State win the Big 12 for the first time in 109 years and to do so while the bully Longhorns and Sooners are still part of it.

As we got closer to the season, I realized it was time to put all that stuff behind me.

This is supposed to be a special season. This is a season we have all been waiting for. I believe there will never be a season like it again in terms of hype and anticipation. Even if Iowa State has better seasons in the future, the Cyclones will never be ranked in the preseason top 10 for *the first time* ever again.

Life only gives you so many of these moments. You need to take them and hold on tight when you get them.

As I write this, 24 hours from now, Iowa State will have played Northern Iowa. The game will be over (we hope … we know weather delays can happen). My outlook will be shaped by moments and outcomes that I don't yet know will occur. Then the season will be underway. We'll find out if Iowa State really is a top 10 team. We'll find out if Iowa State really has improved in September and gotten strong enough to win in November. We'll find out if Iowa State really is good enough to beat Oklahoma. We'll find out if the things we have been dreaming of will come true.

As I write this, I am living in the last moments of the bliss of the offseason. Anything can happen, and all possibilities are on the table. I can dream of beating Iowa, going undefeated, winning the Big 12 title and traveling to the College Football Playoff to watch the Cyclones. At this moment, nobody can tell me different.

CHAPTER THREE

IOWA STATE VS. NORTHERN IOWA PREVIEW

IT'S NEVER TOO EASY FOR IOWA STATE

Sept. 2, 2021

I apologize in advance for the heartburn I am about to cause any Cyclone fans who read this. The conversation around this game just wouldn't be quite complete if we didn't go down the road I'm about to go down.

Here we are. Game one. By the time the game kicks off on Saturday, it will have been 245 days since we last saw the Cyclones. We spend eight months waiting for the season — talking, making plans, anticipating.

Anticipating, of course, the tailgating. Getting into Jack Trice Stadium for the first time in the season. Seeing the team play. This year, the anticipation is higher. This is the special season. The season we have been waiting for.

We think. We hope.

Before we get into the negative stuff, let me start by saying this. If I was a betting man (which, by writing a book about *this* season I am making a bet of sorts), I would pick Iowa State to win on Saturday. I would probably pick Iowa State to win comfortably, by at least two scores. Keep that in mind.

OK, here we go.

There is a certain reality to Saturday's game. All our hopes and dreams can get crushed in one afternoon.

Sure, a loss to the Northern Iowa Panthers does not prevent Iowa State from having a shot to get to the Big 12 Championship. It does not even necessarily take away all hope of a College Football Playoff berth.

However, it would be awfully disappointing. Devastating, even.

The diehards know this, but for anyone who may be a novice college football fan reading this, let me explain. Anytime you see a team in Iowa State's level — a Power 5 conference in the Football Bowl Subdivision — play against a team in Northern Iowa's level — the Football Championship Subdivision — it should be an almost automatic win. Throw in the fact that Iowa State is a top 10 team in the FBS, and well, the thought of losing should not honestly cross my mind.

The Iowa State vs. UNI series, however, has been anything but automatic.

This series parallels the Iowa vs. Iowa State series in some ways. As much as Cyclone fans do not always want to admit it, for much of history, Iowa State has been the little brother, so to speak, to Iowa. Whenever we win it's considered an upset. It's widely expected that we will play with more emotion in that game than most games on our schedule. Some seasons, a win against Iowa is the highlight of the season. (That has probably, finally, changed in the Matt Campbell era.) My perception has always been UNI fans feel the same way about the game with Iowa State. Throw everything at it. Pull the upset. Beat up your big brother.

In my mind, it shouldn't be this way. No offense to my Panther friends, but UNI *shouldn't* be able to defeat Iowa State. It should be *easy* for the Cyclones.

It's rarely easy.

I am reminded of 2013, when head coach Paul Rhoads entered his fifth season. We caught the end of the Hawkeyes' opener in the tailgate lots. Iowa lost on a last-second field goal to Northern Illinois. Fueled up on adrenaline and beer I declared, "Let's prove this is OUR STATE!"

I believed something special was building in Ames. It was even easier to believe that, as we filed into the stadium full of the optimism of a new season on a warm August evening to watch ISU play UNI.

It's difficult to say exactly when I stopped believing.

The fun, and sometimes maddening, part of when UNI comes to town is there are thousands of Panther fans who travel with them. It creates a rivalry atmosphere and can be quite annoying when the rival (who, again, in my opinion shouldn't really be a rival), is winning. At some point in the first half, UNI running back David Johnson broke off a big gain. It could have been his 37-yard touchdown run in the first quarter to give UNI the lead. It could have been early in the second when he caught a nine-yard touchdown pass. Heck, it could have been his 27-yard touchdown to give UNI a 21-7 lead midway through the second quarter. It doesn't matter. Whatever point it was, at some point a UNI fan a few rows away from us stood up to cheer, and he waved a white towel, or maybe it was a t-shirt. The fans had plenty of reason to cheer loudly, and he was the loudest.

"It's too easy!" he yelled.

The first time, I was slightly annoyed. *OK buddy, it's the first half. Just chill.*

The second time, my annoyance grew into what could only be described as anger. Anger over a mixture of factors, I'm sure. The score, the UNI fans around us cheering ("It's too easy!!!"), the fact that some running back from an FCS school was running untouched on our field.

It was probably about the time that Johnson caught a 29-yard touchdown pass in the fourth quarter that my anger turned to shame. As our new acquaintance a few rows away waved his white t-shirt in the air, yelling "It's too easy! It's too easy!" it was impossible not to agree. It *was* too easy.

Johnson ended up with 199 rushing yards and four touchdowns. We didn't yet know that he would go on to play in the NFL and amass more than 6,000 all-purpose yards (and counting). All we knew was that somehow the best player on the field played for the team that was literally in a lesser subdivision than Iowa State. He, and UNI, just made it look so easy in a 28-20 win.

This was not the first time I had seen UNI come to Ames and look like the better team. In 2006, my second year in the ISU marching band, I couldn't believe my eyes as I watched the Panthers put themselves in position to win before missing a last-minute field goal. In 2007, UNI broke through and won in Gene Chizik's second game as ISU's coach. In 2011 against UNI, the same Iowa State team that went on to beat the No. 2 team in the country later needed a near-miracle from Steele Jantz to Josh Lenz, and then another game-winning drive to save a 20-19 victory.

And for as much good as ISU coach Matt Campbell has done, he has not been immune to the UNI slipup.

The 2016 UNI game was the first game that I ever went to with my now-wife, Paige. It also led to one of the biggest fights we probably have ever had. During the first game with Campbell as coach, the excitement of a new era was quickly doused with cold water as UNI won, 25-20. After a rough start, it looked like all was going to be OK after a 33-yard touchdown pass to Allen Lazard in the fourth quarter gave the Cyclones a 20-19 lead.

I high-fived everyone around me, and noticed Paige doing the same thing. *This is great,* I thought, so thankful that I could share my love of Iowa State football with her.

A few minutes later, after the Panthers had regained the lead, Iowa State threw an interception with 1:10 left, down 25-20. The game was effectively over as Iowa State could no longer stop the clock. I could feel my body temperature rise with my level of frustration.

I had always been taught by my dad that we stay until the end of the game, and he and my mom sat through some miserable games when I was in the marching band. Paige's dad had taught her the same thing. Everyone around us started filing out, our group included.

Perhaps the worst feeling in the college football world is watching a rival, even a rival who you feel shouldn't be a rival, win on your team's field and celebrate after the game. The opposing fans cheer raucously. The opposing marching band plays the fight song. The players run over to face the stands where all their fans are standing and cheering and share the beautiful experience. When Iowa State is on the losing end of this, it makes me want to scream.

As Paige and I stood there, suddenly with empty seats surrounding us, I turned to Paige and said, "Let's go." I didn't want to stick around for the celebration. I wanted to get out of that stadium as fast as possible.

"No. We stay until the end of the game."

"The game is over."

"No, they are still playing. See?" she said as UNI players took a knee to run out the clock. She didn't seem to understand that the last few snaps did not matter.

"But the game is OVER!" I said.

"I'm not going to leave."

I had no choice. As frustrated as I was, I wasn't going to leave her.

When we got back to the car, my friend Chris and I began our favorite ritual after a loss: dissecting our every emotion about what we just witnessed.

"I can't BELIEVE we lost to UNI!"

"How embarrassing. The new coach lays an egg his first game."

Paige didn't get it. In her mind, she had seen an entertaining, back-and-forth game that our team just happened to lose. She didn't see our perspective: Iowa State should never lose to UNI.

"Would you guys stop talking about it? It wasn't that bad."

If Chris's head could have exploded, there would have been brains everywhere. I listened in horror as my best friend of 10-plus years got into an argument with my girlfriend of a year.

"It *is* embarrassing. We should never lose that game."

"No, it's not. It was a five-point loss."

Silence. Uncomfortable, squirmy silence.

I'm happy to report that eventually everyone cooled down. Nobody's relationship or friendship ended that evening. We can all look back and laugh about it now. In recalling this story to Paige, she's pretty sure we turned on Taylor Swift's "Shake It Off" to lighten the mood.

We were all still together, older but not wiser, in 2019. I stood in the stands at Jack Trice Stadium as the Cyclone Marching Band played the fight song prior to Iowa State's season opener vs. Northern Iowa. Chris looked at me and said, "Just think, we could win the national championship this year."

I think we both had chills at that thought. I know I did. Neither one of us would have *predicted* Iowa State to win the national championship (and indeed, the Cyclones lost a number of close games in what was ultimately a 7-6 season). But at that moment, the sky was the limit. The team hadn't yet played, or lost, a game. It was coming off two straight seasons of contending for a spot in the Big 12 Championship Game, beating top 10 teams and going to bowl games. There was a sense that if everything fell right, Iowa State could have a special season.

Our feelings in that moment were peak opening day optimism. And a few hours later, they were gone as UNI held a lead in the fourth quarter.

It took a Connor Assalley field goal in the final minute of regulation to send the game to overtime. As Assalley lined up for the kick, Chris left our seating area because he couldn't bear the thought of being in the stands if the kick was no good. He eventually came back, but when the same scenario happened in the first overtime, I had the same feeling. I left our seating area and stood by the exit as the kick sailed through the uprights. Slightly embarrassed by my actions and highly superstitious, I came to the conclusion that I had no choice but to stay in that same spot. After all, if Iowa State needed another field goal to tie or win, one of us would need to be standing there (sounds logical, right?), and we couldn't just keep inconveniently walking by our neighbors in the stands every time we had to leave and stand by the exit. Time might as well have stopped moving as I awkwardly watched the next two overtimes from the area by the exit.

In the third overtime, with the Cyclones down by three points and needing to score to stave off defeat, Iowa State appeared to be in prime scoring position when running back Sheldon Croney Jr. fumbled near the one-yard line. In my mind, I had already taken two steps toward the exit, believing in my gut we were about to lose. Knowing I wanted to get as far away from the stands as quickly as possible. Paige wasn't there to stop me this time. (She had, ironically, left the game early for another engagement.) The ball was on the ground, and in the ensuing scramble ISU quarterback Brock Purdy dove into the pile to come up with it. I realized I had stopped breathing for a few seconds. On the next play, Croney was thankfully able to get into the endzone for the walk-off OT win. I put my hands in the air, laughed weakly, looked up toward Chris who was still in the stands and shook my head in disbelief. Iowa State survived, but just barely.

As I prepare for the 2021 season opener against Northern Iowa, there's a scary reality to this game. I have been planning for months to write a book. I've told my family, friends, coworkers and the universe that I'm writing a book. Because this is the special season. This is the one we've been waiting for. For the past eight months we have been basking in the glow of the seemingly never-ending offseason. The real games start Saturday, and with that the anxiety.

Campbell's teams have not exactly been lights out in Week 1, even outside the UNI games. Iowa State is just 2-3 in openers under Campbell.

To be fair, there have also been some comfortable wins in the UNI series for Iowa State over the years. And to try to ease my anxiety, I am reminding myself that all rational signs point to this being one of those games.

This Iowa State team is returning almost all its starters from the best season in school history. It has a player in Breece Hall who was arguably the best player on the field in almost every game he played last year against major conference competition, and he is running behind an offensive line regarded as one of the strongest nationally. The defense has stars all over the field. If you trust the process, as Campbell likes to say, the process says this game should be wrapped up by early in the third quarter.

Still, UNI is a well-coached team. The Panthers had a losing record in spring football, but also reportedly dealt with health issues that made it difficult to find any consistency. Based on history, UNI players, coaches and fans have earned every right to believe they can come into Ames and ruin our special season.

There will be a lot of emotions Saturday afternoon. Among them will be the familiar feelings of the excitement of a new season coupled with the joy of finally being in the stadium after the pandemic-altered season of 2020. Once the game kicks off, though, it will feel just like every other Iowa State vs. UNI game, at least until the Cyclones hopefully take control. As shocked as I will be if UNI has a chance to win this game in the fourth quarter, in some ways I won't be shocked at all.

Here's hoping all my worry is for nothing.

CHAPTER FOUR

IOWA STATE VS. NORTHERN IOWA RECAP

A DREAMY TAILGATE AS THE DREAM SEASON HUNG IN THE BALANCE

Sept. 7, 2021

"Hey Opie, I have a question for you."

My friend Nancy, who was sitting in front of me with her husband Eric, had just turned around to start a conversation as we sat in our seats at Jack Trice Stadium. I have known them both since college marching band and have tailgated with and sat next to them at games for years (and yes, Opie was a college nickname). They are two of the nicest people I know. In this case, I knew what Nancy was about to ask.

Iowa State was in a slog of a game with Northern Iowa. At this point about halfway through the fourth quarter, the Cyclones were up by only six points, a tenuous lead to say the least. It was a game that on paper favored the Cyclones by nearly 30 points, and in reality was going to go down to the final minutes.

I knew what question Nancy, who knew I was writing a book, was about to ask. It would have been something like "What are you going to do if UNI wins?" or maybe "Are you still going to write a book if UNI wins?" (That answer would have been yes.)

She was about to ask the question I had been trying not to think about since the first quarter began and it became obvious the Cyclones weren't going to run away with a 30-point win. *What the heck am I going to say if we lose?* I had spent eight months telling everyone I was writing a book about this season, and the special feeling could be gone after one game. My anxiety level had been elevated the entire game. The vibes of seeing the stadium packed at kickoff, the feeling of euphoria after being in the stadium for the first time since November of 2019, had long since turned into feelings of restlessness and worry among the sellout crowd of 61,500 packed inside Jack Trice Stadium.

What if we lose? I didn't have an answer.

"Nancy," I replied. "I just can't right now."

She understood.

—

The day up until kickoff had been nearly perfect. In fact, the week leading up to the game was full of the traditional hype, hope and anticipation that comes with the opening game, ramped up a notch due to the overall expectations of a special season.

On Monday, the ISU athletics department released a video narrated by former Cyclone and current Green Bay Packer wide receiver Allen Lazard titled "WE WILL," a nod to the legacy of Jack Trice, the first black football player in Iowa State history who famously wrote a letter the night before he tragically died in a football game against the University of Minnesota (more on this story to come). Also on Monday, the first email arrived from someone in our tailgate group beginning to make plans for the weekend. It was here and it was real. There was going to be Cyclone football.

To underscore the excitement, on Tuesday Iowa State declared the first two games would feature sellout crowds, thanks in large part to the more than 49,000 season tickets sold, a record.

On Wednesday, they released the uniform combination that the team would be wearing: white helmet, cardinal jersey, white pants. I'm not going to pretend this didn't affect my decision-making on gameday attire.

Then on Thursday and Friday, the countdown began. Two more days … one more day …

The first gameday of the season is a special occasion. I have found few things in life that match my level of giddiness to go to Jack Trice Stadium for the first time.

The first few minutes of any tailgate remind me of when I was a kid and we all gathered in the living room on Christmas morning to open presents.

You spend days (weeks? months?) waiting, looking forward to this thing you so desire. Finally, the day is here. You wake up in the morning with butterflies. Everyone gathers. The moment is so close you can taste it. And then … someone needs to hand out the gifts. One by one, the gifts are handed out. "This one says it's to mom. … Here's one for Kent. … Oh, here's one for Kyle."

What takes five minutes feels like an hour. The presents are right there in front of you, piling up. Right there. You can feel the wrapping paper. You can see the slit where, in just a few seconds, you will rip it open like you're stranded on a desert island and it contains a 32-ounce bottle of water.

In the same way, once I wake up for gameday, I am ready to be, at that moment, standing in the parking lot, looking at the stadium with the first beer of the day in my hand, surrounded by the 15-or-so people who I have shared this experience with for more than a decade. Instead, there are still a few steps to take before you can settle in for the tailgate. You have to pack the cooler, pack the car, pick out the perfect outfit, coordinate the carpool, drive to Ames, wait in line to get into the parking lot and then finally pull into the parking lot of the tailgate.

At this point, I'm bursting with anticipation.

We grab our coolers out of the trunks of our vehicles, set up the tent and table quickly, and then I grab that first beer out of the cooler, sliding it into a koozie. The anticipation is over. It's time to rip open that present.

It's time for fun.

For a night game, this process starts around noon or 12:30 p.m. For a mid-afternoon game, the tailgate starts sometime between 8:30 and 10 a.m. This is a little more unusual, but you can still convince your body that this is semi-normal. Then there's the 11 a.m. kickoff. There's nothing normal about this.

The tailgate lots open six hours before the game. If you are doing the math, that's 5 a.m. This means, driving from Des Moines, we need to leave around 4 to meet up with the group. Which means we need to be awake no later than 3:30. If you're anything like me, it's not exactly easy to get to bed before 10:30, and if I know I need to get up early, I don't necessarily sleep well. I'll wake up and look at the clock. *1 a.m. Now it's 2:30. I'll never get back to sleep … what's that sound? Oh my gosh it's the alarm? Why? Oh yeah, it's GAMEDAY!!!*

Regardless of excitement level, it's literally like getting up in the middle of the night.

Once I'm at the tailgate, it's easy to lose track of the time. Outside, surrounded by Cyclone fans, not thinking about anything else in the world. My body is on vacation time. It simultaneously feels like we've been out there forever and also the tailgate just began. Time moves at a different speed.

Regardless of the time of day, tailgating evokes a feeling like few other things do for me. The first tailgate of the year, especially, is always like opening that first present on Christmas morning.

Of course, as we get older, life comes with more responsibilities. That's how planning for Cyclone football Christmas morning (aka the first tailgate of the season) began during UNI week. My friend Chris, who I have gone to nearly every home game with since 2011, and his wife Kaci now have a nearly two-year-old son. Due to childcare considerations, they let me know they wouldn't be able to get to the tailgate until a little after 11 a.m., even though the lots would open at 9:30.

I had a decision to make. Would my wife, Paige, and I meet up with the early birds in the group to get into the lots as soon as they opened? Or would I wait for my best friend and miss an hour-and-half of precious tailgate time? I weighed my options. On one hand, I wanted to be there for every moment of that first tailgate. This would be the first time we had gotten to do this in nearly two years. On the other hand, we hadn't gotten to do this in nearly two years for a reason. I knew there would be so much extra emotion around this experience, beyond the normal opening game feelings. I thought back to 2020, watching games in Chris's backyard due to the pandemic, being respectful of each other's distance. We stood the entire time during the Big 12 Championship and Fiesta Bowl, bundled up and trying to keep warm in the unforgiving Iowa winter. Both of us were taking a cautious approach regarding the pandemic. It would have been easier for each of us to watch inside, alone, but we wanted to watch together.

When I thought about the entire gameday experience — driving to Ames, talking about the game, pulling into the tailgate lots — I knew it would be emotional for both of us. I wanted to experience it together. What's the point of the journey if you're not sharing it with the people closest to you? We decided to go just a little later than normal and ride up with Chris and Kaci.

Chris and I got together Friday evening to talk about the season. I had anticipated being there an hour or two, but we ended up talking until past midnight. By the time I got home and got into bed, it was around 1 a.m. I optimistically set my alarm for 7:30, but it was no later than 7 a.m. when I was awake.

It's gameday! Time to get up!

As we got ready for the day, I knew I had to wear red. I picked out my new cardinal shirt with the Jack Trice logo: five stripes to depict the design of the jersey worn in the days when Jack Trice played. The team was wearing white helmets, but I didn't have any white hats. The closest was a yellow hat with an I-State logo on the front. *That's the one.*

Then it was time to pack the cooler. I like to bring an Iowa craft beer or two with me to sip on and enjoy early in the tailgate. I also packed some New Glarus Spotted Cow, a beer only available to purchase in Wisconsin, which increases its marketability due to its scarcity. And for any drinking games, I packed some Coors Light. (Many Iowa State fans would choose Busch Light for this purpose, I realize. I've always been a Coors guy.) To fill out the cooler, we also threw in some waters and cold brew coffees. For food, we packed some hot dogs and hamburgers, chips and other snacks. It had been so long, and yet preparing for the tailgate felt like old hat for me.

As the four of us — Chris, Kaci, my wife Paige and I — rode up to the tailgate, we talked about times past. Such as: "Remember when Chris and Paige got into a fight after the first UNI game Paige went to?" We pulled into our traditional grass lot a little after 11 a.m., and the scene was there in front of us. Cars and tents everywhere. Flags flying in the gentle breeze. People playing bags and other such games. Grills fired up. Rap music, country music, oldies, pop hits blaring from all different directions, fighting for attention. Everyone dressed in Cyclone gear, with a handful of Panther fans mixed in.

In the words of the "Field of Dreams" movie, *Is this Heaven?*

We found a parking spot and then rolled our coolers over to the area where our group was tailgating. The cooler was heavy, but I was so close to that first sip I could practically feel it hitting my lips.

"At least the cooler will be lighter when we roll it back," I remarked.

We were about to see friends that we hadn't seen since before the pandemic. We just had to find them. We rolled the coolers along, and Paige walked in front of us, looking in between parked cars in search of our group. Then she pointed. We had found them. We caught up with Paige, turned to our right and there they were. The next few moments were kind of a blur of noise and greetings and handshakes and hugs. We were all together again.

Time for that first beer … but before I could even think about taking one out of the cooler, I heard "RICOCHEEEEEET!!" Ricochet is a game we play that involves, well, drinking beer quickly. This was no time for a craft beer. I dug out one of the Coors Lights. A few minutes later, in the midst of a game and excitement and adrenalin, I still took a half-second to consciously appreciate that I was now tailgating.

The next three hours were spent catching up with old friends. More people showed up over the course of the day. People who hadn't been part of this group as long as many of us had, but had at some point or another become integrated in. As one person, Dave, put it, "I told my other friends that I need to come to this tailgate because it's so much fun."

For as long as I can remember, about halfway through our tailgates we throw some pizza rolls on the grill. A few years ago, a local news cameraperson was roaming around the lots and saw us grilling pizza rolls. This made the newscast, and our little tradition became just a little bit famous. "Yeah, we're the group that makes pizza rolls on the grill." Pro tip: If you ever try this, DO NOT bite straight into the pizza roll. If you want to taste anything the rest of the day, let it cool down first, and then take a bite off the end to let the steam roll out of the inside.

After the pizza rolls were devoured, I grilled my hot dogs and hamburgers. Standing around the grill as multiple people had items scattered around it, we talked about what we were each making, followed by "Oh that sounds delicious," followed by "Oh you can have one, I brought extras." This is a community.

A little while later, I grabbed a Spotted Cow out of the cooler.

"Spotted Cow? No way!" my friend Tyler exclaimed.

"I have another one," I answered. "Do you want it?"

"Are you sure?"

"Of course."

Tyler later made a point to tell Paige that I am a great guy for sharing my beer and vowed he would pay me back. I told him don't sweat it. We were just happy to be there. It was a perfect 75-degree day and we were tailgating. What could be better?

There is usually a moment in the tailgate where I begin to transition from fun festival mode to ready to get in the stadium mode. For this game, knowing it would be a little extra emotional to see the band march and see the team entrance, I wanted to go in a little early. A little after 2:30, we began packing up. We still had to bring our coolers back to the car, and I knew from experience that it is tough to get people to move in the right direction at this point of a tailgate. I had long ago accepted that I don't always need to be in the stadium for the band's pregame show, but today I really wanted it. As we arrived back to the car with a couple of other friends who were also storing their stuff in the trunk, the group was still moving with a little less urgency than I preferred. I clapped my hands.

"Let's go!" I shouted.

We walked across the street and approached the gates. I heard the public address announcer reading off the starting lineups. What looked like thousands of people were in line to get in. *We're never going to make it in time …* More quickly than I expected we were at the front of the line, getting our tickets scanned. Paige's bag got checked, and … *We're in. We're in the stadium!* We took a few steps toward the ramp behind the Sukup End Zone Club that would lead us to our seats. Before we went, I looked back to see Chris and Kaci were just a few spots behind us in line.

"Let's wait," I said.

The four of us walked up together toward our seats in Section M, in the upper deck of the southwest corner of the stadium. Just as we were nearing the entrance of the seating area, I heard the band's pregame entrance playing. We were going to get up to our seats just in time.

The next several minutes were again a blur of taking in the scene around me. Sixty thousand-plus people back together for the first time in so long. Clapping to the fight song. Cheering after the National Anthem. Yelling "Cyclone Power." Watching the Cyclone Weather Alert. My face welled up with tears as Kanye West's "POWER" came on and the team began its walk from the locker room to the entrance to the field, every step being chronicled on the giant videoboards.

The team ran onto the field as we cheered. The loudspeakers blared a pump-up song as the crowed clapped in unison. The crescendo had reached its peak. I looked at Chris, also knowing he would be emotional. We let ourselves feel it for a second.

"OK, I'm ready now," he declared with a steely resolve in his voice.

It was time for Iowa State to win a football game.

The crowd was still at a fever pitch as Iowa State kicked off to Northern Iowa and senior Rory Walling made the first tackle of the season. It stayed that way as fans came to their feet to cheer on the Cyclone defense on a third-and-10 play. Will McDonald, who tied for the nation's lead in sacks in 2020, recorded his first sack of 2021 on Northern Iowa's Will McElvain.

I jumped up and pumped my fist.

Football was back, baby!

Unfortunately, nobody told the Iowa State offense, which failed to pick up a first down on either of its first two drives.

Not ideal.

UNI took the ball for its third possession and faced a third-and-11 backed all the way up at its 12-yard line. This is when the vibes from the day so far dissipated. McElvain scrambled and found Deion McShane for a 37-yard gain to midfield. (This was also my first irrational moment of the day as I yelled for a penalty. I thought McElvain had crossed the line of scrimmage before throwing his pass. I later realized I was wrong. It was just a very good play.)

Two plays later, McElvain found Quan Hampton, who grabbed the ball just out of reach of ISU defender Mike Rose, broke a tackle and was off to the races for a 52-yard touchdown. As he ran toward our endzone, for the first time that day I really noticed the cheers from the Panther fans, including the people in the row right behind me who I didn't even realize were there until just that moment. A younger, perhaps college-age or just out of college, fan was yelling at the top of his lungs. It brought me back to ghosts of the past and "It's too easy!" It was a sobering reminder that UNI was excited for the season too, and their fans were also hoping to win. The offseason hype for Iowa State was now a moment of the past and the real games had begun.

During the timeout between the extra point and kickoff, Chris turned to me.

"We're in a close game now. We need to accept it."

He was right. I did not want to accept it. Despite all the words I wrote earlier in the week about past UNI heartburn, in my gut I didn't actually think it would be a close game.

Luckily, Iowa State scored a field goal on its next possession, and then put together a 14-play, 59-yard drive to score its first touchdown of the season and take a 10-7 lead. UNI answered with its own field goal before Iowa State hit another field goal to end the half up 13-10. We were in a close game indeed.

Nothing changed in the third quarter, either in the type of game being played or in the score. Iowa State seemed to be content with playing a conservative offense and relying on its defense, a trend during opening games under Campbell. The problem for me was that the game continued to be much closer than anyone expected. Heading into the fourth, Iowa State's dream season was very much hanging in the balance. I knew from having watched ISU coach Matt Campbell's teams for the past five years that he, and the team, were generally very comfortable being in a close game, even if the fans weren't. Which oddly enough gave me comfort. I doubted they were freaking out on the sidelines, but I was trying to keep from freaking out in the stands. As if to prove just how comfortable he was in this game, Campbell chose to punt from the Panther 39-yard line to begin the fourth quarter.

Behind me, one fan wondered aloud before the play "Will they try a field goal?"

To which another fan responded, "You must be new here."

A 57-yard field goal attempt would have been much riskier than punting, a risk Campbell was unlikely to take in this instance even if he did have a kicker who could make it.

Iowa State got the ball back a few minutes later for a first-and-10 from its own 39-yard line with 11:38 to go. I turned to Chris. "This is where we go down and score a touchdown, and then play the 'Juicy Wiggle!'"

The "Juicy Wiggle" is a catchy little song by Redfoo that has become an unofficial anthem for the Cyclones. It is always played after a second half touchdown when the crowd is already happy, and we all clap and dance, and for night games turn on the lights on our cellphones. I wanted to experience that feeling on opening day.

Chris looked at me. He has a … gift … of sorts. When he has a feeling something bad is going to happen in the game, he needs to say it out loud. He can't stand the thought of having to keep it to himself. I recognized from years of knowing him that this was one of those times. "Don't say it. Whatever you are about to say, don't say it! I swear I'm going to punch you in the face if you say it!" (I wouldn't actually have done that.)

"I have to say it," he answered.

"Don't do it. Don't put the negative energy into the world."

"OK fine. I will text it to myself. Just in case."

For a while, it looked like I was going to be right and Iowa State was about to score a touchdown. The Cyclones got down to the UNI eight-yard line after senior quarterback Brock Purdy scrambled for 19 yards. Preseason Heisman Trophy candidate and running back Breece Hall then took it down to the three on the next play.

C'mon "Juicy Wiggle."

Nope.

The next two plays were stuffed, and Iowa State faced a fourth-and-goal from the four.

"Surely they'll go for it here," I said. "A field goal doesn't make any sense."

With less than seven minutes left in the game, UNI's time was running out, but a six-point lead would be very much more stressful than a 10-point lead. And even if the Cyclones didn't score on fourth down, UNI would have to start deep in its own end against the stout Cyclone defense. *Yep, going for it here just makes sense,* I thought.

I groaned as Campbell sent out the field goal unit.

The kick was good, and Iowa State held a 16-10 lead. Northern Iowa was going to get at least one more chance to score a touchdown and win.

This was about the time Nancy turned to me to ask the question I didn't want to think about. I stopped her before she could say the words I was anticipating. *What if we lose to UNI?*

The Panthers started what they hoped would be their game-winning drive at the 25-yard line. The crowd came to its feet as UNI faced a third-and-six and stayed on its feet for fourth-and-two. *Get us the ball back, defense. Please.* No such luck. The Panther running back moved the chains forward with a four-yard run. Just three plays later, though, UNI faced a third-and-12. McElvain threw a deep ball that missed the receiver by a wide margin and was intercepted by Iowa State's Datrone Young. The crowd cheered thunderously for one of the few times in the afternoon. Iowa State had the ball back with 2:05 left. During the ensuing timeout, the stadium bumped as music played over the loudspeaker. I looked around to the nearly full stadium and took in the scene of people bobbing their heads in some cases, moving their bodies to the beat in some cases and clapping in rhythm. I saw UNI fans heading toward the exits. It was almost over.

But not quite.

Iowa State predictably ran the ball three times. Northern Iowa was able to stop the clock twice with timeouts, forcing the Cyclones to punt the ball with just over a minute left. A Panther touchdown at this point would essentially win them the game and end Iowa State's dream season before it could really begin.

My friend Eric in front of us, who has a dry sense of humor about these sorts of things, exclaimed, "Great! All we need is to screw up once to lose!"

Ughh.

The Panthers got the ball back at their own 10-yard line, needing to go 90 yards in less than a minute to win. The odds were heavily against them, even as they threw a series of short passes to get to the 42. I still held onto some fear. I was imagining UNI getting one Hail Mary play. I did not want to imagine what it would feel like as that ball hung in the air. With 14 seconds left, McElvain threw in the direction of Hampton on the Cyclone side of the 50-yard line, but Iowa State defender Anthony Johnson was well-positioned and able to knock the ball down.

Six seconds left. Time for one play.

Please don't let something fluky happen.

The world stopped as UNI receiver Sam Schnee caught a short pass and ran forward. The Cyclone defense was playing back, protecting the endzone at all costs. Rose calmly made a tackle 33 yards from the endzone, and I breathed an enormous sigh of relief.

Iowa State 16, Northern Iowa 10. The dream season lived on.

Normally after a win, the loudspeakers play Neil Diamond's "Sweet Caroline" in celebration. Not on Saturday. Nor did they play the "Juicy Wiggle." The overwhelming feeling I sensed among fans filing out was relief, not joy.

As we were walking out of the stadium, I finally asked Chris. "What did you text yourself when I wouldn't let you say it out loud?"

"I said we were going to score a field goal to go up 16-10, and then give up a touchdown to lose."

Thank goodness he was only half right.

So, what if they had lost? How would I have reacted? How would I have continued this journey?

In the moment Nancy was about to ask me that question, in the stands, I really didn't know the answer. After having time to contemplate it, I *still* don't know the answer. It would have changed the trajectory of this season, and by proxy my journey through this season in a way that I never truly let my heart believe could happen, even though I knew on an intellectual level that it could.

When I tried to answer that question, I just couldn't. I was mostly thankful that I just didn't have to.

CHAPTER FIVE

IOWA STATE VS. IOWA PREVIEW

THE RIVALRY THAT COMPLETES ME

Sept. 9, 2021

My brother is seven years older than me and a Hawkeye fan. The fact that he is my big brother mirrors the sentiment prevalent among many fans that Iowa State is the little brother to the Hawkeyes. Growing up and throughout our adult lives, this dynamic has played out similarly. Quite frankly, I've always wanted to be like my brother, and in so many ways Iowa State has always wanted to be like Iowa. Now, in so many ways we are.

Recently, with the news about conference realignment, there has been speculation that the yearly CyHawk rivalry could end. There seem to be some fans on both sides that would be OK with that. It's almost like we go out of our way to act like we don't care about each other.

Not me.

This rivalry reminds me of a scene in the movie "The Dark Night," part of the Batman series. Batman, played by Christian Bale, interrogates the Joker, played brilliantly by the late Heath Ledger. In the scene where Batman asks the Joker, "Then why do you want to kill me," the Joker laughs.

"I don't want to kill you. What would I do without you? ... You, you complete me."

I don't want to kill off the CyHawk series. I need that rival. It completes my fandom.

To be totally honest, as I was beginning to put together this chapter way back in July before the season started (don't feel too special, Hawkeye fans, I started that process for most of the games on the schedule), I was trying to downplay it in my mind. I was trying to convince myself I didn't need it anymore.

After all, if this was once Iowa State's Super Bowl, it is not anymore. Iowa State has now won the Fiesta Bowl. The Cyclones were one drive away from winning the conference championship. They have legitimate playoff hopes. Winning the CyHawk game, I told myself, wasn't nearly as important.

When I was in the marching band, my parents would come to almost every game. In the 2007 season, an 0-2 Iowa State team shocked the Hawkeyes for one of what ultimately turned out to be three wins on the season (and five wins for head coach Gene Chizik's entire Iowa State career). Bret Culbertson (who I also shared a journalism class with during this same semester) hit five field goals, including the game winner with just seconds left, to stun the Hawkeyes. It was one of the most unexpected games I have ever sat through. I'm sure most Iowa fans could say the same. My mom likes to tell the story of a game later that season, a 56-3 Iowa State loss against Texas. As my parents were walking out of the stadium that day, some Cyclone fan remarked, "Well at least we beat Iowa."

For many years, beating Iowa could salvage an otherwise forgettable season. Now that this fact is no longer true, I've been trying to figure out how much I do care or how much I should care. The Cyclones have bigger fish to fry this year than just beating Iowa.

Now that it's game week, I realize that I was wrong back in July. I need this now as much as ever.

So many of my most vivid memories of Iowa State football revolve around the Iowa game. The day I truly became an Iowa State fan in 1997 was the same day I fully realized how embarrassing it was (at the time) to be an Iowa State fan instead of a Hawkeye.

The day my fandom paid off came just a year later in 1998. The Hawkeyes were heavily favored to win their 16th game in a row in the series. Dan McCarney was in his fourth year as head coach and was coming off a 1-10 season. That afternoon, he earned a special place in Iowa State lore as his star running back Darren Davis ran for 244 yards in a blowout win to stun the Hawkeyes. I listened to the game on the radio as the late Pete Taylor brought it to life. It was a major shift in the state. I could feel it even as a kid. Suddenly,

Cyclone fans believed they could beat Iowa. Suddenly, there was optimism. There was some pride in being a Cyclone fan. The 1998 season was ultimately viewed as a success (by me, at least) despite the Cyclones winning only three games. They beat Iowa.

My first true, in-person experience with the Iowa vs. Iowa State rivalry was the 1999 game in Jack Trice Stadium. I attended with some family friends. It was a largely forgettable game between two poor teams. One of the only things I remember is an interaction after the Hawkeyes scored their only touchdown of the game.

At that point in my life, I was a pretty big fan of both teams. I was wearing an ISU shirt that day, and cheering for the Cyclones, but I also regularly watched Hawkeye games and genuinely cheered for them, too. I had no real ill-will toward Iowa. I quickly learned I was in the minority of that opinion.

After the Hawkeyes kicked the extra point, the Iowa cheerleaders prepared to run onto the field carrying their I-O-W-A flags. Members of the crowd started to figure out this was about to happen. I could feel the mood in the stadium change. I didn't quite understand what people were getting upset about, but I could feel it, and something in my gut told me I should be upset too.

Then it happened. The cheerleaders ran onto the field with their flags. The Hawkeye marching band played their fight song. And the crowd booed. The man in front of me stood up and yelled something like, "NOT ON OUR FIELD!" I, all of 12 years old, found myself fired up. "Yeah, not on our field!" I echoed.

Why in the world would I have been so upset about a standard action of college football — cheerleaders leading cheers? That night, I felt the true dislike that exists between rivals, and the tribalism that forms between them. In no world did the Hawkeyes do anything wrong in that situation. In that moment, we just didn't like them.

Iowa State won five games in a row in the series between 1998 and 2002, capped off by a game that still defines the series. In 2002, The Cyclones fought back from a 24-7 halftime deficit to win, 36-31. The Cyclones were led by Seneca Wallace, who at the time was busy turning himself into a Heisman Trophy candidate. As it turned out, this game gave Iowa its only loss of the regular season and likely cost the Hawkeyes a chance at playing for the national championship. (If Iowa State goes 11-1 with a loss to only Iowa, I'll like our chances for the College Football Playoff this year.)

When I attended Iowa State between 2005 and 2009, I got to experience four years of the rivalry in the marching band. When the game was at Jack Trice Stadium, the Iowa band would take the field first for its pregame show. The student section would boo. By the time we would take the field, the crowd was nearly full, and the cheers as we marched onto the field were deafening. The fans appreciated our band more during those games because we were theirs, and we were not the Hawkeyes. The 2005 and 2007 games at Jack Trice Stadium were intense as Iowa State pulled major upsets both years.

In Iowa City during the 2006 season, we watched Iowa State grab a 14-3 lead with just 2:47 left before halftime. It was a warm day, which meant we took off our band jackets during the game. As Iowa State's Bret Meyer completed a nearly seven-minute drive with a nine-yard touchdown run, we were putting our jackets back on to prepare to go down to the field for our halftime show. I had just moments ago put my jacket back on and was now cheering the touchdown when a beer can, still full of at least some beer, hit me in the back, spilling liquid all over my jacket. I didn't see who threw the can, and I didn't even turn around to look. Being in the band, I knew it would be frowned upon to confront an opposing fan. I calmly picked up my sousaphone, put it over my shoulder and headed toward the field. That was the end of my good vibes of the day. I was covered in beer and Iowa immediately went down the field to score before halftime to cut the lead to 14-10, before coming out of the half and cruising to a 27-17 victory.

The first game I attended post-graduation was the 2009 Iowa game. Just a couple months earlier, I had taken a job covering high school sports in the middle of Missouri. It was a five-plus hour drive to Ames, but I was not about to miss the Iowa game. Being a high school sports reporter, this meant I needed to cover a high school football game on the Friday night before the game, and of course the CyHawk game was scheduled for an 11 a.m. kickoff. After the Friday night game, I stopped at home around 10 p.m., dropped off my camera equipment, loaded up my car and took off for Ames. Twenty minutes down the road, I was going through my mental checklist. *Toothpaste? Check. Change of clothes? Check. Ticket? Ticket? AH* **** *I FORGOT MY TICKET.* Around 40 minutes later, I was back at the same spot, ticket in hand. The Black Eyed Peas song "I Gotta Feeling" blared on my radio speakers for the first of what felt like 10 times during the trip. It was now after 11 p.m.

Once I got within 90 minutes or so from Ames, I started feeling less crazy about my decision. It was still the dead of night, and cars were zipping by me with their Iowa State flags flying out the car window. *It's gameday, baby!* "I gotta feeling … that tonight's gonna be a good night …"

I met up with Chris around 5 a.m., and we drove over to the lots shortly after they opened, neither one of us having slept a minute. The Cyclones also looked like they hadn't really slept the night before in a 35-3 loss. It was a giant letdown, and indeed not a good night afterwards.

Two years later in 2011, for another 11 a.m. kickoff, Chris and I both lived in Des Moines and convinced his now-wife, Kaci, to go up early with us. Although the lots technically didn't open until 5 a.m., hundreds or maybe even thousands of students and people who were not too much older than students camped out in their cars, waiting for the lots to open. This included some people in our group, but not the three of us. Instead, we made the sensible decision to get there by 4 a.m.

Kaci, as I recall, wasn't fully on board with this plan. A Florida native, she was not much of a college football fan, nor did she have a strong tie to Iowa State outside of Chris, and she had never experienced a CyHawk game. As we pulled into the tailgate lot just south of University Boulevard (or was it still Elwood Drive?), it was around 4 a.m. And it was like pulling into a nightclub in the form of a grass parking lot.

Stereos were blaring with competing music. Rap, country, oldies, it was all there. Tents were set up, and every sign pointed to people having been there for hours. Nobody was just unpacking their cooler or setting up their tent. They were hanging out, drinks in hand, talking, playing bags and beer pong and other such games. For that moment, it was the parking lot that never sleeps.

Even though I knew what to expect, I was still a little bit in awe. Kaci's eyes might as well have been bulging out of her head.

That day ended well. In what was one of the most memorable games in the series, Iowa State and Iowa fought to three overtimes. In the second overtime, Iowa faced a third-and-long down by seven points. It was a hot day in the 80s, and at this point it had been more than 10 hours since I began tailgating. I was yelling so loud that for a few seconds the sun, heat and fatigue nearly caught up with me as I almost blacked out. Fortunately, I was able to stay upright as Iowa (unfortunately) scored a touchdown to tie it. In the third overtime Iowa State's James White took an option pitch into the endzone to give Iowa State the walk-off win. It was the first time I ever had the opportunity to rush the field at Jack Trice Stadium in celebration of a big win.

In 2012, I witnessed my first Iowa State win on the road. It was a game that the Cyclones seemed to be in control of all day, and yet the Hawkeyes were marching down the field trailing only 9-6 with less than two minutes remaining. Iowa's James Vandenberg threw a pass on first-and-10 from Iowa State's 32-yard line. Iowa State linebacker Jake Knott read the play, tipped the ball into the air, and I temporarily forgot I was surrounded by Hawkeye fans as I jumped and yelled as Knott somehow came down with the football that he tipped to himself to seal the Cyclone win.

Back in Kinnick Stadium in 2014, an 0-2 Cyclone team hung in the game and gave themselves a chance to win late. Quarterback Sam Richardson led Iowa State on a four minute-plus drive to set up Cole Netten's game-winning field goal. The Iowa fans around me were almost deathly quiet. I was afraid to show too much emotion on the outside, but inside I was screaming at the top of my lungs. Walking out of the stadium, it was eerie. Chris and I walked in near silence, hyper-aware that we were wearing Cyclone shirts in a group of mostly Hawkeye fans. We saw a friend from across the crowd, another Cyclone fan. We waved at him and I gave a little, "Woo." The softest little cheer I'd ever given. I got the impression that I was one stray comment away from getting yelled at, cursed at, having beer thrown at me or worse.

That was the last time we beat Iowa. Now seven long years ago.

Before the 2016 game at Kinnick Stadium in Iowa City, I walked around the tailgate lots near the stadium. Iowa State had just lost to UNI in coach Matt Campbell's very first game. Iowa was coming off a historic season and had high aspirations for a repeat performance. Walking around the lots, I couldn't help but feel the irrelevance of my Cyclones. Once the game started, it wasn't much different. Iowa ran Iowa State out of the game 42-3. My now-wife Paige and I made the decision to stay in Iowa City in a camper my brother and cousin, both Hawkeye fans, rented. After the game, as I figuratively licked my wounds, I tried my hardest not to talk about the game or the fact that my team's new coach had just lost by 39 points to its biggest rival. Yes, I'll admit it now, that evening I seriously questioned whether Campbell was the right coach for Iowa State, as my Hawkeye family members teased me about the outcome.

It reminded me of so many years being an Iowa State fan and feeling the sting of knowing my team didn't belong on the same field as Iowa, or most of the rest of the Big 12 teams. The pockets of success since 1998 were interspersed with pockets of great struggle — two-and-three-win seasons, blowouts that were over by halftime. Even though I had mostly been an Iowa State fan post-1998, post-15-game losing streak to Iowa, I still understood the stigma of fandom that developed in the 80s and 90s when Iowa would win by scores like 51-10, 57-3 and 63-20. I still felt the condescension of Hawkeye fans on message boards, social media and sometimes at family gatherings. The belief that despite some success, Iowa State football wasn't really that much better in the mid-2010s than it was in the mid-1990s.

While I was marinating in this spiral of football depression, legend has it that the culture was changing within the Iowa State football program in those very moments. Campbell, as the story goes, challenged his team that evening. Do we want to accept this type of performance? Do we want to have a culture where we believe we deserve to lose? Or do we want to change?

I believe it was a turning point in the modern era of Cyclone football.

What has followed are four straight bowl games since 2017, each progressively better than the prior in prestige. Top 10 wins. Competing for conference championships. Having a team worthy of writing a book about.

But not yet a team that has beaten Iowa.

They've been tantalizingly close.

In 2017, Iowa had just tied the score in the fourth quarter after trailing by 10 points. The Cyclones got the ball back to go on a potential go-ahead drive. After the first-down play, ISU running back David Montgomery was tackled as he was running out of bounds. Somewhere down on the field, I saw someone on the ISU sideline calling for a late hit. I don't know if it was a coach, player, manager, trainer or fan. All I know is it prompted me to stand up and mimic the motion of the referee throwing a flag as I yelled, "COME ON!" Whether it was actually a late hit, I have no idea. In that moment I was in the zone, yelling for my team.

A few rows behind me, I heard a fan yell, "Calm down!" I made a couple assumptions, neither of which I know was actually true. One: This was a Hawkeye fan. Two: This fan was yelling at me.

Luckily, I have become a bit more in control of my emotions since that 1999 game ("Not on our field!"). I stopped myself from turning around and looking for the fan who just yelled in my direction. I stopped myself from saying anything.

The next play, Hakeem Butler caught a long pass and broke free from the Iowa defenders for a 74-yard touchdown. As the ball landed in his hands the crowd gave a deafening cheer. It was pandemonium as Butler ran untouched into the endzone. In that moment, with 50,000-plus ISU fans cheering at the top of their lungs, I let out my frustration. "YOU CALM DOWN!" I yelled, fully aware that not even the person next to me could hear me. In that moment, I was sure Iowa State was going to win. In a cruel twist of fate, Iowa scored a touchdown to bring the game to overtime, and then scored the walk-off touchdown to win 44-41. At this point, I was remarkably calm. Just heartbroken.

The 2019 game was more of the same. ESPN's "College GameDay" made its first visit to Ames. We waited in two hours of traffic starting at 6 a.m. just to park. The game, which began at 3 p.m. was weather delayed twice. Iowa State took a 7-3 lead with 5:44 left in the first quarter and held a lead until Iowa finally grabbed the lead back at 15-14 with 12:10 left in the fourth. The teams traded field goals, resulting in an 18-17 lead for the Hawkeyes, a lead which looked comfortable enough when they got the ball back with two minutes left. The Iowa State defense forced the stop it needed, and Iowa had to punt with 1:37 left. Iowa State was going to have one more shot to go down and win the game … until two Iowa State players ran into each other as one of them was trying to field the punt. The result was a fumble, recovered by Iowa, and my hands going to my head in agony. Every sign, except the final score, pointed to a game Iowa State should have won.

Ouch.

After the game, there were altercations between Iowa State fans and University of Iowa marching band members. Your perspective on who was in the right or wrong probably depends on which team you support, but it was another reminder: Sometimes rivals just don't like each other.

But I still think we need each other.

For me personally, I still follow the Hawkeyes through the eyes of my brother, who has had season tickets at Kinnick Stadium since 2004. For my entire adult life, we have both filled up our fall Saturdays by cheering on our teams. The rivalry is an integral part of my life. The first thing we talk about whenever we see each other in the fall is Iowa and Iowa State football. We text each other to begin every gameday either team has.

I can't get away from the rivalry. So many Cyclone fans have similar stories.

Spouses, siblings, extended family members, close friends and coworkers on opposite sides of the rivalry, forced to interact in everyday life.

This year, it's unquestionably the biggest game between the two teams, and I would make a strong argument that it is one of the top five most meaningful games in Iowa State football history.

The game matters in an entirely different context than it ever has before. I'm reminded of another book/movie reference from the "Harry Potter" series, when Harry hears the prophet on his relationship with Lord Voldemort. "Neither can live while the other survives." Both teams are in the top 10 in the country. Both are true playoff contenders. In the context of this season, neither team's playoff hopes can live while the other team's playoff hopes survive. The winner Saturday can keep dreaming. The loser, while not eliminated, will have an uphill battle. This game may no longer define our season as a success, but a loss would go a long way toward preventing us from having the success we desire.

ESPN's "College GameDay" will be there. The spotlight of the country will be on Ames. It's the kind of opportunity Cyclone fans could barely have imagined 25 years ago. It's the kind of day I dreamt about during the darkest days of the spring of 2020 during the COVID-19 pandemic.

The meaning goes even deeper than that.

This is a rivalry game. It's not the Big 12 Championship Game, it's not the Fiesta Bowl. It *is* the type of rivalry that made me a college football fan in the first place. The kind of rivalry that makes this sport so special. Whatever happens the rest of this season, this game will live in our memories forever. The conversation I have heard so much this offseason goes something like this. "We have to beat Iowa this year. We just have to beat Iowa this year." For as much success as the Cyclones have had, we still don't have the all-important bragging rights over our rival. That still matters.

Coach Campbell likes to say his team is trying to become the best version of themselves. I believe the best version of this Cyclone football team is better than the best version of this Hawkeye football team.

In the same way I'm now a grown adult and on equal footing with my big brother, Iowa State is not the kid brother anymore in this relationship. I don't need this game to prove that. But this game means more than it ever has before.

We just have to beat Iowa this year.

CHAPTER SIX

IOWA STATE VS. IOWA RECAP

THE MORE YOU WANT IT, THE MORE IT HURTS

Sept. 14, 2021

I had a low-grade headache from the time I walked into Jack Trice Stadium for the Iowa State vs. Iowa game. It had been a day full of sun and heat that reached in the 90s, and the last two hours of the tailgate felt like we were just trying to survive. Despite having drank what seemed like a gallon of water, the heat had caught up to me after eight hours outside and my head was beginning to hurt.

Headache or no headache, I was not going to miss this game. I was able to convince myself that my head didn't hurt that bad and that it wasn't really that hot as I watched the Cyclones run out onto the field. I looked around at the crowd. There was a buzz in the stadium I had never felt before. We had a top 10 team in the country. We were playing a top 10 team in the country. They happened to be our biggest rivals who we hadn't beaten since 2014. And by the way, this was the game of the day in college football on the national landscape. I turned to my friend Chris and my wife Paige and my voice was shaky as I said, "I've never felt it quite like this before."

There was no doubt. We wanted it, and we wanted it bad.

This was confirmed for me during a timeout in the first quarter. Iowa had just missed a field goal, a shank by their field goal kicker. Before the kick, the crowd was yelling, trying to distract the kicker. After the kick came off his foot and went nowhere near the goalposts, everyone erupted for the first time that day. I couldn't help but feel like we had gotten in the kicker's head. During the ensuing timeout, the crowd started an impromptu "Let's go State! Let's go State!" chant, followed by a "Cyclone! Power!" cheer. Almost everyone was standing. It was a raucous environment. There was electricity in the air.

I again turned to Chris and said, "I've really never felt it quite like this before. We *want* this game."

A few hours later, I sat in silence, no longer able to convince myself that my headache didn't hurt and taking in a different scene. The few thousand Hawkeye fans had started several "Let's go Hawks! Let's go Hawks!" chants throughout the day, and as the day moved on it became less desirable for the Iowa State fans to boo and drown them out. We lost our mojo watching the Hawkeyes take control of the game. It wasn't the "Let's go Hawks!" chant that really hurt, though. When they chanted "Hawkeye State! Hawkeye State!" it stung but was to be expected. No, the chant that occurred as the fourth quarter was winding down, and Iowa had a sizeable lead, was worse.

"O-ver-ra-ted!" ★Clap clap clap clap clap★ "O-ver-ra-ted!" ★Clap clap clap clap clap★

Indeed, the Cyclones, for this day at least, were overrated as the ninth best team in the country. They would surely drop, and likely far, after this game. And we were left trying to make sense of what this season, which coming into the day had College Football Playoff aspirations and dream season vibes, meant now that the Cyclones were no longer undefeated after just two games.

—

The week leading up to the game had the typical CyHawk banter and, as per usual, a number of storylines seemed to emerge throughout the week to ramp up the rivalry. Immediately after the Cyclones and Hawkeyes opened their seasons with wins in week one, the popular traveling pregame show on ESPN, "College GameDay," announced it would be in Ames for the CyHawk game. For many years, I had dreamed of having "College GameDay" come to Ames and of having a football team worthy of getting this type of attention. Two years ago, that dream came true. It felt like a turning point in the program's prestige when "College GameDay" decided to come for the 2019 CyHawk game. It was a great experience, and at the same time meant that we waited for more than two hours in traffic early in the morning to get into the parking lots. As rumors swirled during the final weeks of the offseason that "College GameDay" might come for the Iowa vs. Iowa State game, my initial thought was, *No thanks*. It felt a little less special this time, and I had no desire to fight that traffic again. After "College GameDay" announced it would indeed come, I changed my attitude. I decided I better embrace the experience. After all, this was a big game in a big season.

On Tuesday, the Associated Press Top 25 poll came out. Iowa State was No. 9, Iowa was No. 10. It would be the first time in the history of the rivalry that both teams were ranked, and now they were both ranked in the top 10.

Also on Tuesday, Iowa running back Tyler Goodson remarked on the game to reporters: "This is like their Super Bowl." It's an age-old criticism in this rivalry that somehow Iowa State cares more than Iowa, and it's like filling out a square on your CyHawk Bingo card every time an opposing player or fan mentions it. If it was at one point ISU's Super Bowl, that day has passed, even though I still care a lot.

On Wednesday, Iowa State unveiled its uniform combination: white helmet, black jersey, white pants. Up until very recently it would have been unthinkable for Iowa State to wear the color black, let alone when playing their rivals who wear black and gold. The black jerseys, however, worked their way into the rotation during ISU coach Matt Campbell's tenure and have been associated with big wins, including the Fiesta Bowl. I was almost sure the Cyclones would wear black against Iowa this year and was not surprised. This was a big game, worthy of a big game jersey. I am also convinced the Cyclone coaches knew exactly the reaction they would get from some Hawkeye fans for wearing black jerseys. Something along the lines of, "How dare you copy our color?" Just a little extra tweaking of the rival.

And then on Friday, things ramped up when ESPN announced its guest picker for "GameDay." The guest picker joins ESPN's analysts on set to give their picks for the biggest games of the week. The game at the site where the show is stationed that week is always picked last. Lee Corso, the popular analyst, has a long-running schtick where he will put on the mascot head of whichever team he is picking in that game. If he picks the home team, the crowd goes crazy. If he picks the away team, the crowd boos. It's great television that plays into the passion of college football fans.

The guest picker adds fuel to this process. Throughout the week, Cyclone fans threw out names such as actor Kevin Costner, who was just in Iowa for a baseball game at the Field of Dreams, or one of the handful of Cyclones in the NBA such as Georges Niang, Monte Morris or Tyrese Haliburton. Rumors began to circulate on Friday that the guest picker would be a Cyclone fan's worst nightmare: Ashton Kutcher, the Iowa-born actor who is an unabashed Hawkeye fan. *No way ESPN would go that route. Just no way.* I couldn't, for the life of me, understand how they could pick a guest who is a known fan of the away team. It seemed like it would be a slap in the face.

And it felt like a slap in the face when ESPN indeed announced it was Kutcher. On the "College GameDay" Facebook post, the account even tagged the Hawkeye Football Facebook account, but not Iowa State. The announcement post included a video of Kutcher wearing a Hawkeye hat, and he ended by saying "Go Hawkeyes!" in a way that seemed purposely obnoxious. Part of me thought we were getting Punk'd, but I have been an Iowa State fan long enough to know that was probably not true. ESPN was playing into the rivalry.

It could be easy to justify that Kutcher is the most famous and relevant person from Iowa for this type of appearance. Sure, that may be true. But it still hit a chord that made it painful for Cyclone fans. Here we were, with (hopefully) the best team we've ever had, hosting our rival and "College GameDay," and ESPN picked our rival's most famous fan to appear on set, at our home stadium. The feelings of irrelevance many of us have felt for years prior to this, the feelings of being the little brother to Iowa, those feelings were hard to escape on the Friday evening before the game. Sometimes it really is Cyclones vs. The World.

None-the-less, I went to bed Friday evening thinking, *Tomorrow could be a special day in my life ... one of those really memorable Cyclone wins.* Although I had set my alarm for 5 a.m., I woke up at 4:45. *Gameday! No going back to sleep now!* Per our usual morning gameday ritual, I texted my brother, the Hawkeye fan. I put on my black t-shirt with the Jack Trice logo, and a red hat with an I-State logo to make sure nobody confused me for a Hawkeye fan. We met Chris and his wife Kaci, as well as our good friend Charles, who had driven down from Minneapolis for the game. We were all in a jovial mood despite the early hour.

All week I had been worried about the possibility of sitting for hours in traffic to get into the parking lots. This time, we had no issue. We arrived a little after 7 a.m., parking pass in hand, and pulled right into the lots. *Time to tailgate!* It already felt like things were going better than the CyHawk gameday two years ago. That feeling would not last.

As we stood around and sipped on our first drinks of the day (for me, a full bottle of water before cracking the first beer), our discussion turned to the game. During the UNI game, Chris and I discovered a great system to prevent him from verbalizing negative predictions. Instead of saying out loud what he feared was going to happen in the game, he texted himself.

We did not learn from that lesson.

"I just have this bad feeling we are going to lose by something like 17 points today," he said.

D'oh!

Around 9:30, Chris, Kaci, Paige and I, along with a few others, headed to the "College GameDay" set located south of Jack Trice Stadium in the Reiman Plaza. As it was two years ago, it was a site to behold. The plaza was packed with Cyclone fans, and of course a few Hawkeyes. As is customary on "College GameDay," there were handmade signs everywhere. Fans try to come up with the most creative signs to get on television. As the morning went on, we continued to point out unique signs to each other (many of which likely pushed the boundaries of appropriateness to be shown on television). Some were straightforward such as "Iowa is Bad at Football." (I wish that would have been proven to be true.) Some were a little more creative, like "Ashton Kutcher Please Take a Shower."

The crowd grew, and the anticipation built as ESPN showed Kutcher's airplane arriving on the big screens next to the set. The weather was heating up, and so were emotions.

Others left to go back to the tailgate, but I wanted to see the picks and Chris was game to keep me company. If there was any less excitement about having "College GameDay" on site in 2021 as opposed to 2019, I wasn't noticing it at that point. The crowd was into it and playing their part to make Cyclone Nation look strong to a national audience.

And, if there was any doubt that ESPN was trying to manufacture drama with its pick of Kutcher, that doubt was erased as a farming combine, painted in all black with a yellow Hawkeye logo, pulled up to the "GameDay" area, Hawkeye flags flying from the top, Kutcher waving from the door. Yep, they were going all in on this bit. As Chris pointed out, there was a WWE aspect to it. Play to (or against) the crowd to manufacture excitement and controversy.

A few minutes later, it came time to pick the game. Although we couldn't hear much from on the set, as Kutcher talked most of the crowd predictably booed. It was a good-natured crowd, but I sensed a tinge of genuine anger that we were getting played as a fanbase having a Hawkeye fan on stage. Looking around me, I also sensed that ESPN's cameras might have a difficult time panning the crowd without catching a few hand gestures.

Then it was Corso's turn. His pick would generate likely the loudest cheer or boo of the day. *C'mon Corso, pick Iowa State,* I thought to myself. We couldn't hear what he was saying, but we saw him reach down and pick up … a Herky mascot head. He was picking the Hawkeyes. As Kutcher and Corso put their arm around each other, Corso still with Herky on his head, Iowa fans cheered and Iowa State fans drowned them out with boos.

I turned to Chris and said, "I've just decided I believe we're going to win!"

Something about the Cyclones vs. The World mentality gave me more confidence. Ah, the irrational optimism created by the emotions of a gameday.

A few hours later, after some more tailgating, I needed to sit in the car for a little bit. The heat had arrived, in the 90s and humid. At that point I had drank eight-to-10 bottles of water, but the heat was still getting to me. There was no way around the fact that it was a long day in the heat and sun. I sat in the air conditioning, drank some more water and mentally prepared myself for the game. I could feel a headache coming on, the type I've felt before after a day in the heat, and I knew it was going to persist. I also had confidence the adrenaline and emotion would help me hold the worst effects at bay until the game was over.

I forgot about the headache as we got into the stadium just in time to see the marching band take the field. The CyHawk game is always the most packed crowd of the year for the band's pregame show, and the crowd was into it. The PA announcer asked for a moment of silence in remembrance of the 20th anniversary of Sept. 11, and after the playing of the National Anthem fans chanted "U-S-A!! U-S-A!", a reminder that although we were Cyclones and Hawkeyes and may have different political beliefs, we also shared a common bond of being Americans.

All of the other familiar stuff happened — the Cyclone Power cheer, the Cyclone Weather Alert and the team entrance. The loudspeakers blared music as the game approached kickoff. I often feel these are the best moments of the day, as excitement reaches its peak and nothing negative has happened during the game yet. The student section looked like a popcorn machine with people jumping up and down. Cyclone fans around the stadium were clapping to the beat, and not just a polite clap. We were using our hands as noise-making machines. The whole scene was chill inducing.

I need to warn readers now that the description of this game gets a bit tedious, because it needs to be to truly convey the suffocating feeling of what it was like to watch. If you like reading about punting and field position, oh boy are you in for a treat!

Iowa took the ball first and the ISU defense immediately held the Hawkeyes to a three-and-out. In came the punter, Tory Taylor. Normally I wouldn't spend much time thinking about the punter. On this day it was inescapable. He belted the kick 58 yards, and it was downed at the Iowa State eight-yard line.

Here's how I would describe Hawkeye football under head coach Kirk Ferentz, who has led Iowa since 1999. The Hawkeyes are not flashy. They do not try to run a hurry-up offense or gamble too much on defense. They play fundamental football. Take care of the ball and don't turn it over. Control the field position with solid punting. Limit big plays on defense and force the offense to earn it with long drives. It's as though they say, "Here's who we are. If you think you can beat us, go ahead and try." They have an identity that has been overall overwhelmingly successful and has won them a lot of games they wouldn't be expected to win if stats are any indication. It keeps them in games against better teams, sometimes keeps inferior opponents in games with them, and sometimes adds up to a perfect combination of being able to destroy the opposing team's will.

From what I can tell, Iowa State, under Campbell's direction, has tried to build a program in the same type of style. As Campbell likes to say, if the Cyclones are going to be good, they need to win in the margins. In conference play, this has been very successful and put Iowa State in positions it has never been in before. In the CyHawk rivalry, it has pitted two teams that want to win the game in exactly the same style, and one has always been better at it than the other.

So, the punter matters in the CyHawk game because field position matters, because that's one way to win in the margins. Iowa's defense was going to make Iowa State's offense earn every yard and every point, and a 92-yard touchdown drive would be a tall task. Iowa State went three-and-out on its first possession and trotted out Corey Dunn for a punt. His punt went 56 yards, and was returned four yards by the Iowa returner, setting up the Hawkeyes at the 39-yard line, five yards ahead of where they punted minutes ago. The Hawkeyes didn't gain a yard on their possession, and Taylor booted a punt 50 yards to be fair caught at the Iowa State six-yard line. Both of the Cyclones' first two possessions began pinned inside their own 10, playing right into Iowa's gameplan.

Iowa State did gain a first down to a loud ovation from a still jacked-up crowd, but then had to punt again. This time, Dunn's punt went just 39 yards and was returned 18 yards. Iowa began possession in Iowa State territory at the 41-yard line. The Hawkeyes had yet to pick up a first down but had effectively moved the ball 31 yards through special teams play and were right at the cusp of field goal range. Having watched my fair share of Iowa games over the years, I knew they were accomplishing exactly what they wanted.

Iowa moved the chains for a first down for the first time that afternoon, but a sack by ISU defensive lineman Will McDonald forced a long field goal attempt of 50 yards. In one of the loudest crowd reactions of the game, the Iowa kicker shanked it. I've always felt there is something extra deflating about watching your team miss a field goal. It feels like a waste to get in position for points and then not capitalize. It is also typically a momentum shift. And Iowa State has had its share of inconsistent field goal kicking over the years, including some really big and bad misses. Iowa, conversely, always seems to be solid in that aspect of the game. When Iowa missed its first kick, it felt like maybe, just maybe, the tide was turning in our favor and it was a little extra satisfying to see our rival miss it. The crowd responded with "Let's go State" and "Cyclone! Power!" chants during the ensuing timeout. It was about the only time in the game Iowa made a mistake, if you can even call missing a field goal from that distance a mistake.

The Cyclones responded, driving down to the five-yard line before needing to settle for a field goal. It was nice to have the lead at 3-0, but there was also a feeling of regret. Scoring in the red zone (inside the opponent's 20-yard line) is one of those winning in the margins moments that Iowa State had just missed.

After another defensive stop, Taylor punted it 46 yards to be fair caught by Iowa State's Tarique Milton at the 10-yard line. Another possession with poor starting field position. The Cyclones decided to take a chance, and quarterback Brock Purdy heaved a throw downfield in the direction of receiver Xavier Hutchinson. The pass was late, and Iowa's Matt Hankins came down with a jump ball interception at the Iowa State 49-yard line. Avoiding turnovers, and conversely forcing them when the opportunity presents itself, are both examples of a team winning in the margins. Iowa again won in the margins on that play, and then put together its first solid drive of the day with a short field. When presented with the opportunity of their own in the red zone, the Hawkeyes scored on a four-yard Tyler Goodson run to make it 7-3 with 8:13 left before halftime.

After another Iowa State punt, the Hawkeyes put together what would ultimately be their best drive of the day capped off by a 26-yard touchdown pass with just 1:01 before halftime. Iowa now led 14-3, and the mood in the stadium turned a little bit somber. This was not what we had all hoped for.

It felt like the game was hanging in the balance when Purdy found Darren Wilson Jr. over the middle, who broke free and ran down the sidelines before finally being pushed out of bounds at the Iowa four-yard line, a gain of 49 yards. On the next play, with just 12 seconds left in the half, Purdy handed it off to running back Breece Hall who powered his way toward the goal line and stretched out his arm to push the ball across. Iowa State had scored to end the half, and the crowd was back into it. Would it be a game-changing, and maybe even a season-changing, drive?

At halftime, Kaci asked me how I felt.

"Pretty good, a lot better with that last drive. I think if we can come out and score right away it could turn this game around," I said.

Iowa State took the ball first. I envisioned the Cyclones marching down the field, scoring a touchdown to take the lead and the loudspeakers playing the "Juicy Wiggle" to a rockin' crowd. It looked promising as Iowa State got near midfield with a couple first downs before being forced to punt. Dunn's punt was fair caught by Iowa's returner at the 10-yard line. Finally Iowa State flipped the field position. The Cyclones forced a three-and-out and Iowa was forced to punt from the six-yard line.

This could be our moment, I thought.

"I think we're going to get the ball back, score and play 'Juicy Wiggle,'" I told Chris.

Even with a 50-yard punt, Iowa State would still get the ball in Iowa territory. If we were going to beat Iowa at its own game, this was the moment.

Milton was hovering around midfield to attempt to field the punt, but the play all around was awkward. For some reason, he could not position himself to make the catch, and the ball bounced right by him and right down the field to be downed at the Iowa State 25 — a 69-yard punt when all was said and done. Somehow, the Cyclones went from needing to go half the field to needing to go three-quarters of the field. Another loss in the margins.

On second down, Purdy was sacked and the Cyclones were ultimately forced to punt from their own 13. Dunn hit it 54 yards, but Jones broke a tackle and returned it 24 yards to the Iowa State 43. The Hawkeyes had again won in the margins and flipped field position. I've, somehow, gone this far without mentioning how great the Iowa State defense was, and indeed they again forced an Iowa punt, which was again downed … at the six-yard line.

"My gosh. Unbelievable," I muttered.

I never anticipated writing in this much detail about punting and field position.

That's when the game went from frustrating to nearly unbearable. Hall, Iowa State's superstar running back, had the ball knocked away by the Iowa defender, which was scooped up by Iowa's Jack Campbell for a touchdown. The momentum had fully turned now as Iowa went up 21-10. Iowa State had again lost in the margins with its second turnover of the day. "Let's go Hawks! Let's go Hawks!" rang through the air.

On Iowa State's next possession, Purdy threw a pass that went right through the hands of Hutchinson, and right into the hands of Iowa defender Seth Benson for another turnover. Iowa took possession at the Iowa State 25. After another three-and-out forced by the ISU defense, Iowa drilled a 51-yard field goal to make it 24-10.

Some of the most memorable games are the unexpected comebacks, and I told myself that maybe this could be one of those as Iowa State began to drive on its next possession, making it into Iowa territory. I couldn't believe my eyes as Purdy's pass was again intercepted by Hankins and returned 41 yards all the way to the Iowa State 22-yard line. That was four turnovers for the Cyclones. Three given up by senior quarterback Purdy (with a major assist to go-to receiver Hutchinson), one given up by Heisman Trophy hopeful Hall. Iowa State had gone from losing in the margins to handing the game to Iowa on a silver platter.

Iowa was again only able to convert the turnover into a field goal, but the damage was all but done. Iowa 27, Iowa State 10 with 12:53 to go. Some Iowa State fans began filing out of the stadium. This was not how any of us pictured this day going. Except Chris, who apologized to me for having verbalized his prediction earlier in the day. The air had been let out of the stadium, except for the Iowa fans cheering as their cheer squad waved the I-O-W-A flags.

The game took on a different feel at this point. On the next possession, it wasn't the senior quarterback Purdy who trotted out to lead the Cyclone offense. It was his backup, Hunter Dekkers. Some in the crowd applauded, I suspect for a combination of wanting to show support for the new quarterback in the game but also out of frustration with Purdy's game. Right or wrong, it seems football fans often want to see the backup quarterback when things are going poorly. The offense, on cue, immediately went three-and-out.

For most of the fourth quarter, I couldn't tell if Iowa State was actually still trying to win. A Campbell saying that we all know well is, "Trust the process." When Iowa State is not playing well, and more importantly not doing the little things well, or — say it with me — winning in the margins, Campbell sometimes does not force the issue, especially during the non-conference portion of the season. It's almost as if he's saying, "If we don't do the things we need to do to deserve to win, we just aren't going to win." It's kind of like a parent who declines to bail their teenager out of jail because they don't deserve it. As the fourth quarter wore on, I sensed little urgency. The play-calling didn't seem to change. The backup quarterback Dekkers remained in the game. Freshman running back Eli Sanders was getting snaps. I don't know if Campbell saw the game as a blowout and this was an opportunity to give his backups experience, or if he was sending a message to his star players, or a little bit of both. (The reasoning given by Campbell after the game for Dekkers replacing Purdy was that it seemed like the right move to "settle the game back down.") As unlikely as a comeback seemed with Purdy and Hall in the game, it seemed overwhelmingly unlikely without them. It sort of felt like Iowa State had conceded the game. "We're going to work on us now, and if we happen to come back, great."

I have seen Campbell have enough success to give him the benefit of the doubt, knowing it's a long season. But it was so depressing. As more and more Cyclone fans left during each timeout on the field, I sat silently seething as my head continued to throb a little more painfully.

"Let's go Hawks! Let's go Hawks! ..."

I couldn't help but think about the emotions going into this game. How much I wanted it. How much the fans wanted it. How much it meant to not only beat our rival, but to beat a top 10 team, and do it in what was supposed to be our best season ever. The script in my head said, *Of course we'll beat Iowa. That's what is supposed to happen this year.*

I asked a few people around me if this was the most disappointing game they could remember.

"Nah, we got blown out by Kansas at home before, and we lost those games that could have gotten us to the Big 12 Championship [back in 2004 and 2005]," one person said.

"We've had some pretty bad games," another said.

I agreed, and yet when I thought about the expectations of this year, the Iowa fans all around me having a party as they let the air out of our dream season, I'm pretty sure I've never been more disappointed in a single game. At some point, the "O-ver-ra-ted!" chant started up, and it was almost too much to take in.

Of course, right after I felt like Iowa State had conceded the game, Dekkers led the Cyclones on an 83-yard touchdown drive to make the score 27-17 with 3:27 left. Iowa State came agonizingly close to recovering an onside kick. Iowa finally didn't make a play in the margins as the ball bounced off a Hawkeye player's hands … right past Chase Allen and out of bounds. Hawkeye football. Iowa State again forced a three-and-out and got the ball back for one last-ditch effort. (The Cyclone defense, it should be noted, gave up only 173 yards, an incredible performance.) A few solid plays took the Cyclones within field goal range. If they could make it, they'd have one more chance at an onside kick and a couple plays to force a miracle comeback. In poetic fashion, kicker Andrew Mevis had his own shank, wide left.

"Well, hopefully we just got our missed kick out of the way," I joked sarcastically, fully aware of the schadenfreude I had felt earlier when Iowa's kicker missed.

That was the game.

As we walked out of the stadium, I was dejected but calm, having mentally accepted for quite a while that Iowa State was going to lose. I looked at my phone and had a text message from my mom.

"We love you!!" she wrote.

Since their two sons (me and my brother) are on opposite sides of the rivalry, my mom and dad tend to cheer for both Iowa and Iowa State. They want to see us happy. They will never admit who they are cheering for in this game to keep the peace, and I suspect they really don't enjoy the game knowing one of us will be disappointed. She knew I would be pretty down after that loss. Her message was well-timed. I needed to feel some love right then.

After a lot of games, we'll listen to the postgame show on the radio on the drive home. Sometimes I'll scroll through Twitter, which I usually can't access while in the stadium, to catch up on what other Cyclone fans think. As we sat in traffic, my headache feeling much stronger than it did four hours ago, I didn't do any of that. I made a deal with myself: *No scrolling Twitter until at least tomorrow.* This was just a good night to not think about the game. I was numb from the letdown of not getting what I so badly wanted, and I didn't think I could handle seeing the inevitable trash talk from fans. I was stuck in my thoughts. The dreamiest of dream seasons was now over, after two games. Iowa State's offense had looked like a shell of its former self despite almost all the same players. The vibes would now be different.

I used to let an Iowa State loss ruin my entire weekend. At some point, I realized that was probably unhealthy, so I learned to compartmentalize better and let the losses go. This was not one of those times. I knew this was going to stick with me. It was a similar feeling to the loss at the beginning of the season against Louisiana in 2020. All the hype and hope were deflated quickly. Except this time it was to the Hawkeyes, which was even worse. This had now become a memorable day in Hawkeye history, from having Kutcher pick the Hawkeyes on "College GameDay" to dominating their rivals to earning a spot near the top of the college football rankings. *Can't you let us have it just this once??*

I walked my dog that evening before calling it a night, and I thought about the new reality of my journey as my headache subsided. The Vegas game, which so many people had been so excited for, wouldn't feel quite the same. It just couldn't. The madness of college football is that the entire offseason of excitement can be doused with cold water very early.

I was also reminded that the best season in school history happened after that Louisiana loss. It didn't feel like Iowa State was going to be very good after the Louisiana game and, at least on offense, the 2021 Iowa game gave me many of the same feelings. In 2020 things turned around quickly. In 2021 there are still 10 opportunities remaining. The story of this season is still very much in progress, and I always knew there would be adversity.

The sun still came up on Sunday morning (in a manner of speaking; it was a cloudy day, which coincidentally would have been a perfect day for tailgating without the threat of heat exhaustion). I was reminded that living the worst days as a fan makes the best days even better. It's still Cyclones vs. The World. Let's hope for some better days.

CHAPTER SEVEN

UNLV PREVIEW

TAKING OUR SHOW ON THE ROAD

Sept. 16, 2021

It's time for the trip I have been dreaming about for nearly a year-and-a-half.

The frustration, and also part of the beauty, of college football is how much is hurts when your team loses, especially to your rival and especially early in a season where you have high hopes and expectations. But it's over now. It's time to move on. And what better way to move on than joining thousands of Cyclones fans on a road trip.

There's something special about these experiences.

One of the best examples of this is when Iowa State fans take over Kansas City's Power & Light District most years during the Big 12 men's basketball tournament. Hilton South, as we call it. For years, I had heard stories of how much fun it was to go to the tournament. I would listen to the stories of people who were old enough to experience it as adults in the 1990s and 2000s, who saw Iowa State win it in 2000, who spent days and nights at Kelly's losing track of how many drinks they'd consumed.

The age of social media brought this to life for me. When Iowa State started its men's basketball resurgence in the early 2010s, right around the time the tournament moved back to Kansas City, I experienced a couple years of FOMO seeing the Facebook and Twitter posts of the cardinal and gold sea in the Power & Light District. In 2014, the Cyclones played Kansas in the semifinals. A couple of friends and I decided that if ISU won the game, we'd drive down the next day for the championship. Iowa State, led by Georges Niang, Melvin Ejim and others who would come to be remembered as Cyclone legends, defeated Kansas in the semifinals and earned a spot in the championship. My friends Chris, Charles and I drove down on Saturday morning, along with hordes of other Cyclone fans who made the same decision, to take in the experience in person.

When we walked into the Power & Light District that afternoon, fresh off a filling meal at Jack Stack BBQ, it was everything I ever wanted. Cyclone fans everywhere. A sunny 70-degree day in March. My team playing for a championship. A festival-like atmosphere. It was like a giant tailgate for basketball.

There was something a little different in the air. I had been to many ISU football and basketball games and had even traveled to road games and postseason games. There was an anticipation for this one I had never felt before. We had a chance to be champions. A chance to win a trophy. A chance to create an experience that we'd never forget, that would live on — and we were all there for it. I knew it was the kind of day that we would all share stories about for the next 20 years. This was most crystalized for me when, during the pregame pep rally, organizers handed out Band-Aids that fans could wear above their eyes, a tribute to Niang who had received a cut above his eye the night before. It was an inside joke moment among 10,000 or so people, the kind of moment that only gets created when you are all part of something special.

Soaking up the warmth of early spring and the vibes of fellow Cyclone fans, it felt impossible that Iowa State could lose that evening. Indeed, the Cyclones won their first Big 12 tournament championship in 14 years. It didn't matter that we were too cheap to buy tickets to the game; we watched with hundreds of others on the big screen outside the stadium. It didn't matter that the temperature dropped and the sunny daytime sky turned into a snowy night. It didn't matter that I was still wearing shorts and a t-shirt. What mattered was that we were champions. What mattered was that we had a memory that would last beyond that night.

There are still stories we tell from that night in 2014. It was a defining night in my life, the kind of night that other nights get compared to. "Did it live up to that first Big 12 Championship in KC?" No other experience quite has.

As we head to Las Vegas, I think Iowa State's game against UNLV will have many of the same feelings. We aren't playing for a championship this weekend, and unfortunately the Iowa game left a little bit of a cloud over our emotions coming into this one. But this is still a potential special season in the most successful era in Iowa State football history. We still believe this team has a chance to create memories just like that 2014 Cyclone men's basketball team did. In the same way we remember those feelings of traveling with fellow fans to watch Niang, Ejim and others, this weekend we get to travel to watch players like Brock Purdy, Breece Hall, Mike Rose and others who will likely ultimately be fondly remembered as Cyclone legends. Rare is the chance that we get to experience this type of in-season celebration.

When this game first came out on the schedule a few years ago, I really didn't think much of it. *OK, cool, a road game at UNLV.* At some point it dawned on me that some Cyclone fans might be excited to take a trip to Vegas to see Iowa State play. Similar to stories you hear about prior tournaments in Kansas City, many people have fun memories of ISU's football games at UNLV in 1999 and 2008. Still, it didn't really rise to the point where I felt like I needed to, or even necessarily wanted to, attend.

Then the pandemic hit. In the early months of the era of social distancing, I found myself starting to dream of that next big trip I could take. In my mind, I started to imagine what it could be like in Las Vegas if Iowa State had a strong 2020 season (keeping in mind that at the time, we didn't even know if there would be a 2020 season), and then we descended upon Vegas as the world opened up in 2021. As early as May or June 2020, I would go on walks around Gray's Lake in Des Moines and daydream about that long weekend in Las Vegas with Cyclone fans.

In my daydreams, it always involved Iowa State coming off some sort of special season the year before. Maybe a Big 12 Championship Game appearance. Maybe a major bowl victory. Whatever it was, it would set us up for an unprecedented level of excitement in 2021. We'd enter the UNLV game as a team with championship aspirations. Thousands — maybe even tens of thousands — of fans would be there. We'd take over the opposing team's stadium. We'd be loud and proud. I can still see the Gray's Lake bike path and the bridge set against the late spring and early summer sun, and Des Moines' downtown skyline — the images my eyes were actually seeing — while my imagination showed me pictures of Purdy finding Charlie Kolar in the endzone and thousands of Cyclone fans cheering like we were the home team.

Rarely in life do things work out exactly as you hope they will in your wildest dreams. In my daydreams in 2020, I always imagined we would be taking this trip after a win against Iowa. It never fit into my plans to be coming off a disappointing loss in game two of the season. Sitting in Jack Trice Stadium last Saturday, watching the crowd slowly empty during the fourth quarter, I will admit that even my excitement level waned. To be honest, I've been trying to come to terms with the fact that it's not quite going to feel like a Big 12 Championship in Kansas City on Saturday.

When I step back, I recognize it's still a big deal, and still remarkably close to everything I dreamed of. Iowa State is still coming off a Fiesta Bowl win, is still a top 15 team, and is still a Big 12 title contender. Last year, we didn't get to experience taking over Phoenix for the Fiesta Bowl. This will feel like a bowl game, with the exception we still get the entire conference season to see what this team can become.

I'm also reminded the lengths I have taken to make this trip a reality. At some point early in 2021, it became clear that pandemic restrictions were going to be eased. Life would begin to get back to at least a semi-normal place. College football stadiums would be full in the fall.

People with money to make figured this out as well. Flight tickets from Des Moines to Las Vegas skyrocketed for the weekend of the game. As flights out of Des Moines approached $650, I thought I was going to need to strap myself to the airplane and just ride along.

At the same time, the UNLV athletics department began playing a game of chicken, declining to announce when single-game tickets would go on sale, or even how many tickets would go on sale in the stadium. The urgency of finding tickets increased.

As a result, a good number of Iowa State fans began buying season tickets to UNLV football games to guarantee they could get in. Early in the summer, UNLV released the allotment of 4,000 to Iowa State to sell to their fans. Prices for these tickets were higher than the lowest ticket package for season tickets (which by this point were sold out).

For a little while, I thought I was going to be taking the trip by myself. The excitement my friends felt about going was tempered, understandably, by the cost. I myself questioned whether it was worth it, but I knew I couldn't miss this experience.

The first major hurdle was passed after my friend James was able to secure tickets through his dad, who was high enough on the donor list to have a chance to purchase seats.

Then there was the hurdle of travel costs. This took some creative thinking. Since my friend Chris was originally from the Chicagoland area, we could look at flights out of O'Hare, which were in the $200 range. This would solve another potential challenge — since Chris and his wife Kaci have a soon-to-be-two-year-old son, they would need to find childcare for the long weekend. If we flew out of Chicago, the thinking went, their son could stay with his grandparents. Problem solved.

We booked tickets out of Chicago, meaning the trip would look something like this: Drive to Chicago from Des Moines, fly from Chicago to Las Vegas, fly back to Chicago from Las Vegas, and drive back to Des Moines from Chicago. Simple.

Whatever it takes to be there. Life only gives you so many opportunities to enjoy experiences like this one.

The game itself isn't expected to be much of a game. With Iowa State's style of play, I could always see it being closer than expected. But the thought of losing isn't really crossing my mind. Maybe that's a dangerous way of thinking, but I think this group of seniors and the coaching staff will be ready to prove something.

As I embark on the trip to Las Vegas, in my mind's eye I'm envisioning a beautiful sunny day, surrounded by cardinal and gold, believing that there is nothing better in the world than being a Cyclone fan on this day. Maybe it will give me a touch of the feelings that I have felt on spring days in the Power & Light District, with new memories to be made as I cheer on the Cyclones.

CHAPTER EIGHT

IOWA STATE VS. UNLV RECAP

A BIG GROUP THERAPY SESSION

Sept. 21, 2021

"What an incredible scene," I said as I took in the sight of thousands of Cyclone fans on the walk back from Allegiant Stadium to the Las Vegas strip.

Iowa State had just defeated UNLV in convincing fashion. Iowa State fans outnumbered UNLV fans by a wide margin. Some estimates said 25,000 to 30,000 Cyclone fans made the trip to watch their team play in Las Vegas.

It was a jovial crowd walking out of the game after a 48-3 win by Iowa State. It felt like a get-right game after a disappointing start of the season. The feelings of the Iowa game had now fully worn off as we celebrated Cyclone fandom and our team, together, over a long weekend in the desert. We were walking across West Hacienda Avenue, on a bridge over the interstate that runs through the city, a bridge that connects Allegiant Stadium to the nearest resorts, Mandalay Bay and Luxor, where the majority of Cyclone fans were staying. There were Cyclone fans as far as the eye could see in front of and behind me, against the backdrop of the bright lights of Las Vegas. As I walked, the pyramid structure of the Luxor emitted a bright blue light into the air and the golden lights of Mandalay Bay seemed to be inviting us to celebrate just a little longer that evening.

One group near us began singing "Sweet Caroline," the unofficial victory tune of the Cyclones.

"Sweeeeeet Car-o-liiiine," they began. "Bah bah bahhhhhhhhh!!" hundreds of us answered. "Good tiiiimes never seemed so good," followed by "SO GOOD! SO GOOD! SO GOOD!"

At that moment, I couldn't help but think about the offseason. When the University of Texas and University of Oklahoma decided to leave the Big 12 Conference for the SEC, the eight remaining Big 12 schools, including Iowa State, were left with an uncertain future. The conversation around college football circles seemed to focus on the fact that the Angry Eight, as we were informally called, added no value to a college football conference. Article after article, tweet after tweet, seemed to take some twisted pleasure in pointing out that the Angry Eight just didn't belong in a major conference. That we were just not good enough. That we didn't bring in the television ratings or major markets that a major network, such as ESPN, would look for.

I thought of the pictures from the UCLA vs. Hawaii game at the start of the season, which showed what looked like only hundreds of fans, maybe a few thousand, in a 90,000-seat stadium. UCLA was a top 15-ranked team in the country, and considered a brand name, but couldn't come close to filling its historic, picturesque stadium. (One national writer tried to justify this by pointing out that it was hot and there are beaches in California, as though that adds more value to a college football team.) I thought of earlier in the day when we watched the Miami Hurricanes, ranked in the top 25, play a big home game against Michigan State. As they panned the stadium, there appeared to be thousands of empty seats. Sure, I'm cherry-picking examples, but my hunch is a lot of places around the country would have a similar story.

And so, as I surveyed the scene of thousands of Cyclone fans around me, I felt a surge of pride. I knew there was something special about this fanbase, something more valuable than the national college football world has found a way to quantify. This experience was everything I had wanted. It was everything I had dreamed about for a year-and-a-half. Cyclone fans had shown up and had a party, making a noticeable presence in one of the tourist capitals of the world. The team had responded in-kind. It was a great night to be a Cyclone.

I turned to my friend Chris.

"Look at this. Any conference that doesn't want this is crazy."

As it was a week ago, and is so often, that night in Vegas was again Cyclones vs. The World. This time, the Cyclones won.

—

Thursday seemed to be the day Cyclone fans began to descend on the Sin City as I began to see Cyclone fans posting on Twitter about their travels. ISU Director of Athletics Jamie Pollard tweeted a picture from Des Moines International Airport showing the terminal full of Cyclone fans. Stephanie Copley, host of Cyclone Fanatic's "Title IX Podcast," shared the flight staff on her airplane, full of Cyclone fans, played the Iowa State fight song upon landing in Las Vegas.

I traveled to Chicago with Chris and Kaci late Thursday evening. Although it wasn't the scene that I saw on social media posts from Des Moines, our flight did include a few Cyclone fans. We also saw a group of Iowa fans in the airport. I averted my gaze to avoid eye contact. The sting of losing to the Hawkeyes was still too fresh.

We arrived at our hotel, the Luxor, a little after midnight Pacific Time. As we waited in line to check in, we met up briefly with another friend, Dave, who had gotten in earlier in the week. Dave had traveled with some other friends the week prior, and they had driven to Las Vegas on Wednesday. They had not had much in the way of cell phone service while in a more remote area of California and had not been able to watch the Iowa vs. Iowa State game, or even see the score, until Wednesday.

"Oh no," I said. "I feel your pain."

At that point in the wee hours of Friday morning, I had already taken more than five days to come to terms with the loss to Iowa. Poor Dave was still reeling.

"You'll never believe this," I told him. "While we were in the tailgate lot on Saturday, Chris told me he was feeling like we were going to lose by 17."

"DUDE!" Dave exclaimed angrily.

"I can't help it. I just had a bad feeling," Chris replied.

"How are you feeling this week?"

"I haven't decided yet."

"OK, we're going to bed," Dave said. "You need to make this right."

I have no idea what Dave expected Chris to do to make this right, but whatever it was I couldn't help but agree. We needed a win.

Sometimes when Cyclone fans travel to different cities for games, there are obvious moments when you realize Cyclone Nation has arrived. I think of the Power & Light District in Kansas City or Beale Street in Memphis.

Once you arrive, you are surrounded by thousands of Cyclones. As we got up after a short night of sleep on Friday morning and began exploring Las Vegas, it felt more like a trickle of Iowa State fans here and there.

My first true encounter began as I was walking toward Allegiant Stadium. I had a 10 a.m. interview with the Iowa State University Alumni Association to talk about the on-the-ground experience in Las Vegas. As I was walking in a mostly unpopulated area, I saw a man in a black I-State shirt walking toward me, presumably having already decided to walk by the stadium himself. This was my moment. "Go Cyclones," I said. "Go State!" he answered. It now felt a little more like I had arrived.

This scene repeated itself throughout Friday afternoon and evening. As we made our way up the Las Vegas strip for lunch, we discussed our strategy for when we would run into Iowa State fans. *What do we say? How do we acknowledge each other?* Turns out, we were overthinking it. Most Cyclone fans, I found, would initiate the greeting. "Go State!" or "Go Cyclones!" or just "CYCLONES!!!"

We grabbed lunch at a place called Beer Park, a rooftop patio. To that point, the Cyclone fans we saw had been scattered. As I looked around at Beer Park, I realized almost every table was full of Iowa State fans. I hypothesized that if you advertise your restaurant as an outdoor area to drink beer, Cyclone fans are probably going to find it. We sat at the bar next to a couple who were Iowa State fans and struck up a conversation.

"We've got a group of 45 people here," he said.

We discovered that we both lived in the Greater Des Moines region and had mutual acquaintances. In more than 10 years of living in the area, I had never met him, but here we were in Vegas brought together through a mutual interest.

We walked back to our hotel at the Luxor (with lots of "Go State!" and "Go Cyclones!" encounters) and decided to meet up with Dave to hit the pool. It was tough to tell how many people there were Cyclone fans as people were in their pool gear, but there were a few clues.

One man waded over to us and said, "I had to say hello to my fellow Cyclone fans. I can tell because of your farmer tans."

Later, a "Cyclone! Power!" chant broke out.

The conversation between Dave, Chris and I turned to the next day's game, and wondering if Iowa State could cover the betting spread, which had now reached 30 points in favor of the Cyclones. Would it feel like the UNI and Iowa games, when something just wasn't quite right with the offense? The consensus seemed to be that none of us would have bet on the Cyclones to cover (and I long ago learned my lesson about not betting money on the Cyclones). The way they play can sometimes tend to keep a game close even when they are comfortably in control. In a counterargument, I brought up a game from 2019 against Louisiana-Monroe, which the Cyclones won 72-20.

"It could happen," I said.

Our friend James, who was staying with us, got in shortly after that and we said goodbye to Dave and the pool to head back up the Vegas strip for dinner. The Cyclone fans we met along the way seemed to be feeling more festive. "CYCLOOOONES!!" One time, as we walked through a casino, where everyone was required to wear masks, I made eye contact with a fellow fan. He greeted me with a little fist pump, and I returned the greeting with a thumbs up. We had this greeting thing figured out.

It was difficult to tell exactly how many Cyclone fans were there. Vegas is an international tourist destination; we weren't the only show in town. That said, we were making an impression. Every now and again we would hear someone say, "What's up with all these Iowa people here?"

On our walk back from dinner, we met up with some friends from college. The day prior, my friend Nate, who attended Iowa State and now lives in Minneapolis, had sent me a text message to let me know he and another friend were going to be there. I had not seen Nate in five years. I suspect a lot of Cyclone fans would be able to tell this kind of story. In the days leading up to this trip, I learned of more and more random connections that were also making the pilgrimage.

Saturday morning arrived. "Gameday!" my brother texted me from back in Iowa. It was time for the crucial decision of what shirt I was going to wear. Iowa State's jersey combination was set to be cardinal helmets, white shirts and cardinal pants. Since I don't own a white Cyclone shirt, I figured I'd go with a cardinal shirt with a Walking Cy logo.

To start the day, we headed to the sportsbook area in the Luxor. The cardinal and gold was definitely noticeable now. The sportsbooks in Las Vegas are a college football fan's dream on a Saturday in the fall. Televisions everywhere, all showing different games. Even if you don't bet, which I don't, it's one of the best ways I have ever found to experience a college football Saturday. Nearly everyone watching the games had ISU gear on. A little while later as we walked to our breakfast spot, we passed a number of Cyclone fans. At this point, it felt like there was no need to acknowledge each other. The novelty of seeing ISU fans had evaporated a bit. There were so many of us that it wasn't as unique anymore to run across any individual Cyclone fan.

After watching the fourth quarters of a number of the early games, we headed up to the room to chill and prepare for the evening. For every UNLV or Las Vegas Raiders home game at Allegiant Stadium, there is a pregame beer garden outside of the Luxor and Mandalay Bay. It was scheduled to begin at 3:30 p.m. A little before 4, Chris, Kaci, James and I decided to head down for the pregame festivities and the game. This is when it really began to feel like a Cyclone takeover.

We got to the lobby of the Luxor, and a mass of Cyclone fans had arrived. No longer was it just a fan here or a group of fans there; it began to feel like Cyclones Everywhere, as my friends at the Alumni Association would say. Outside the casino, hundreds of people were just perched up, hanging out. We soon discovered this area was serving as an overflow of sorts. As we arrived at the beer garden, for the first time that weekend, it felt like we were all collectively together as one Cyclone Nation.

The line to get into the beer garden was long. We figured it may have been at capacity, but we decided to try the VIP entrance. They let us right in.

"This feels just like Power & Light District," Kaci said, referring to the scene when thousands of Cyclone fans gather before Big 12 basketball tournament games.

The area was packed with Cyclone fans, listening to a band, watching a college football game on a giant video screen. And the beer lines were long. I got the impression that maybe they didn't account for just how many fans would show up and want to buy drinks. It's a common mistake; there are plenty of stories from past bowl game experiences of Iowa State fans overwhelming bar staffs.

After waiting in line for five minutes or so, it felt like we hadn't moved. "Let's just head back to the casino," I said.

We stopped in a convenience store just inside the Luxor, bought a few drinks and headed in the general direction of the stadium. There was a little bit of ... frustration ... at this point. The pregame beer garden idea hadn't worked out like we hoped. We felt a little bit directionless. Kaci, sensing this, convinced us to stop and take a shot. I can't remember the last time I had taken a shot, nor is it something I normally enjoy. But when in Vegas, right? We found a spot nowhere near other people to stop, got out mini bottles of whiskey Chris had bought at the convenience store and said a cheers to friendship and the Cyclones. For the next 45 minutes or so, it was just the four of us, all close friends who were laughing, joking and having heartfelt conversation. As we've gotten near our mid-30s, these types of moments have been fewer and further between, and you enjoy them together when you get them.

We began our walk through the tunnel connecting the Luxor to Mandalay Bay, in the direction of the stadium. At this point, we were joining countless other Iowa Staters heading in the same direction, talking and joking. For the first time that day, it truly felt like gameday to me.

This is when one of the quintessential moments of the trip happened, a moment many of us will remember when we think back to Las Vegas 2021. We exited the casino and began the walk over the bridge elevated above the interstate. The road we were on was closed to traffic other than pedestrians. Even though it was just a little after 6 p.m., and the game didn't begin until 7:30, there were thousands of Cyclone fans walking in the direction of the stadium. There was only one path to get there from where we were, so everyone had no choice but to walk the same direction. As we got to the top of the sloped bridge, we stopped and stood for a while. It was a warm evening in the desert, and the early evening sun seemed to shine down at just the right angle to illuminate the scene in front of us. The mountains in the background looked like a painting. It was a surreal site, seeing a sea of Cyclone fans methodically walk toward the stadium, all in the same direction, almost glowing in the desert sun. "It looks like a bunch of zombies," Chris said.

He wasn't the only one feeling that way. Over the next couple days I would see plenty of social media references to the zombie-like crowd. We, the Zombie Cyclones, came in peace, but we definitely came to take over and we were fueled by beer and Cyclone football.

All week, I had been trying to get a good feel for the game. Would Iowa State rebound from a loss? Would the Cyclones finally get back on track and look more like the team we expected to see preseason? Or would they struggle in a game they were very much expected to win, and win big? As we joined the Zombie Cyclones in reaching the outside of the stadium, the sun shining in my eyes, I felt it. This was like those times in Kansas City where we just knew our men's basketball team was going to win. In that moment, it felt impossible to me that Iowa State could lose.

We made our way inside and began to search for the 200-level. Allegiant

Stadium is a brand-new stadium built for the NFL's Las Vegas Raiders, who relocated from Oakland after the 2019 season. The outside sort of looks like a spaceship. The inside feels much more like an NFL stadium than most college stadiums I have been to. It's hard to get lost in a place like Jack Trice Stadium, but we discovered it to be relatively easy to do in Allegiant Stadium. We felt a little bit like fish out of water as we looked for our seats in the 200-level. We found a stairwell that seemed to lead us in the right direction, until we realized we were in the suite area. We went back down and then up another stairwell, which we realized was still the wrong section, apparently with no access to our real seats.

"What a maze," I grumbled.

The third try was a charm. We found our seats, which were on the side of the field overlooking the endzone to the left of the 50-yard line.

I went back out to the concourse to grab some food and realized Chris was talking to Dave and our friend Tyler. Two weeks ago at the tailgate for the UNI game, I had given Tyler one of my New Glarus Spotted Cow beers. He vowed he was going to pay me back, and sure enough he remembered.

"Kyle! I owe you a beer! What do you want?"

The choices at the nearest beer stand were Negra Modelo and Coors Light.

"Oh, I'll do a Coors Light and a water," I said.

"OK, but I still owe you. I'm not paying you for Spotted Cow with a Coors Light."

I tried to argue to no avail.

By the time I returned, it was nearly game time, and the section and stadium had filled out with Cyclone fans. As far as I can tell, nearly all fans in the 200- and 300-level were Cyclone fans, and in the 100-level it appeared that all fans behind the Iowa State sideline and in one of the endzones were cheering for the Cyclones. There was a scattering of what appeared to be UNLV fans in the seats behind the UNLV sideline and in the other endzone. No doubt it was a home game atmosphere for Iowa State. (After the game, UNLV announced that the crowd of 35,193 was the seventh largest in history to attend a UNLV football game.)

The Iowa State crowd felt festive to me. Most fans had been in Las Vegas for at least a couple of days at this point, and we were ready to keep the fun going as the team took the field. The Iowa game the week before had the feel of a gladiator fight. This one was more like a party that broke out into a football game. As UNLV's players ran onto the field, I couldn't help but feel a little bit sorry for them knowing that what felt like 85% of the fans in their home stadium were cheering against them. Iowa State players then made their entrance to a roaring crowd.

If the party was to continue, now it would be up to the team to keep it going.

Iowa State took the ball first and it became clear the Cyclones were going to live up to their end of the deal. Iowa State's offense had an energy, and a pace, that we hadn't yet felt during the season. The Cyclones gained first down after first down to the cheers of an approving crowd. It dawned on me that even though it felt like we were the home team, we would not have our home announcer declaring "That's another Cyclone ... first down!" So, I improvised.

"That's another Cyclone ..." I yelled.

"First down!" a handful of people around me shouted.

Iowa State drove it down to the one-yard line before running back Breece Hall, who had a slower start to the season than expected, pushed it into the endzone for the Cyclone touchdown. It capped off a 12-play, 72-yard touchdown drive that took six minutes and 51 seconds to complete. We were nearly halfway through the first quarter and UNLV hadn't had the ball yet and would now be losing 7-0 when they first touched it. Any slim hopes the Rebels had of an upset had taken a major hit.

It would take even more of a hit as they failed to move the ball themselves and were forced to punt it away. Iowa State again calmly and methodically took the ball down the field and found its way into the endzone to begin the second quarter, capped off by another one-yard run by Hall. It was 14-0 Cyclones, and the party was on.

The rest of the first half was a dominant performance by the Cyclones. Of course, no game is perfect. Iowa State got the ball back and took it down to the one-yard line before Hall got stopped trying to dive into the endzone on fourth-and-one. On another drive inside the Rebel 20-yard line, Purdy got popped on a run play and lost the ball in a fumble recovered by UNLV. What realistically should have been a four-touchdown lead was still just 14-0.

The Iowa State defense, however, didn't really need the extra help. We got the impression UNLV wasn't going to score any points, let alone 14. The typical suffocating Cyclone defense wouldn't even let UNLV pick up a first down. Iowa State's offense recovered from its own miscues to score a couple more times; first on a 20-yard pass from Purdy to Xavier Hutchinson, and then on a 40-yard field goal by Andrew Mavis to make it 24-0 at half-time. UNLV's offense, meanwhile, tallied only 18 total yards in the first half, meaning Iowa State's offense scored more points than UNLV's defense gained in yards. That's about as dominating as it can get.

To begin the second half, the crowd was significantly more subdued, but this time in a relaxed way as opposed to a disappointed or worried way. Iowa State had effectively won the game in the first half, and now we could peacefully and happily watch the Cyclones coast to a win. The Coors Light I was still sipping on tasted a little sweeter.

A surreal moment happened for me in the second half. A year-and-a-half ago during the beginning of the pandemic, I had daydreamed about this trip, this game and a convincing Iowa State victory. In my daydreams, the play that would put the game decisively in Iowa State's favor was a pass from Purdy to tight end Charlie Kolar. As Iowa State drove down the field already up 24-0, I had the urge to take one more photo to document my seat in the stadium that was full of Iowa State fans. I got my cell phone out and focused on a view of the field. As I was clicking the photo, I heard the crowd around me cheering. I looked up from the screen of my phone to see in live action, Kolar was indeed running into the endzone for a touchdown. Purdy had found him on a 33-yard pass play that worked to perfection. It felt a little bit like divine intervention that I just happened to take a photo of the play I had been dreaming about for so long. It was a crystalizing moment. *I am supposed to be following this team, and going on this journey,* I thought.

UNLV, now down 31-0, put together its only good drive of the evening, getting itself into field goal range. As the Rebels faced a fourth-down play, we speculated that they would surely go for the first down. When losing 31-0 in the third quarter, the only way to have a whiff of a chance to win the game would be to score a touchdown in this spot. Instead, the field goal team came onto the field. It was a move that said, "We don't believe we can win, but we don't want to be scoreless." UNLV unofficially waved the white flag as the kick went through the uprights to cut the deficit to 31-3.

Much to our delight, Iowa State wasn't done scoring. Less than two minutes later, Purdy again found Hutchinson for a 17-yard touchdown pass to make it 38-3. In the fourth quarter, Iowa State, as it did the week prior, but a number of backups into the game, this time in much happier circumstances as the Cyclones were winning big. Mevis drilled a 54-yard field goal (sometimes it really is your night) and freshman running back Deon Silas capped off the scoring with a one-yard touchdown run. UNLV never threatened again. Iowa State 48, UNLV 3. The Cyclones covered the 30-point betting spread.

The game felt exactly like what the team needed, and what we needed for our psyche as fans. Purdy finished with 21 completions on 24 pass attempts for 288 yards and became the school's all-time leader in total yards gained (one of quite a few records he now held). Hall hit the 100-yard mark for the first time of the season. And the defense gave up only 134 total yards in another lights-out effort.

As the team got ready to go back to the locker room, they stopped in our corner of the field to salute the fans. We put our hands together and cheered our players. There is something a little extra special about sharing that moment between the team and fans after a road win. *I hope I get to experience this a few more times this season,* I thought to myself.

We exited the stadium and joined the Zombie Cyclone procession back toward the casinos. The words from Sweet Caroline rang through the air ("Bah! Bah! Bahhhh!"). It was a perfect evening to be a Cyclone. I had another crystalizing moment as I thought about how much the ISU fanbase cares, how much we have supported our team despite a history that includes more losing than winning. How even in our most anticipated season ever, one of the dominant storylines coming in revolved around conference realignment and the perception from others that we didn't really belong. I thought about how much we wanted it the week prior, and how disappointing it had been to walk out of the stadium after a loss to Iowa, and how we were quickly forced to come to terms with a less-than-perfect season.

One game doesn't change all that, and there was still a lot left for the team to accomplish. For one night, though, all was right in the world. We were all together, celebrating a Cyclone win, making the kind of memories we would likely talk about for years to come.

CHAPTER NINE

IOWA STATE VS. BAYLOR PREVIEW

SAVE YOUR BETS, BRING YOUR TENTS

Sept. 23, 2021

Let me tell you a story about why I will never bet money on Cyclone football.

The year was 2013. I went on a trip to Las Vegas with my close friends for a bachelor party. Having never bet on sports, it was extra exciting to be there for a college football weekend to be able to place some small bets on a handful of games. We eagerly headed to the nearest sportsbook on Friday evening to check out the betting lines and make our picks.

That weekend, Iowa State was set to play at Baylor. The Cyclones had started the season poorly, and Baylor was a ranked team with an explosive offense. Still, when we saw the line of Baylor being favored by somewhere around 35 points, all of the Cyclone fans in our group felt irrationally over-confident. *No way does Iowa State lose by more than 35 to Baylor.* As we all placed our bet, one member of our group, a Hawkeye fan, saw an opportunity.

"Wait, you guys are all betting on Iowa State to cover?" he asked. "Something isn't right here. I'm taking Baylor."

I'm used to Hawkeye fans disparaging Iowa State. It didn't really phase me. It should have.

The next day, my friend James and I were in one of the larger sportsbooks, which had countless televisions of all different sizes hanging on the wall.

College football was everywhere, but as kickoff drew near, the Iowa State vs. Baylor game was hard to find anywhere. Finally, we found a small television in the corner set to the broadcast. James and I found spots to stand, right next to a lone Baylor fan. This wasn't exactly a game people were clamoring to find.

There were probably dozens or even hundreds of people watching games at that point. Every now and then you'd hear a simultaneous cheer and groan as a big play would happen in one of the other games being shown. Some people were winning money, some were losing. I couldn't help but feel jealous of everyone who was cheering as we watched our game unfold.

The 35-point spread in favor of Baylor, as it turns out, was laughable. I don't remember a single thing about the game other than Baylor touchdown after Baylor touchdown. By halftime, the point spread was covered and it became quite obvious there was no reason to keep watching. I basically never quit watching at halftime, no matter how bad the game is. That day I did. It's almost embarrassing to type, but Iowa State lost 71-7. It was the type of loss that makes me appreciate the hype of this season even more.

Like I said, I never bet money on Cyclone football.

The players and coaching staffs involved in that game have moved on, but this series has produced memorable games in each of the last three years that make this year's matchup intriguing and fuel a little bit (maybe a lot) of dislike toward Baylor by Cyclone fans.

In 2018, I was sitting in a bar in Green Bay, Wis., just outside of Lambeau Field, to watch the Iowa State vs. Baylor game. It was one of the few home games I've missed in the last 16 years (besides 2020). The Cyclones were on cruise control when David Montgomery was driven out of bounds and tackled very late into the bench. Over the next few minutes, and next few plays, fights broke out that ended up with Montgomery being ejected and kept him out for the first half in a big game at Texas the following week. At least Iowa State held on for a fairly comfortable victory.

The one that really stung was the 2019 game in Waco. There are a few unfortunate similarities between the setup to that year's game and the setup for this year's game. For the 2019 game, Iowa State entered with a 2-1 record (just like this year), with a loss to Iowa (just like this year). Baylor was 3-0 (just like this year).

I was in Galena, Ill., with family. One of the fun things about a college football Saturday in a neutral area like Galena is walking around with your team gear on, like a badge of pride, a show of loyalty. You see and interact with other people who are out with friends and family, but have one eye on their team's game, wearing team gear from schools across the Midwest.

We ate a late lunch at a sports bar and restaurant in the main shopping area. It was well-known by my family that I wanted to post up and watch the Cyclone game. Since we had a larger group, they sat us upstairs at a long table. Everyone ordered lunch and drinks as the game began. As we wrapped up lunch, one by one everyone got up to go on their separate ways to do more shopping or just walk around the downtown area. I ordered a drink and settled in for the long haul, sitting all by myself at a table originally set for nine.

The game was a slog as the Cyclones couldn't get anything going offensively. As I checked Twitter, I noticed the storyline forming: On a blazing hot day in Waco, Iowa State had not gotten permission to set up its tents on the sideline and was forced to take them down and lose the shade they provided. As the afternoon sun placed the Baylor sideline fully in the shade, the Cyclone players stood on their sideline with no protection. Common sense and any care about player safety may have dictated that Baylor should make an exception and let Iowa State put up its tents. No such exception was made.

My mood was also a slog as I sat alone, and my temper (internally) was about as hot as the players on the field looked. The waitress checked up on me every now and again. She may have wanted to ask, "Are you OK?" Instead, she just offered to bring me refills.

Early in the fourth quarter, Baylor scored a touchdown to go up 20-0. I'd had enough. I no longer wanted to be sitting in a bar alone watching the Cyclones lose. I paid my tab and walked downstairs. *Maybe I'll walk back to the hotel and catch the rest of the fourth quarter in our room,* I thought.

As I walked toward the door … my dad walked in.

"Want to watch the rest of the game?" he asked cheerily, blissfully unaware of the score.

"Uhhh, sure," I said. I wasn't going to turn down this nice gesture and the opportunity to sit and have a drink with my dad, even if I was upset. "I just left our table upstairs. Let's grab another."

This time, they put us in a room on the main floor. The room was set up primarily for tables of four. There were televisions on, but nobody seemed overly interested in the games. I positioned myself to watch the TV showing the Cyclone game. About that time, another small group walked in and sat down.

"Shoot, the Cyclones are losing," a man said. "Oh well." It was clear he was not as emotionally invested as I was.

The next few minutes were thrilling.

Iowa State, down 20-0, finally got things going. The sun began to set. It wasn't quite as unforgiving on the Iowa State sideline. Suddenly, everything worked. The Cyclones scored on three straight possessions to take a 21-20 lead, capped off by a 20-yard touchdown pass from Cyclone quarterback Brock Purdy to tight end Charlie Kolar, which caused me to audibly yell "YES!" in a way that made a few people look in my direction. The Cyclone non-superfan a few tables over noticed.

"Sorry," I said, pointing at the television. "I'm excited."

He was pleasantly surprised. I was ecstatic, having watched one of the most thrilling 12 minutes of Iowa State football I had ever seen.

I went from being distraught to believing that maybe this Cyclone team was the team of destiny. The team to come back from 20 points down on the road when everything else had gone against them. This could be the team to make something special happen.

Who needed tents anyway?

Baylor had one last chance and marched down the field, setting themselves up for a 38-yard field goal try to win the game. In entered a kicker who had never made a field goal at the collegiate level, and who had missed a kick already that day. *Come on, miss it. Please.* When it counted the most, he put it right through the uprights. Baylor 23, Iowa State 21.

I put on a brave face.

"Shoot. What a great game. Can't be upset by that comeback," I said to my dad and my new acquaintances, wishing internally that I could be more like the casual fan who didn't let this type of loss ruin his day.

As we left the bar to walk back toward the hotel, the scene was much the same as earlier but felt completely different to me. I was hyper-aware that I was walking around in an Iowa State shirt, and I was sure that all the other college football fans with their Hawkeye and Gopher and Badger shirts were either pitying me or silently laughing at me. In reality, the game had just ended and they likely had no idea the Cyclones just lost. But I knew.

In hindsight, that game was typical of how both teams' seasons went. Baylor won close game after close game. Iowa State lost close game after close game. I think it's fair to say I will not be able to get the 2019 game, and its ultimate negative impact on the season, out of my mind as I travel to Waco for Saturday's game.

Last year's game didn't exactly help. By the time the 2020 game rolled around, Baylor had a new head coach in Dave Aranda and Iowa State was in the midst of its best season in school history. Yet the Bears almost derailed Iowa State's quest to make the Big 12 Championship. Brock Purdy threw three first-half interceptions, the last of which was returned for a touchdown to give the Bears a 21-7 lead. It felt like the Iowa State of old when the Cyclones fumbled a punt return early in the third quarter. With a 21-10 lead, the Bears had a chance to score another touchdown and really deflate the Cyclones' hopes. In another sign of many that these Cyclones were different, Iowa State held Baylor to a field goal and then, led by a rejuvenated Purdy, scored the next four touchdowns to take a 38-24 lead. Linebacker Mike Rose intercepted a pass in the endzone in the final minute to preserve a 38-31 victory.

Of the four games Iowa State has played so far this season, in some ways this one has the least hype around it. The UNI game was the first in front of a full stadium since 2019. The Iowa game brought out the emotions that can only be caused by a rivalry. The trip to Las Vegas was a giant party. This weekend's game, though, is probably the most important so far. This is game one of the Big 12 season, and therefore the first game that counts toward getting back to the Big 12 Championship. After a rollercoaster in the first three weeks, this game will provide its own unique challenge that Iowa State hasn't faced in nearly two seasons: a true road game in a full stadium where the crowd will be heavily against the Cyclones.

It's easy to feel good about Iowa State's chances. The team played loose and seemed to have fun at UNLV, and a veteran group like this one might respond well to a true road environment in a way younger teams could struggle with. Unlike the game at Baylor in 2013, this year's betting line is slightly in favor of the Cyclones. Unlike the game at Baylor in 2019, Iowa State players should have tents to block the sun this year.

Still, this does not feel like the gimme I was hoping it would be when the schedule came out. Baylor is coming off a 2-7 season but has started strong at 3-0 this year (albeit against easy competition). Last year, the Bears proved they were capable of winning if Iowa State doesn't bring its A-game from the get-go.

The nature of a college football game is that the sample size — 12 games

— is so small that one or two games can really swing a season. This one feels like a swing game. There's still a nervousness from the start of the season that couldn't be fully erased in a game against a poor UNLV team. A win, and the hype will start to build back up. A loss, and this team will have a lot of work to salvage its goal of getting back to the Big 12 Championship.

Simply put, for Iowa State to have the special season we are still hoping for, it has to find a way to win these types of games. If I was a betting man, I would put money on it.

CHAPTER TEN

IOWA STATE VS. BAYLOR RECAP

IT'S ALL PART OF THE JOURNEY

Sept. 28, 2021

Perspective. It can be tough to keep in life sometimes, particularly when you really want something.

On Saturday in Waco, Texas, I was reminded of how important it is to keep perspective. Surrounded by hundreds of Iowa State fans at the Cyclone Club of Dallas/Fort Worth's tailgate party, Iowa State Director of Athletics Jamie Pollard said a few words to the crowd.

Pollard shared an anecdote about his experience at the Fiesta Bowl to cap the 2020 season. How for years he had dreamed of that experience and having 30,000-plus Cyclone fans in attendance to celebrate, but instead the stadium was nearly empty due to pandemic protocols. He reminded us that sometimes we, as humans, focus so much on the destination that we forget to enjoy the journey. The destination can be great but may not live up to what you build it up to be in your mind.

The journey is what makes the destination worthwhile.

The words hit home with me as I continued my own journey as a fan following my favorite team. I looked around and thought about where I was. I had taken a trip, by myself, to a town in the middle of Texas to watch a game. I went on the trip not knowing anyone who would be there and trusting that I'd be able to make friends. At that moment I was enjoying a beautiful day surrounded by Cyclone fans who were just happy to be there, many of whom do not get the chance to attend games as often as I do living in Iowa. It was the kind of experience I would never have dared take just a couple years ago.

Enjoy the journey. Don't worry about the destination, I told myself. Indeed, as I wrote way back in the forward, I chose this season for what it could be, not what I knew it was going to be. There was never any guarantee that Iowa State would live up to preseason hype, but I was going all in this season regardless. It was a perfect storm of factors for this season and for my life to take this journey.

A few hours later, I again reminded myself to enjoy the journey. Iowa State was down by eight to Baylor in the final minutes but had the ball and was driving down the field. It wasn't the greatest position to be in, for sure. My anxiety was telling me that even if Iowa State managed to score a touchdown, it would still need to make a two-point conversion just to tie the game — essentially a 50/50 proposition. And if the Cyclones did tie the game, they'd need to stop Baylor from getting into field goal range in the final seconds. And if they did that, they'd still need to go into overtime, where anything could happen. A lot had to go right for Iowa State to win.

I took a deep breath and reminded myself I couldn't control the outcome. I could only enjoy the journey. I was surrounded by hundreds of passionate Cyclone fans in a road venue (Cyclones vs. The World!) and I was watching a team led by some all-time great Cyclones try to lead an all-time great moment. This was exactly the type of situation I had in mind when I decided to write about this season. The chance to see my team do something improbable, and great, in a situation that just maybe would become an all-time great moment in my fandom.

It had been a frustrating game, but maybe, just maybe, these Cyclones could make magic happen.

They did. And then they didn't. We got a brief few moments of cheering and high-fiving when Iowa State scored a touchdown with less than 30 seconds left. And then my fears came to fruition on a regrettable two-point conversion attempt. Just four weeks ago we were dreaming of the College Football Playoff. Now, after a 31-29 loss, Iowa State was 2-2, 0-1 in the Big 12, and the dream season was becoming considerably less dreamy.

As we walked out of the stadium, a group of what appeared to be Baylor students were heckling Iowa State fans as they walked by. I was walking with my new friends Adam and Nicole, who hosted me for the weekend. To our surprise, Nicole walked up to the group. *Oh no,* I thought. I was worried about a verbal argument. Instead, Nicole offered to chug a beer with them. I immediately knew this was a story Adam and Nicole would tell for years, and I was again reminded about the nature of the journey. We were disappointed, but we don't do this just to see our team win championships (as much as we want that to happen). We do this to enjoy being part of a community of fans, to feel emotions about the outcome of a game, and to make memories. Even in a loss, we made memories that would keep us coming back for more.

———

Despite the fact that I had made plans to go to every game in 2021, there was an asterisk all offseason due to a personal conflict during the Iowa State road trip to Baylor. I spent most of my encounters telling people, "Yeah, I'm going to every game, except one." The "except one" was a qualifier I had to continue to throw in when describing these plans.

The reason was a good reason. A good friend of our family was set to get married on the day of the Baylor game. My wife, Paige, was a bridesmaid. I was torn. Do I go to a friend's wedding, or do I go to the Iowa State game? Normally, it wouldn't even be a question. However, I'm only doing a journey like this once, not to mention writing a book about it.

As the season started, I had become set on going to the wedding. Until the week after the Northern Iowa game, when my thought process began to change.

Now, as I've gone through this journey, I have tried my hardest to not let the fact that I'm writing a book influence the interactions I have with friends, family and Cyclone fans. The stories I have told are authentic, which I thought was of utmost importance for the integrity of this journey. That said, it's difficult to get around the fact that publicly stating I was writing a book about this season led to an opportunity that is now part of the journey, and therefore part of the story.

Anyway, the week between the UNI and Iowa games, someone who read my UNI recap online reached out to me. He let me know he lived in Waco with his young family, was an Iowa State graduate and was helping plan a tailgate party for the Iowa State game at Baylor. If we needed a place to stay for the game, he said, we were welcome to stay with him.

A free place to stay and a road tailgate with Cyclone fans? It seemed like a great opportunity, exactly the kind of experience I was hoping to have when I set out to go all in on this season.

I was now even more torn.

The other factor is that I was discovering how much of this journey was contingent on being there. Seeing the tailgate lots fill up for the first time in two seasons for the UNI game. Feeling the anticipation for the Iowa game, the type I've rarely if ever felt before. Seeing the Zombie Cyclones make their way to and from Allegiant Stadium in Las Vegas. These were once-in-a-lifetime experiences that I will not soon forget. To do this right, I began to feel like I had to be there.

After quite a few conversations with my wife, and the sincerest apologies to my friends, I decided the day after getting back from Las Vegas to take the trip. Even as I typed these words I still felt a little guilty and more than a little melancholy to be missing a special day — a once-in-a-lifetime opportunity for dear friends. I also felt extra grateful for the encouragement and understanding they showed in supporting me as I chased a dream of writing this book.

After all that, on two days' notice, my wife, Paige, helped me book a flight out of Des Moines International Airport into Austin, Texas, and a car rental from Austin to drive the 90 minutes or so to Waco. My new friend Adam, the Iowa State grad who so graciously offered me a place to stay, let me know to book a spot at the Cyclone Club of Dallas/Fort Worth tailgate. As I looked into it more, I discovered that it seemed the DFW Cyclones took great pride in putting on a party for the Iowa State fans in the area who may not get to Jack Trice Stadium on a regular basis. In the past, they had hosted 700 people at this tailgate. They pointed out that for the cost of admission, they would provide the food and drinks, removing the need for tailgaters to worry about packing a cooler. This sounded like a perfect option for someone like me. Furthermore, there was an option to buy tickets through their group where we could all sit together. Perhaps the best part was that proceeds would go to support the DFW Cyclones Scholarship Endowment Fund and the Texas Firewalkers Disaster Assistance Fund. It was a no-brainer to register for the tailgate and purchase tickets through this group.

I particularly enjoyed how organized the group was and how seriously they took their role in supporting the Cyclones. In a follow-up email after I registered, the club reminded fans that Baylor tends to wear gold, green and black (they announced the day before the game that it would be an all-gold uniform, and that Bears fans were encouraged to wear gold). Therefore, we should "color it cardinal."

"We will have a really nice contingent and we want those TV cameras to see us in full force," the email said.

That made my wardrobe decision easier. The Cyclones were set to wear cardinal helmets, white jerseys and white pants. I, however, would be wearing a cardinal t-shirt. (In fact, it would be the same Walking Cy logo t-shirt I had worn to the UNLV game. *Keep the good luck going,* I figured.)

The email also reminded fans to be respectful of opposing fans and represent our university well — always a good reminder. It pointed out that a number of parents of players were expected to be at the tailgate, another fun bonus. And they encouraged locals to bring a few extra lawn chairs for those of us who were flying in for the game and therefore would be unable to pack one ourselves. Much appreciated.

I found my gate at Des Moines International Airport on Friday afternoon. It didn't quite resemble the pictures I saw from the trip to Las Vegas, but there were a handful of people wearing Iowa State gear. My decision to make this flight was feeling a little less crazy.

Ironically, my brother and his wife were traveling with some friends to Las Vegas. Our time at the airport overlapped by just a few minutes.

I begged him: "Please don't bet on Iowa State."

I reminded him of what happened when I bet on the Cyclones in a game that ended up 71-7 in favor of Baylor. I didn't need that bad mojo. As a Hawkeye fan, he didn't seem that concerned. "New era. New coach," was his mindset. I couldn't help but wonder if he just enjoyed seeing me superstitiously fret.

I was seated on the airplane across from a couple who was also on their way to the game.

"Go Cyclones," we said to each other, followed by a brief "Cyclone! Power!" chant between the two of them.

I was enjoying the festive atmosphere already. We struck up a conversation for a few minutes. Although they typically went to only a couple home games a year, they had never been to Waco and thought it would be a fun road game to see. *Perhaps someday I'll be more like these fans and just go to a few games a season,* I thought. But not today.

We landed, pulled into an airstrip away from the main terminal, and took a shuttle mostly full of Cyclone fans to the main terminal, which took what felt like a half hour. It gave me a chance to be around a few Cyclone fans, one of whom was a player's parent. It was great to hear that his son enjoyed playing for ISU coach Matt Campbell and reminded me that these players were still college students, younger than me by more than 10 years. It was perspective I needed to keep following the next day's game.

I made the 90-minute-or-so drive to Waco and met up with my hosts, Adam and Nicole. I was slightly nervous, taking a chance on staying with people I didn't know. My fears were immediately eased. It's difficult to explain how I knew, but I just knew they were good people and we clicked.

Adam and I took an Uber to a bar in downtown Waco, where the DFW Cyclones had hosted a happy hour earlier in the evening. A few people were still hanging out. A group that had also flown from Des Moines met up with us, and one person in the group knew Adam from Twitter. A Baylor student came up to our group to let us know she was from Iowa and was happy to see us here. We asked who she was cheering for.

"Baylor, but I also hope Iowa State does well," she said.

That wasn't quite the answer our group wanted to hear as a few people gave her a hard time (all in good fun, of course). I'm pretty sure her friend — with no Iowa ties — had no idea what she was getting into.

Adam and I checked out Waco Ale Company, a brewery with a nice selection of IPA's and friendly bartenders. Some more Cyclone fans who Adam knew came to our table to catch up. I could tell this was a reunion of sorts for Cyclone fans living in Dallas/Fort Worth, Austin, Waco and surrounding areas.

The next morning, we got up early to head to the tailgate. Despite the fact it was a 2:30 p.m. game and the tailgate didn't officially begin until 9:30 a.m., Adam wanted to get there early to help with setup. We left his house around 7 a.m., with me wondering how I was ever going to catch up on sleep after the trip the week prior to Las Vegas and now an early tailgate start in Waco. All part of the journey.

As we drove, I checked in with my brother.

"Gameday!" I texted.

He let me know he was up placing his bets. Including one on … Iowa State to cover. I tried to warn him, but as he later pointed out, "I figured I would win either way," with a wink-face emoji. As a Hawkeye fan, it didn't bother him that much if Iowa State were to lose.

We arrived at the tailgate and began helping with setup with the handful of other volunteers. Adam was a great friend to have, as he introduced me to a number of the volunteers. I was struck by the pride the DFW Cyclones took in being part of this group. They even had merchandise with the I-State logo modified to include the design of the Texas flag. I, of course, had to buy a t-shirt.

I met one fan who lived in Texas and had season tickets to Jack Trice Stadium.

"How do you make it to all the games," I asked, feeling impressed at this dedication.

"We are able to plan our schedule and travel around it," she said.

Another fan still had family in Iowa and had just made it to the UNI game.

The tailgate began to fill up as more people arrived. I noticed a lot of the people seemed to know each other. They planned similar tailgates whenever Iowa State played road games against other Texas schools, and I suspect a community has formed between them. For some, I imagined this game had to be similar to the feeling I feel on the opening game each season, like it was Christmas morning and they could barely hide their anticipation. Hundreds of people showed up. It felt like a home game.

I ran into a friend and former coworker, a big Iowa State fan who has traveled to most road games for years. He introduced me to a few of his traveling buddies.

One of them told me, "It's fun to cheer for a good team. But if they weren't good, I would be here anyway. It's an addiction."

A little while later, one of the organizers announced over the speakers the team buses were on the way and would be driving by any second.

"Let's go wave at them," he encouraged us.

People headed toward the side of the road, and there came the buses. People waved and cheered as a number of buses pulled through. The scene made me swell with pride. I'm a sucker for those sorts of things.

I saw the same people I had met at the bar the night before who had flown from Des Moines. We took in the scene and remarked how amazing it was that so many people had shown up to a road game tailgate. Across the crowd, I saw someone who I was almost sure was a former marching band mate. *Is that her?* She began to walk over and I realized it was. She and her husband, who live in Iowa, had also decided to make the trip for the weekend. I also struck up a conversation with a man who was in the marching band years before me and is still heavily involved in the Iowa State

Alumni Band. We swapped old band stories — such as having cans of beer or other projectiles thrown at us at opposing stadiums. We could laugh about it all these years later.

Pollard showed up and gave his remarks. He mentioned that normally he was on the team bus when it pulled through and assured us the players notice the fans when they gather and cheer as the buses pull by. He reminded us to enjoy the journey.

A few minutes later, Jeff Johnson with the ISU Alumni Association led the crowd in cheers. When I was a student in the band, Johnson would come on the field before games and lead the crowd in cheers like "I-S-U!" or "Cyclone! Power!" It was a shot in the arm for the stadium at that time. I don't know how else to explain it other than … we just didn't really know how to do that sort of thing all that well. Eventually, we learned how to do it ourselves and Johnson wasn't needed in that role anymore. I also remember when we would play as a band at pep rallies or donor events before games or student orientation that Johnson would also be there leading cheers. Seeing him do it for the DFW Cyclone tailgate brought me back. It felt just like it did before as Johnson pointed at different sections of the crowd to direct them when to cheer.

"We're going to do Cyclone Power. Watch where I point to know when to say your line!"

He would jokingly chide us if we weren't paying enough attention. Every now and again he'd stop and encourage us to be louder. By the end of it, everyone was in the gameday mood.

A little after 2 p.m., we headed to the stadium. As we got closer to the gates, I began to truly realize for the first time that day that Iowa State was the road team. Although the tailgate felt similar to the experience in Las Vegas in terms of being surrounded by Cyclone fans, the stadium would be hostile toward Iowa State.

I was struck by the beauty of McClane Stadium. It is located on the Brazos River, and Nicole pointed out it was just one of a few stadiums where people could "sailgate" on boats before the game.

We filed in and mixed in with the Baylor fans. It felt a little bit like we were on the strip in Las Vegas as every now and then we'd see other Iowa State fans and say, "Go Cyclones!" The DFW Cyclone sections were in the 300-level at the very back of the stadium behind the endzone. Adam and Nicole's seats were a section over, so we went on our separate ways. I walked (and walked) all the way up to row 18, with just a few rows behind me. The other end of the stadium was open, and we could see the river in the background. I didn't notice any sailgaters that day. It could have been too hot to be out on a boat in the sun on a day in the upper 80s. It was nice where I was, surrounded by Cyclone fans in the road team stadium, and in seats that were covered by the stadium's overhang. A little lower and we would have been stuck in the sun as many people on our half of the stadium were. I noticed this year Iowa State was allowed to have its tents on the sideline.

I took my seat next to some other Cyclone fans. Over the course of the game, I got to know them a bit. One man was from the Dallas/Fort Worth area, one from Houston and one from San Antonio. The San Antonio Cyclone told me he had always wanted to come to a DFW event and decided to make the drive for this game. We discovered that we both had Pella ties (my hometown, his college town). He talked about how much fun it had been to have Iowa State play in the Alamo Bowl in San Antonio in 2018.

We cheered as the Cyclones ran onto the field, being as loud as we could in the road stadium. Iowa State took the ball first. *Let's go score, and we can take control of this game early,* I thought. Iowa State began driving down the field but faced a fourth-and-two at the Baylor 26-yard line. I expected Campbell to send the field goal unit out, but he didn't flinch. Iowa State was going for it, a sign in my mind that the team was going to show more urgency in conference play. Running back Breece Hall picked up a nine-yard gain to pick up the first down and scored three plays later on a two-yard run to loud cheers from our section. Iowa State 7, Baylor 0.

"Best drive of the season so far!" I texted my friends watching from home.

I was feeling good. Iowa State's defense had been lights out so far during the season. I didn't think Baylor would have the lead during this game. I was wrong.

The defense looked the worst it had all season giving up an eight-play, 75-yard drive to allow Baylor to tie the game at 7-7. *Ouch.* On their next possession, the Cyclones picked up a first down, but were forced to punt. *That's OK,* I thought. *Reverse the field.*

If there was a Bingo card on Iowa State miscues it feels like we have seen too often over the years, the next play would have checked a box. The punt went only 16 yards. (In the stands, we thought he just shanked it, but later I learned it was partially blocked. Either way it's a play that just can't happen for Iowa State.) Baylor took the ball near midfield, and again began to drive.

The Baylor crowd was very much enjoying this, with many fans giving an enthusiastic standing ovation as the first quarter ended. On the first play of the second quarter, Baylor again found the endzone on a 21-yard pass from Gerry Bohanon to Tyquan Thornton to take a 14-7 lead. This was not the defense we were accustomed to seeing.

I still had confidence. It became a trend during 2020 that the Iowa State defense would give up drives and points early but tighten up as they adjusted to the opposing team's gameplan. After the Cyclones answered with a field goal drive to make it 14-10, I remarked that now would be a great time for the defense to do what they do. Instead, Baylor marched right down the field again for a nine-play, 75-yard drive, capped by a 33-yard touchdown pass to a wide open Ben Sims. A long touchdown pass, so rare in the Campbell era, felt too familiar to other less successful periods of Cyclone football. *Check another square on the Bingo card.* The Bears were seemingly doing whatever they wanted offensively, and Iowa State hadn't found an answer yet.

Now down 21-10 with just more than five minutes to play in the half, we had the feeling Iowa State really needed to answer going into the locker room. The Cyclones put together another good drive, which stalled as they faced a fourth-and-11 from the 30-yard line of Baylor. This time Campbell sent the field goal unit out for a 47-yard attempt. The Baylor crowd made noise to try and distract the kicker, and the crowd's cheers told me it was no good even before I saw the ball go wide left. Missed field goal. *Another box on the Bingo card.*

Iowa State's defense finally made a three-and-out stop to force Baylor to punt.

"This is a tough spot for a freshman," the fan next to me said, referring to Cyclone punt returner Jaylin Noel, who had just begun fielding punts a week ago at UNLV.

A cannon of a punt went 58 yards and Noel had to chase it backwards … and dropped it around the 15-yard line. *What a disaster!* It looked like the Baylor defender was going to pounce, but somehow Noel fought for the ball and recovered it. The Bingo card box of fumbling a punt return had been checked, but the disaster was averted due to a gutsy effort by the freshman to make the play.

Iowa State again put together a good drive, settling for a 38-yard field goal that went through with four seconds left in the half to cut the deficit to 21-13.

For as poor as the first half had felt at times, the Cyclones were still very much in it. *Now is the time for the defense to tighten up!* I thought. Instead, Baylor again moved the ball down the field before Iowa State's Isheem Young forced Bohanon to fumble. Iowa State's Kym-Mani King recovered to give the Cyclones new life.

Iowa State again drove down the field, but on third-and-six Purdy missed an open Xavier Hutchinson, again forcing Iowa State to settle for a field goal attempt. This time, kicker Andrew Mevis put it through the uprights to cut the lead to 21-16. Slowly but surely, Iowa State seemed to be turning the tide.

I went down to the restroom and tried to get back to my seat before the game resumed. As I returned to the concourse, I knew what was happening before I saw it. I heard the crowd cheer and looked through the openings in the concourse to see Baylor fans come to their feet. Baylor was returning a kickoff — and far. I was able to catch the feed on the stadium video board just in time to catch Baylor's Trestan Ebner complete a 98-yard touchdown return. Kickoff return coverage had been an Achilles heel for Iowa State in 2020 and was widely considered one of the top areas the team would have to fix if it was to compete for a championship in 2021. Most kicks on the day went for touchbacks, exactly to plan. This one did not, and it cost Iowa State dearly. *Another box checked on the Cyclone miscue Bingo card.* I got back up to my seat and sarcastically asked my seat neighbor from Austin if I missed anything. He started to answer seriously, and I cut him off. "I know … I saw it."

Iowa State was now down 28-16, and — as I had in the UNI game, as I had in the Iowa game — I was again forced to begin to come to terms with what an Iowa State loss would mean in this journey.

Nothing good.

It looked even more dire when Iowa State went three-and-out and was forced to punt. This time, though, the Iowa State defense had begun to find its groove and forced a return punt (another tricky punt this time caught cleanly by Noel). The Cyclones were able to put thoughts of losing out of my mind. Hall, who had not performed quite as well as the high level we had expected coming into the season, broke a 42-yard run. In a game that seemed to get wackier as it went, the Cyclones were called for a 15-yard penalty when the referee tripped over someone on the Iowa State sideline. From my seat, Campbell appeared to be furious with the ref as we all wondered if we had ever seen a call quite like that. No matter. The next play Purdy found Chase Allen for a 24-yard gain, and two plays later found Charlie Kolar for

30 yards down to the two-yard line. Hall ran it in for a touchdown from the two, and Iowa State was back in it down 28-23. A few minutes later, as the game headed to the fourth quarter, the hundreds of Cyclone fans in our area of the stadium made our voices heard.

"Let's go State! Let's go State! Let's go State!" we chanted.

The momentum was on our side. Adam, sitting a section over, texted me "30-28," referencing that he thought the Cyclones were going to score another touchdown and win the game.

I returned the text: "37-28." I was feeling good.

Time for a Cyclone win.

That's when we saw two plays that I am convinced would have led to an Iowa State win had they gone the Cyclones' way.

First, on third-and-11, with the Cyclone fans making noise, Bohanon was sacked by ISU defender Will McDonald and fumbled the ball around the 15-yard line. We held our breath as the players fought for the ball. *Could this finally be the really big turnover we've been waiting for??* And then the referee signaled: Baylor ball. Still, we cheered the defense off the field for fourth down. On Iowa State's second play of the possession, Hall broke free again for 34 yards. On second-and-six from the Baylor 22, Purdy wound up to throw to Kolar, who was wide open heading to the endzone. I'm pretty sure I started cheering as I saw the pass released, and I looked at Kolar with nobody around him. I was just waiting for the ball to fall into his hands.

Where's the ball?

I heard a cheer, and my brain registered, *This is too loud to be a cheer for Iowa State.* I hadn't even seen a Baylor defender tip the ball at the line of scrimmage and another defender intercept the pass. A sure touchdown turned into a costly turnover.

Another Bingo square checked.

The Cyclone defense had found its game now, forcing another punt (which Noel again fielded nicely while running backwards). Iowa State was forced to punt it right back, and Ebner fielded a line drive with space around him. The Baylor crowd again came to its feet as Ebner broke a long gain. It felt as though this might be the final blow, but Iowa State forced him out of bounds at the 16-yard line — the same spot where the punt had originally occurred. It was going to take another great defensive effort to keep the Cyclones in the game, and it was. Iowa State forced a field goal, making the score 31-23 with just over 5:30 remaining.

My normal seatmate, Chris, was back in Iowa for this game and was watching on delay and therefore not texting me during the game. A section over, Adam took his spot.

"Somehow we are still in this," I texted him, trying to put positivity into the world.

"It's a tease," he responded. *Bad omen, dude!*

He wasn't wrong, unfortunately.

Iowa State took the ball back, and it became clear the Cyclones were in no hurry. Their plan seemed to be score on this possession, tie the game with a two-point conversion and go to overtime. I would argue what happened next would be remembered as one of the great drives in Iowa State football history, in the moment it needed to happen the most … if only the game outcome would have turned out differently.

With the Baylor crowd roaring (or at least what was left, as a number of fans on the sunny side of the stadium had exited early), Iowa State put together a methodical drive. Purdy found Allen for a 21-yard gain to start it. On third-and-one, he found Kolar again for a two-yard gain to move the sticks. Iowa State faced a fourth-and-one, with the game hanging in the balance. Hall powered ahead for two to keep the drive alive. *Enjoy the journey*, I told myself. Purdy ran for 10 yards for another first down to the 22. The clock ticked under a minute. On third-and-six, Purdy found Hall for seven yards and a first down at the Baylor 11. Purdy then threw to Kolar who got into the endzone as we erupted in cheers.

But wait.

"There's a flag down," my neighbor from San Antonio pointed out.

The referees talked for an agonizingly long time. The call was ineligible man downfield against Iowa State. It was another losing in the margins play, and another Bingo card box checked.

Instead of scoring, Iowa State had to run a play from the 16-yard line. Purdy threw it to Hall, who slipped a defender and walked calmly into the endzone. Iowa State had scored again, this time with no penalty, to make it 31-29 and give itself a chance to tie with a two-point conversion.

I was simultaneously impressed, ecstatic and quite nervous. I had been so close to mentally giving up a few times that day. Iowa State had seemed to overcome mistake after mistake, and multiple times had narrowly avoided completely getting blown out. Now it was down to one play to keep the game alive. I had a bad feeling; my perception has long been that the Cyclones for some reason struggle in short-yardage situations close to the goal line. I have no data to back this up, but it just feels like it.

I felt a little more confident as Iowa State came to the line. The players seemed to have a purpose. Purdy lined up under center, which is very unusual (he usually lines up in a shotgun formation a few yards behind the center). They seemed to be trying something outside the box. Immediately it became clear the play wasn't going to work. The snap was clunky, and Purdy had a difficult time handling it. By the time he had a firm grip on the football, he was under pressure from a Baylor defender and had to heave it desperately toward the endzone, where it was intercepted by another Baylor defender as the crowd let out a roar.

It struck me just how much the players wanted it as I saw Kolar and others sit on the ground dejected for a few seconds. As upset as I was, I knew they had to be heartbroken.

Still, Iowa State had one more chance. Baylor was called for unsportsmanlike conduct on the two-point attempt, meaning the kickoff with 0:24 left would be moved up 15 yards. If Iowa State could recover, it could get into position for a field goal with one or two strong plays. Having seen the Cyclones nearly convert an onside kick successfully against Iowa, there was reason to believe it was possible. The kick, however, went right into the hands of a Baylor receiver. My seatmates began to leave, until ... "Offside, on the receiving team." Iowa State would get to move up five more yards and try again.

"How many times has this gone against us? Maybe just this once it can go our way," one fan said.

Unfortunately for Iowa State, it was the same result. Baylor ran out the clock for a 31-29 win.

My text message chain was devastated (besides Chris who wouldn't be devastated for a few more hours). I was numb. As we filed out, I caught up with Adam and Nicole and the same friends we had met the night prior at the brewery, who asked how I was going to put this into words. I didn't know yet.

The reality I needed to come to terms with was that Iowa State was no longer a playoff contender. That possible destination was gone by September. Nobody envisioned this. It was pretty much the worst possible scenario to begin the season (other than a loss against UNI). The whole backdrop of this being a special season, for now, was off the table. Iowa State would have a lot of work to do even to make it back to the Big 12 Championship Game, which now felt like the ceiling for the season. One of the reasons I had picked this season to take this journey was now proving to backfire.

Baylor fans were happy, now at 4-0 with a win over a ranked team (though Iowa State dropped out of the AP rankings the next day). It's a special kind of sports misery being forced to walk out of a road team stadium after their team wins and your team loses. Luckily their fans were good-natured.

I checked my phone and had a text message from my mom. "So sorry! Love you!!" She is the best.

We walked by one spot outside the stadium where a number of Cyclone fans were standing around. I realized this must have been the players' parents as a number of them were wearing jerseys and they were standing by what looked to be a potential entrance to the locker room. I couldn't recall ever having seen the players' parents after a loss. It's something I likely wouldn't have noticed at Jack Trice Stadium but was more noticeable in the road venue. Perhaps I was projecting my own feelings, but they seemed dejected. I thought about how difficult it would feel to be as invested as they are and witness a heartbreaking loss, knowing the pain their sons were feeling. I reminded myself again: As bad as I felt, they felt worse.

As we got ready to cross the street, we noticed some Baylor college students who seemed to be in an animated conversation with a few Iowa State fans that were walking by. It was a close game, with one team scoring a thrilling win and the other a frustrating loss. Naturally, all it would take would be a few ill-timed words to flare tempers a bit. I pointed out the scene to Adam and Nicole when a Baylor fan approached us.

"I hope you don't make judgements based on that," he said.

"Nah," I replied.

"Did you have fun?" he asked. "Well, other than the outcome at least?"

"Yeah, it was actually a lot of fun," I replied. "You have a nice stadium and that was a really entertaining game. I can't complain."

Around that time, Nicole was on her way to have a few words, or rather, a drink, with the college-aged fans.

"That's one way to make peace!" I told our new Baylor friend as we went our separate ways.

We got back to the tailgate as it was being torn down. The energy was considerably down from earlier. There's something so deflating about a loss like we just witnessed, especially after what had been a wonderful day, and especially while there was still work to be done in tearing down the tail-gate party.

The mood was bittersweet. The letdown from the game was interspersed with the feeling of a successful tailgate and the recognition that a good time was had by all. After merchandise was packed up and tables were put away, everyone began to say their goodbyes. The common refrain was, "Great tail-gate." I wholeheartedly agreed.

As we drove away, Adam and I discussed the game a bit more. We were frustrated by the special teams play, questioned the two-point conversion attempt play call and were generally distraught that Iowa State had ultimately outgained Baylor by nearly 200 total yards, had gained 12 more first downs than the Bears and had held onto possession for 11 more minutes than Baylor. And still lost. The Cyclone miscue Bingo card items — the kickoff return for a touchdown, the missed field goal, the ill-timed interception and the rest — cost Iowa State the game. I should have stayed off Twitter but I couldn't help but scroll through. It was not a happy place.

"I think it's time to readjust expectations," I said.

We agreed that there was still a lot of hope for this team, but the margin for error was gone.

The next morning, I flew out of Austin early and had a four-hour layover in Charlotte, where I reflected and wrote much of this chapter.

I had to accept reality. This team was not going to make the College Football Playoff. This team could ultimately be significantly less successful than we hoped. All offseason I had assumed 9-3 was going to be the worst Iowa State could possibly do. Now a worse record didn't seem to be out of the question. I thought again about the fact that I had chosen to write a book about this season, the season I was hoping was going to be so special.

And for some reason, I was relaxed.

Pollard's words rung true. Enjoy the journey. Saturday's journey, outside of the outcome of the game, was a great and memorable day in my life. I truly had a fun time and I wouldn't have done it without the pull of the Cyclones and this particular Cyclone team. I thought of the fan who told me he'd be there whether or not the team was good. I thought of the pride I had in the team itself, which kept coming back despite so many times it could have given up. The group of seniors who had given so much to the program, and the parents who surely had to comfort their sons after a tough loss. They would all be there next week.

And I was reminded that the Cyclones were 13-2 in the month of October since 2017. There was still time to make this a good season, or even a great season, or even a special season.

I decided it was time to enjoy the journey without worrying about the destination. For better or worse, I was part of this and this was part of me. Whatever happened, I was going to be there to cheer on the Cyclones.

CHAPTER ELEVEN

A MUST-WIN AGAINST A LONG-TIME CONFERENCE FOE

Sept. 30, 2021

There have been some memorable moments for Iowa State against Kansas over the years. Some of my favorites include the 2015 game when ESPN's "College GameDay" came to Hilton Coliseum to witness a Cyclone win over the Jayhawks. Later that season, Iowa State defeated Kansas for the Big 12 tournament title in Kansas City. Then, there was the time in 2017 when Deonte Burton hit a shot in transition from near halfcourt and Donovan Jackson made a three-pointer from the corner to give Iowa State a season-changing win and make Allen Fieldhouse "just another gym." Oh, and the 2019 Big 12 tournament title win against the Jayhawks was also pretty sweet. I also remember Iowa State winning five in a row against Kansas between 1999 and 2001. And a lot of fans fondly remember Iowa State knocking off Kansas in the final Big Eight tournament in 1996.

Wait a second.

Those were men's basketball-related memories. This is a book about football.

I joke because for one, I enjoy thinking about those memories, and more importantly for the purposes of this story, the Iowa State vs. Kansas men's basketball series has been more of a rivalry — and more relevant — than the football series, at least during my time as a fan dating back to the mid-1990s.

Kansas has typically not been good at football, and in the last decade has been very poor. Iowa State has had some good years and bad years in that time. Every game these two teams have played since 2010 has felt like a reprieve for the Cyclones, an almost automatic win. Some years it ended up being the difference between bowl eligibility and staying at home. Some years, it ended up being one of only three wins in the entire season, a battle to avoid last place in the Big 12. Most years for ISU head coach Matt Campbell, it has served as a get-things-right game to work out any kinks in the middle of the season during a nice boring win. And when the Cyclones have a closer-than-expected game (2019), or lose (2014), it stands out as a blip on the radar.

It was a different story in the late 2000s as Kansas had things rolling while Iowa State was in a poor stretch. Over the last 20 years or so, the teams have rarely been good at the same time.

Then again, the game to me that most epitomizes the awesomeness of being an Iowa State fan was in an otherwise meaningless late-season game in 2013.

It was Senior Night in Ames. The Cyclones were 1-9 coming into the game. Kansas was 3-7. And it was a night game. In November. On the final Saturday before Thanksgiving. It was literally the coldest game in Iowa State football history with a kickoff temperature of eight degrees.

As we were getting ready to drive to Ames that day, I couldn't help but think to myself, *Why am I doing this?* I was going to park myself in a frigid stadium to watch two teams with poor records in a game in which there seemed to be next to no excitement for the fans. I was imagining a mostly empty Jack Trice Stadium and a lethargic crowd.

Adding to that feeling of indifference, we elected not to tailgate that day, a rare choice for our group. Instead we decided to all meet up at a bar on Main Street in Ames for a few hours before the game.

As we pulled into the parking lot at the stadium a few minutes before the game, with layer upon layer of Cyclone gear piled over my body, I steeled myself for the cold I was about to experience. We began the short walk to the stadium and discovered that at least someone had been tailgating. There was a mostly full 24-pack of Bud Light sitting in the grass. My friend Chris decided to help himself. The beer was slushy. He instead poured it out, and it was literally frozen by the time it hit the ground. Did I mention it was cold?

We walked into the stadium just a few minutes after kickoff, and I realized

… there were actually people in the stadium. I'm always bad at judging the size of a crowd, but I can say for a November game for two teams with losing records, it was a decent showing. And as the Cyclones ran for a first down, the ballcarrier (I believe it was Jeff Woody) breaking a couple tackles along the way, I realized something else: These people were excited to be here. From my seats in the south endzone (before it was renovated into the Sukup End Zone Club), I looked toward the east side of the stands and noticed people standing, putting their fists in the air and hollering as the play was ongoing. We collectively had two choices that evening. We could either bundle up and try to keep the cold out, or we could decide we wanted to be there, cheer like crazy and try to keep warm through movement and energy. I knew my choice. I stood and cheered the entire game.

The Cyclone players took the same positive energy approach. Kansas players, it became obvious, did not take that approach. The Cyclones took a 10-0 lead into the halftime locker room and then poured it on with 17 third quarter points to go up 27-0.

Around this time, I started to get a little worried. Not about the game. The fact that my feet were uncomfortably cold. I didn't exactly have the best insulation. I was wearing tennis shoes and two pairs of socks, hoping that would keep me warm enough. In reality, it was just cutting off my circulation. (I can feel my wife, Paige, rolling her eyes at me. We met a few years later, and she convinced me to buy warm boots and wool socks for these types of games.)

I thought about asking Chris if we could leave, but I just couldn't bring myself to do it. We don't leave games early. I needed to figure something out. I walked out of the stands in search of a solution, someplace I could go to warm up. And right there in front of me was my answer: the porta-potty. This was as good as it was going to get. I entered, and immediately felt the warm embrace of my new environment. My nose was running enough that I probably couldn't smell anything anyway. I sat down, took one shoe off, and started massaging my foot. It was a slow relief over the next several minutes as feeling gradually came back, and the pain from the cold subsided. I proceeded to the same process on the other foot. Twenty minutes later, I was ready to go back to the stands to awkwardly explain my long absence to the group.

As it turns out, I am beyond grateful I didn't leave the game early. After Iowa State wrapped up a dominating 34-0 win, the players lined up on the perimeter of the field, right near the stands. Stadium staff opened the gates from the stands to the field so fans could go onto field level to greet the players. I had never seen this before. The players proceeded to walk around the entire field in a line, high-fiving the fans who were still around and thanking them for their support. I wasn't about to miss this opportunity. We went down to field level. I clapped and cheered for my team. And there was Woody, the hero who had scored the game-winning touchdown against Oklahoma State two years before, a senior experiencing his last game at Jack Trice Stadium. I went in for the high-five and felt my gloved hand match his. I am five years older than him, but I felt like a kid high-fiving a child-hood hero.

"Go beat West Virginia," I tried to say, though I was having a difficult time actually saying coherent words due to the cold. I'd like to think he heard me though, because the next week the Cyclones *did* go beat West Virginia, but that's a story for a different day.

In what could have been a day to forget, we decided to make it memorable.

How many Division I major conference programs would have that kind of interaction between players and fans following a game? I'm willing to bet not many, and maybe only this one. That night, we were all in it together and we were grateful for each other.

Thinking of that story makes me appreciate that although this season hasn't yet lived up to the special status we've all hoped for, Saturday's game against Kansas presents another opportunity for us to gather and watch our favorite team at Jack Trice Stadium.

And we get to watch a historic matchup. As the conference realignment discussion started over the summer, I was sad at the thought of Iowa State and Kansas possibly being split up (and also had similar emotions about Kansas State and Oklahoma State). I'm nostalgic about the fact that Iowa State and Kansas have played more than 100 times.

Kansas has a new coach this year with Lance Leipold, and there seems to be a lot of respect around the game for him. As much as in many ways I'd like Kansas to always be bad, it would also be fun to have this game not only be competitive, but have some importance placed on it within each team's season. When Kansas comes to Hilton Coliseum for men's basketball, the game is circled by Cyclone fans, and I'd guess at least some years Jayhawk fans feel the same way.

A perfect example of when this game did have significant meaning is the 2005 season. In a game most of us would love to forget, Iowa State entered the final weekend of the season on the road in Lawrence needing only to beat Kansas to earn its first ever spot in the Big 12 Championship Game.

Many Iowa State fans remember watching the second half of this game as slow torture. The Cyclones led 14-3 at the half, and Kansas came back to tie the game twice before winning on a field goal in overtime. My memory is a little different. I was a freshman at Iowa State, and I was home for Thanksgiving break. I watched the first half before I went to a wedding during the second half. As a member of the Cyclone Marching Band, I knew if we won I'd get to take a road trip the next weekend to the Big 12 Championship in Houston. I felt confident. Iowa State had seemed to clearly be the better team in the first half. I was mentally planning my first trip with the band to see Iowa State play for a championship.

This was before the days of smartphones, so I had no way of monitoring the game in the second half. After the wedding, I called my dad to find out what happened. Looking back, I feel bad for him that he had to be the one to break the news to me. He knew I was going to be upset.

"So, am I going to Houston next weekend?"

"No. [Pause] They lost."

I heard his words but didn't believe them. *No way we lost that game.*

"Are you serious?"

"I'm serious. I'm sorry bud. They lost in overtime."

In writing this passage, I went back and watched highlights from that game from 2005. It struck me how much intensity was present in that game. Iowa State fans, as I remembered, traveled well to Lawrence. Kansas was playing for bowl eligibility, and the home crowd was very much into it. The game meant something. It would be fun to see more matchups like that in the future.

For this year, though, I hope for a comfortable Iowa State win. I hope we get to see backups play a good portion of the second half.

Since Iowa State began the week as a 33-point favorite, this projects to be the final game on the schedule that's not stressful. At least, we hope it's not stressful. Kansas did show the ability to keep it close two years ago.

After the unexpected and — quite frankly, deflating — 2-2 start to the season, this game is beyond a must-win for the Cyclones to keep hopes alive for a Big 12 Championship Game appearance.

This is a tough game in some ways for fans. There's no way the excitement will be anywhere close to what it was for the first two home games of the season. That was true even before the subpar start. Beyond that, there is almost nothing the team can do this week to make us feel better about the loss to Baylor. If they win big, that's what they are supposed to do. If they win close, the heartburn levels among fans will not go down. If they lose — nope, I just can't bring myself to consider that thought.

The Cyclones get a bye week after this game and then play a gauntlet of seven games in a row against most of the toughest teams on the schedule. Take care of business Saturday, the Cyclones can be fresh going into mid-October and we as a fan base can regroup with at least something positive to hang onto. My mindset, though, goes something like this: *Enjoy the tailgate. We only get so many of these a year. Cheer loud for Iowa State to win. Don't worry about the next seven games — or even the next game.*

The old coaching cliche is, "We are just going to take it one game at a time." That's how I'm choosing to experience the rest of this season, starting Saturday night. Enjoy the journey, don't worry about the destination. Beat Kansas, and then I'll worry about the next one.

CHAPTER TWELVE

IOWA STATE VS. KANSAS RECAP

A JUICY WIN

Oct. 5, 2021

Iowa State was rolling, but there was still just a little bit of drama.

The Cyclones had jumped to a 38-0 lead at halftime. The near-sellout crowd at Jack Trice Stadium was enjoying every minute. When I wrote my preview for this game, I wrote that it would be difficult for fans to be truly satisfied no matter what happened. A big win was expected; anything less would cause worry.

I was wrong, at least speaking for myself. Even for a team favored to win by 30-plus points, it was impressive to see Iowa State's ability to take complete control of the game from the opening kick. The crowd showed up and cheered loud, despite a 2-2 start to the season that began with so much hype. It was a nearly picture-perfect fall night in Jack Trice Stadium. The team responded by scoring four touchdowns in the opening quarter and delivering the kind of dominant win that we have rarely seen at Iowa State even in the era of coach Matt Campbell.

As we looked forward to the second half, there was still one check-the-box moment that could make it even better. All offseason — and, for most people, all of 2020 — we had waited longingly for the chance to hear "Juicy Wiggle," a song by Redfoo. "Juicy Wiggle" is a dance tune that gets the crowd standing, clapping, bobbing to the beat. (My wife, Paige, simply describes the song by pumping her fist in the air.) I could try to describe it better, but if you know, you know. And if you don't know, YouTube is your friend.

The first time I think I remember hearing the song was during the 2016 season. They began playing it every now and again after an Iowa State touchdown. I seem to remember people clapping along and generally enjoying it but didn't think too much more of it. The first time I really remember registering the juice (pun intended) it seemed to add into the stadium was during the 2017 Iowa game when Iowa State took a second half lead. At some point in time, the people who run the video board and sound system at Jack Trice Stadium seemed to figure out they had something in this song that Cyclone fans responded to, and they could take the fans' excitement to another level if they timed it right. I think they figured this out before I ever fully realized it. I knew I liked the song, but it wasn't yet an anticipated moment on gameday.

That changed in 2018. Top 10 and undefeated West Virginia came to town on an October evening. It was ISU quarterback Brock Purdy's first ever start after coming into the game off the bench and leading Iowa State to a road win the week prior. The stadium atmosphere was raucous from the get-go; we could smell an upset. In the fourth quarter, Purdy found wide receiver Deshaunte Jones for a 32-yard touchdown pass to grab a 28-14 lead. In the ensuing timeout, "Juicy Wiggle" played over the loudspeakers. I, along with 60,000-plus others in the stadium, danced and clapped, thrilled at watching our Cyclones take a commanding lead over a top-ranked team. At some point, a few people — likely in the student section, but I can't confirm that — turned on their cell phone flashlights as though they were at a concert. They were waving their lights back and forth to the beat. Like wildfire, the lights spread as more and more people saw what was happening and caught on. In a matter of moments, the entire stadium was filled with the cell phone lights going back and forth to the beat. It was a totally organic and unexpected moment and would have to rank as one of the top five best moments I've ever seen in Jack Trice Stadium (if not THE top).

From then on, the song has played almost every game, always after a second half touchdown, usually when the crowd is already in a frenzy. The biggest challenge seems to be simply timing it right. Nobody has a crystal ball to know exactly what is going to happen, and when it is going to happen, within a game; therefore, finding the right timing to play "Juicy Wiggle" requires some luck. Some games it is obvious. For the West Virginia game in 2018, the moment couldn't have been more perfect. Sometimes the song plays at a point that feels like it's too early in the second half, when the game is still way too much up in the air. One game it played after a missed extra point. Not ideal. And in the worst of times, we do not get to hear it at all if the score and situation never necessitate it (or Iowa State fails to score a second-half touchdown).

At its best, though, the "Juicy Wiggle" experience brings the stadium to a fever pitch at just the right moment. In the 2018 game against Kansas State at the end of the season, the song played after the Cyclones cut a 17-point Wildcat lead down to three in the fourth quarter. In the 2019 game against TCU, the song played after a fourth-quarter touchdown put the game squarely in Iowa State's favor. On the ensuing kickoff, TCU's returner fumbled the ball back to Iowa State, and the song came back onto the loudspeakers after the play to keep the celebration going. In 2019 against Texas, the song played after the game was over when the Cyclones made a walk-off field goal to win.

Going into the home opener against UNI, hearing the "Juicy Wiggle" and dancing with fellow Cyclone fans was on my bucket list for the day. After so long of having not been in the stadium, I couldn't wait to have that moment. I had built it up in my mind. It was the same sort of anticipation I had felt for pulling into the tailgate lots, seeing the marching band and yelling, "Cyclone! Power!"

We didn't get to hear it that day.

The following week against Iowa, we did hear it but it was after thousands of people had already left the stadium and a Hawkeye victory was all but assured. Nobody felt much like dancing.

Back to Saturday night in 2021 against Kansas. My dad was with me at the game and had never witnessed the "Juicy Wiggle." I tried my best to explain what it was, but knew it was one of those things you just had to see for yourself to understand. I wondered a few times whether they would play the song in the first half after one of Iowa State's five touchdowns, sensing the moment would be right. My friend Chris, who was not sitting next to me that night, was calling for it in our group text message chain. After one touchdown, people brought out their cell phone lights just to wave them to a different song. People clearly wanted their "Juicy Wiggle" moment tonight. They had to wait for the second half.

Iowa State took the ball first to start the third quarter, and for only the second time that night was forced to punt. It would need to wait a little longer. Kansas then put together its only scoring drive of the evening to cut the lead to 38-7. The thought occurred to me: *What if we don't score in the second half?* What a letdown it would have been not to hear the song.

Then the magic happened. Iowa State took the ball, went down the field in seven plays and capped off the drive with a Breece Hall one-yard run on fourth-and-goal. Iowa State was up 45-7, but the score didn't really matter as there had been no doubt in the outcome for quite some time. What mattered was what was about to happen. The band played one of the school fight songs after the extra point was good. And then we heard the familiar bass line, followed by the piano, followed by tens of thousands of people waving their cell phone lights. I briefly thought about taking a picture, or a video, but instead I turned on my own cell phone flashlight and waved it to the beat.

A nearly perfect night at Jack Trice Stadium had reached its peak.

—

About a week before the game, my friend James let Chris and I know that his dad's seats in the Jack Trice Club would be open for the Kansas game. I had never sat in these seats before and it sounded like it would be a fun time.

Separately, near the beginning of game week, I found out we had some extra tickets available in our group. I offered them to my parents to see if they wanted to join. On Thursday, my dad decided he would join. By this time, the extra tickets were spoken for, but both Chris and Paige generously agreed to let my dad and me join James in using the club tickets.

My dad took me to my first major college football game when Iowa played against Tulsa in 1997. The next year, he took me to my first Iowa State game, a 38-0 win over Ball State in 1998. A few years later he braved one of the coldest games I can remember going to, a 2003 game against Kansas State. According to ESPN's recap, the wind chill that day was one degree. One. Iowa State got thumped by the Wildcats, 45-0. My dad and I refused to leave early.

In my marching band days, my parents made it to almost every game, buying season tickets for my last three years in the band. They sat through hot games and cold games, thrillers and more than a few blowouts. They always stayed until the bitter end.

Over the years, I have gone to quite a few games of all types with my dad. In addition to sharing games at Jack Trice Stadium with him, he took me to my first NASCAR race and he and my mom also took me to my first Chicago Cubs game. In 2016, I convinced him to skip a day of our family vacation in the Wisconsin Dells to catch a Cubs game in Milwaukee. In 2017, my brother and I took dad for a "once-in-a-lifetime" trip to Green Bay to see a Packers game. (We then took second and third annual "once-in-a-lifetime" trips the next two years.) I've been lucky enough to share with him a good number of Cyclone, Hawkeye, Cubs and Packers games as well as races over the years. He has seen me in some of my most passionate moments (good and bad), and I'm always grateful when he joins us for a day of tailgating and football in Ames.

Saturday arrived. Iowa State's uniforms for the day were set to be cardinal helmet, cardinal jersey and white pants. I wasn't wearing cardinal today, however. A couple weeks before the game, a fan on Twitter encouraged people to stripe the stadium, with some sections being cardinal and some being yellow. I thought it was a cool concept and decided to wear a yellow shirt. Over the summer, I had purchased a Welcome to Brocktober shirt produced by Cyclone Fanatic in collaboration with quarterback Brock Purdy. The shirt was produced as part of the new name, image and likeness rules that made it OK for athletes to benefit from their name on merchandise. Brocktober had become a folk legend of sorts for Iowa State football after Purdy played in his first game during the first weekend of October in 2018, and led the Cyclones to a 4-0 record in the month. The Cyclones had a 3-1 October record each year in 2019 and 2020 with Purdy as quarterback. I figured since it was Purdy's senior year, it was now October and the shirt was yellow, I better wear it to at least one game.

I made a grocery run in the morning to grab some beers. My dad was bringing pork tenderloins to grill along with some meat sticks and donut holes from the meat market and bakery in our hometown of Pella.

We pulled into the tailgate lot around 2 p.m. along with Paige, Chris and his wife Kaci, and Paige's sister Erin who was also attending her first game. The weather was in the 70s — a beautiful fall day in Iowa. This was the kind of day that was made for college football and tailgating. We met up with the group and commenced some of our normal games. It felt like less than a minute before someone yelled "RICOCHEEEEET!" It was another fun tailgate with close friends and family.

Around 5:30 p.m., we began to make our way to the stadium. Since this would likely be the only home game my dad would attend in 2021, I wanted to give him the chance to see the marching band. We arrived at the gates and said goodbye to the rest of the group heading to our normal section as we went in search of the Jack Trice Club.

We found the club and made our way to our seats. We were in the back row of the section, which was underneath the first few rows of the upper deck stands. We had a perfect view of the field from the 50-yard line. Just a few steps behind us were a bar and a couple buffet lines with food and desserts. *I could get used to this*, I thought. We took in the band and cheered as the team began to make its way to the field. Although not everyone got the memo about which color shirt to wear, I was none-the-less impressed at the number of people who did wear yellow in the sections designated as yellow by the fans on Twitter. It made me hope Iowa State's athletics department would officially try something like this in the future as it would be a great look in pictures and on television.

The Cyclones needed a win, and Kansas was the right team to play to all but guarantee it would happen. According to ESPN's win probability tracker, the Cyclones began the game with a win probability of 98.4%. The probability never dipped below that.

Kansas took the ball first and was immediately held to a three-and-out and forced to punt to Iowa State. The Cyclones promptly moved the ball 70 yards in six plays, capped by a 36-yard touchdown pass from Purdy to Xavier Hutchinson, on a play in which the Kansas defender aggressively went for the ball, missed it and left Hutchinson with nothing but green grass in front of him. I high-fived my dad and James who were sitting next to me as the crowd roared.

A few plays later, the Jayhawks quarterback put the ball on the ground unforced and Iowa State's Zach Petersen pounced on it. On the ensuing possession, Purdy scrambled and found Charlie Kolar in the back of the endzone. Kolar was able to get separation from the defender, reach out and snatch the ball out of the air while keeping a foot down in the corner of the endzone to complete the catch. I joined the crowd in erupting out of my seat as he made the catch and watched the replay on the in-stadium televisions (the giant video boards were blocked from our view) in awe.

The route was on. Kansas went for it on fourth down from its own 45-yard line on its next possession and got stuffed by the Cyclone defense. Purdy came out and threw a 44-yard touchdown pass to Joe Scates, who caught the ball in stride on his way into the endzone, to give Iowa State a 21-0 lead. On its ensuing possession, Kansas had some success moving the ball, setting up a 34-yard field goal attempt — which was blocked. Iowa State's Greg Eisworth returned it all the way to the Kansas 32-yard line, setting up three straight runs by Breece Hall down to the seven-yard line and a seven-yard pass from Purdy to Jirehl Brock for a touchdown and 28-0 lead. All told, Purdy threw four touchdown passes in the first quarter.

Brocktober had arrived. The game was, for all intents and purposes, over in the first 15 minutes.

As I looked around at a full Jack Trice Stadium on a beautiful October evening, I couldn't help but think about how far this stadium had come since I first came to a game in 1998. The most visible change is the addition of seats in the southwest and southeast corner of the stadium, as well as the addition of the Sukup End Zone Club in the south endzone.

I had a history in those seats before they became club seats. During my first year in the Cyclone Marching Band in 2005 we sat in the south endzone. Normally, we had an entire section to ourselves. The exception was the Colorado game, the final home game of the season. There was enough demand for tickets in the stadium for the athletics department to sell tickets for the seats behind us, which were normally empty. We all had the perfect view as Brent "Big Play" Curvey grabbed an interception from Colorado quarterback Joel Klatt and came rumbling toward us to score the game-clinching touchdown.

The next year, the athletics department decided to sell all of the south endzone seats, moving the band to its own makeshift section in the north endzone. A few years later, I re-joined the crowd of paying ticketholders in the south endzone for the 2011 season, just in time for the new videoboard to be installed in the north endzone. At the time they were great seats for me. I got to be close to the field, and when the game action was on the other side of the 50-yard line I could watch the giant videoboard. Not to mention they were truly the cheap seats. Although the price went up over the years, I am certain I didn't pay much more than $150 for season tickets in those seats during the first season, which was about the only way I could have afforded tickets at the time.

For years, dating back to 2006 when I was a freshman at Iowa State, the plan had been to eventually bowl-in the south endzone, adding permanent seats where the hillside seating used to be, and renovating the existing seats. In spring of 2013, as a young reporter at the Des Moines Business Record and a season ticket holder, I got curious and asked ISU Director of Athletics Jamie Pollard what it would take to complete the project. The Cyclones at the time were coming off the best two seasons of attendance in school history with more than 50,000 fans each game. He told me then it would take a lead donor, and perhaps as importantly, continued strong attendance even when times were not good in terms of the on-field performance by the football team.

Times were indeed not good in the 2013 season, with Iowa State finishing 3-9. But the crowds kept coming, and so did the donation: $25 million from Roy and Bobbi Reiman. In November 2013, just a couple days after I stood through the coldest game in Jack Trice Stadium history in a win against Kansas, Iowa State announced it would take on the stadium addition with a goal to be complete by the 2015 season. An additional gift by the Sukup family brought the Sukup End Zone Club to life.

The addition is a striking difference to the eye from both inside and outside the stadium. The Reiman Plaza seamlessly connects the Reiman Gardens to the stadium's south entrance. As fans file in from the south, the glass façade of the club gives an inviting feeling. From the inside, it completely revitalizes the stadium. It makes Jack Trice Stadium finally look and feel like the big-time college football stadium it is.

As the adaptation of the old "Field of Dreams" quote goes, "If you build it, they will come."

The crowds have indeed shown up. In the 1990s and 2000s, it was difficult to imagine Iowa State could sell out a game in a 61,500-seat stadium against a team not named Iowa, Northern Iowa or Nebraska (a conference rival for many years that often brought thousands of fans to Ames). After Iowa State's loss to Baylor to open the 2021 Big 12 season, I was worried the momentum would disappear enough that a good amount of people might not show up for the Kansas game. Yet, as I sat there watching the Cyclones play the worst program in the Big 12, the stadium seats I could see around me were almost all full. I couldn't see the entire stadium from my view, but I could tell how full the stadium was later when I saw wide-angle photos. The official attendance was 60,446, at 98% capacity, to watch a 2-2 team coming off a heart-wrenching loss against a 1-3 team. (I later learned this was the largest crowd ever to attend an Iowa State vs. Kansas game.)

Over the summer before the 2021 season, the newest renovation was completed outside the stadium. A plaza was added to the north side of the stadium where fans can mingle before the game, and the Stark Performance Center was completed just outside the northwest corner, made possible by the Richard and Joan Stark family.

My favorite part of this building is the addition of a logo visible from parts of the stadium's seating area. The five-stripe logo is made to look similar to the pattern that was on Jack Trice's jersey. Most Iowa Staters likely know Trice's story, but for anyone reading who does not know, here is the short version.

Trice was the first Black person to play football for Iowa State, and tragically died after just his second football game in 1923 at Minnesota after breaking his collarbone and being trampled by Minnesota players. Nobody knows for sure, but there is plenty of speculation that opposing players were targeting Trice due to his skin color.

The school in recent years has done a good job of honoring Trice's memory. The stadium is of course named after him and is the only Division I Football Bowl Subdivision stadium named after a Black man. In 2013, the Cyclones wore a replica jersey for their game against Iowa as a way to honor Trice's memory, and in following years the five-stripe pattern became a secondary logo of sorts for the program. The logo seemed to become even more prominent on merchandise heading into the 2021 season. I bought two such shirts and a hat that incorporates the logo. I have enjoyed seeing Iowa State embrace this symbol of Trice.

As I watched Iowa State take on the Jayhawks, I thought about the fact I was in the Jack Trice Club and reminded myself I was wearing my Jack Trice logo hat. I felt a little extra surge of pride.

My dad and I were still in awe we were sitting in club seats. I walked out with a sandwich and he expressed his surprise when I told him it was complimentary. Like I said, *We could get used to this.* We remarked how different the view was. Though it was open-air, it almost felt like we were inside since we were sitting underneath the upper deck, which blocked our view of the sky. I remarked that in some ways, I almost liked our normal seats better as you could see the entire stadium better. He pointed out there were heaters above us.

"I bet those are nice during cold games," he said.

Almost as if on cue, a few minutes later we were indeed grateful to be protected from the elements as the rain began to fall.

"Huh. Looks like some people in the stands are looking for cover," I remarked as we remained completely dry.

Meanwhile, on the field, Iowa State continued to dominate. Hall capped an 80-yard drive with a seven-yard touchdown run to make it 35-0. With time ticking down in the first half, Purdy was sacked at the Kansas nine-yard line. Iowa State had no timeouts to stop the clock. The Cyclones calmly ran in the field goal unit, and Connor Assalley nailed a 26-yard field goal as time expired. Iowa State took a 38-0 lead in the half. The only element in question was when "Juicy Wiggle" would be played.

That moment came after Hall's touchdown run with little more than five minutes left in the third quarter, with the score 45-7 Iowa State. The moment we had waited so long for finally arrived. It was therapeutic to celebrate a blowout by dancing to the "Juicy Wiggle."

Just as I had hoped, Iowa State began to put its backups into the game. Backup quarterback Hunter Dekkers wasted no time making his presence felt, breaking a 41-yard run to the endzone to give the Cyclones a 52-7 lead.

With the game safely in hand and having enjoyed a successful "Juicy Wiggle" experience, my thoughts turned elsewhere: dessert.

"Did you know they have free Clone Cones?" one of our seatmates asked, referring to the red and yellow ice cream sold at Jack Trice Stadium and Hilton Coliseum.

"What!? I had no idea!" I answered.

"Yeah," he said. "They even have toppings."

We decided to scope it out and found that yes, there was free ice cream. My dad and I each filled our bowls and I put some chocolate candy and cookies on top of mine. Around that time, we looked outside.

"Looks like it's raining again," my dad said as I took a bite of ice cream.

We returned to our seats to watch the Iowa State defense continue to shut down Kansas, and backups including Dekkers and running backs Brock, Eli Sanders and Dion Silas lead the Cyclone offense.

Paige sent me a message. "How is it being dry?"

After I told her it was really nice, she sent me a photo of Chris and Kaci sitting under an umbrella, and a selfie of her and Erin, all looking a little damp and wearing sour facial expressions. I sent a selfie of my dad and me (nice and dry) and a photo of James eating ice cream. Yep, the suite life wasn't all bad. I knew this could be the last time I ever sat in these seats; I figured I might as well enjoy it. I also wondered what bad weather I would potentially need to sit through the rest of the season to make up for my little jokes.

Iowa State capped off the scoring with a 16-yard touchdown run by Silas to make the final Iowa State 59, Kansas 7. My dad and I said goodbye to James and walked back to the car. By this time the rain had stopped (sometimes it really is your night). As we loaded up to head home, everyone seemed in good spirits despite some having sat through rain. There was good-natured ribbing toward my dad and me for having lived the suite life for a night. At least I think it was good-natured.

We talked about the game and wondered aloud if we had ever seen Iowa State score 28 points in the first quarter. (It turned out we had not. Iowa State's 28 first quarter points were the most in school history.) We remarked how much fun it was to see Iowa State win big, and to enjoy the "Juicy Wiggle."

"I wish we could play Kansas one more time this season," I said, thinking about the challenge that awaited Iowa State in its final seven games and the fact there were no obvious easy wins left.

Iowa State was coming up to its bye week with a record of 3-2 and 1-1 in the Big 12. Following the bye would be a seven-game stretch that would include Kansas State, Oklahoma State, West Virginia, Texas, Texas Tech, Oklahoma and TCU.

"I think they can win any game left on their schedule," I said, fully well knowing they could also lose any game left on their schedule.

None of it mattered that evening. We arrived at what had been our meet-up point in Ankeny earlier in the day and unpacked our coolers and other items from my dad's SUV. My dad had sat through some pretty miserable Iowa State games; I got the impression he had enjoyed the entire experience of this one. I was grateful to have shared it with him. It was another reminder to focus on the journey, not the destination.

CHAPTER THIRTEEN

IOWA STATE VS. KANSAS STATE PREVIEW

A SWING GAME IN FARMAGEDDON

Oct. 14, 2021

It has been a long, mostly troubled road for Iowa State against Kansas State in recent years.

I consider the Wildcats to be Iowa State's biggest football rival in the Big 12 Conference. This game doesn't elicit quite the same strong emotions as when the Cyclones play Iowa, but it still stands a tick above other games in terms of how much I want Iowa State to win. In fact, the game has even taken on an unofficial rivalry game moniker: Farmageddon, named for the schools' shared focus on agriculture.

The importance of the rivalry became clearer to me in 2012. I was working as a reporter for the Des Moines Business Record. That summer, before the start of the football season, we hosted a panel discussion that included then-ISU football coach Paul Rhoads. This was likely the peak of Rhoads' popularity. The previous season, the Cyclones had pulled one of the largest upsets in college football history against the undefeated No. 2-ranked Oklahoma State Cowboys to make their second bowl game in three years.

In casual conversation, he told an attendee something to this effect: "We need to beat Kansas State."

The point he made, as I remember it, is that Iowa State and Kansas State have similar profiles within the conference, and that for Iowa State to get to the championship level it aspired to be at, it needed to win this game on a regular basis.

The Wildcats were led by legendary head coach Bill Snyder. He had turned K-State's program from an afterthought to a championship winner. It was the kind of trajectory Iowa State is still trying to follow, and at the time in 2012 I thought Rhoads could be the coach to get us there. So to me, it always felt a little extra heartbreaking that Rhoads could never get over the Kansas State hurdle.

The trouble started all the way back in 2009, Rhoads' first season. The Cyclones tied the game in the closing minutes in the Big 12 opener against K-State at Arrowhead Stadium in Kansas City. Or so we thought. As most people in the stands were still celebrating and high-fiving, my friend Chris pointed out that ISU still needed to kick the extra point. *Relax — those are automatic*, I thought to myself, seconds before the extra point was blocked. It took a couple of seconds for my brain to register what my eyes were seeing as I watched the purple-clad K-State fans in the stands across the field jump around in excitement. To this day, it still feels jarring to think about that roar as everyone around me fell completely silent, leaving no noise to block out the opposing fans' cheers.

Seriously. How many games have ever been decided by a blocked extra point?

After close, hard-fought losses in 2010, 2011 and 2012, and a less close loss in 2013, Iowa State entered the 2014 contest needing a win after losing to FCS North Dakota State the week prior. It was a warm September day. In our car on the way to the game, Chris's wife introduced us to a new Taylor Swift song, "Shake It Off." We were immediately hooked by the catchy tune. Who was to say Iowa State couldn't shake it off from the opening week loss and beat K-State?

The Cyclones jumped out to a 28-13 lead following a trick play that featured receiver Jarvis West taking a reverse and throwing a touchdown pass to Allen Lazard. I have rarely heard a crowd in that type of frenzy.

Right before the first half ended, Kansas State put together a drive that culminated with receiver Tyler Lockett making a catch at the one-yard line. Lockett appeared as though he may have been out of bounds before making the catch, but the Wildcats hurried up to the line, ran a play and scored a touchdown before the referees could review it. The Big 12 later announced that it had suspended replay officials for not stopping the game for a review, but it didn't matter. K-State stole the momentum back before the half, and Iowa State fans felt they were robbed. (In reality, the Wildcats were likely to score on that drive anyway. I've come to terms with this seven years later, but at the time, I was furious.)

Early in the fourth quarter, Iowa State was still clinging to a 28-20 lead when the Cyclones made a fourth-and-inches stop, and then picked up a first down near midfield. A third-and-three pass appeared like it was going to be complete to West for another first down, but in a turn of events I still don't truly understand, the K-State defender ripped the ball away from West before he could complete the catch. An argument could be made that West should have been ruled down with the ball before it was wrestled away, and that's exactly the argument I, and thousands of others, made with our voices in the stands. Again, it didn't matter. The Wildcats eventually went on to win 32-28.

It was among the angriest moments I have ever had as I walked out of Jack Trice Stadium. When we got back to the car, instead of listening to the post-game show, we listened to "Shake It Off" on loop the entire way home from Ames to Des Moines. The. Entire. Way.

The next year was worse.

In the second-to-last game of the 2015 season, Iowa State had a 3-7 record but had played better in recent weeks. Rhoads was at this point in danger of losing his job, but there was a sense he could save it with a strong finish to the season. That was the outcome I was hoping for. I was a big fan of Rhoads as ISU's coach.

Iowa State jumped out to a 21-point lead over the rival Wildcats. I happened to be watching the game with a group of people in a party room at a friend's Thanksgiving party. One person, making casual small talk, remarked that it looked like an easy Iowa State win. I immediately scolded him. We had seen plenty of these games go the wrong way. My mind flashed back to some of the ghosts of recent K-State losses, not to mention losses like the one in 1999 when Iowa State blew a 28-7 halftime lead.

While I didn't feel a 21-point lead was a sure thing for Iowa State, I did feel confident, even when the Wildcats pulled within seven points and had the ball late in the fourth quarter. Iowa State made a fourth down stop and took the ball back with 1:31 to play. Iowa State was *finally* going to end the losing streak.

And then came one of the most maddening sequences I have ever seen.

With 1:31 left, most fans expected Iowa State to line up in the victory formation and take a knee to let the clock run down. The only issue was the Cyclones would have likely had to run a fourth down play, likely a punt. Instead of having the team take a knee, Rhoads elected to try and run a play instead in order to run more clock and maybe pick up a first down to remove all ambiguity. Iowa State handed it off to the running back. Here's how I remember the play going:

MY FRIEND CHRIS: "Why are they running a play?"

ME: *Shrugs*

CHRIS: "Oh my … he fumbled it." Dejection in his voice. "He fumbled it."

ME: *Hands on my head*

CHRIS: "K-State got it."

ME: "No … just no …"

After K-State predictably scored to tie the game, ISU had one more chance. As I was watching the ISU quarterback go back for a pass, I already knew what was about to happen. It was too predictable. He got hit, fumbled and the Wildcats recovered in field goal range to kick a game-winner. Kansas State 38, Iowa State 35.

There I was, surrounded by a party of people, half of whom did not care a bit about the game. I was having a meltdown. I remember watching Rhoads walk off the field and feeling numb as I knew he had just sealed his fate at ISU.

Iowa State announced the next day it would part ways with Rhoads. Had his team taken a knee, who knows what would have happened? As it was, Iowa State announced Matt Campbell as its head football coach a week later.

You might think it would be difficult to top the pain of seeing your team lose because it failed to take a knee with the game in hand, but you'd be wrong.

Two years later, Campbell had the Cyclones rolling going into the final game of the season at Kansas State. Iowa State had flirted with a Big 12 Championship Game appearance before back-to-back November losses, but there was still a sense that this team could accomplish something special by ending its losing streak to Kansas State, now at nine games.

I watched the game with my future father-in-law at an ISU Alumni Association game-watch in downtown Denver. We ordered a pitcher and settled in to watch a 7-6 first half. When my girlfriend (now wife) Paige and her mom joined us shortly before the start of the second half, I said, "Iowa State is losing, but they are playing well."

I had a good feeling.

I was right, for a while. The Cyclones stopped Kansas State in three plays to start the third quarter, and then marched down the field for an 11-play, 85-yard touchdown drive to take the lead on a nine-yard pass to Marchie Murdock. When the Cyclones scored again on a three-yard pass from Kyle Kempt to Hakeem Butler early in the fourth quarter, they made it a 19-7 game. Butler casually flipped the ball to the defender he had just beat, who was still lying on the ground. It was a move of swag, and it drew a 15-yard penalty. I loved every second of it.

K-State scored on its next drive to make it 19-14. I was nervous again. But Iowa State was getting the ball back with a chance to run out the clock. That's when the chaos started.

The Cyclones got a first down, and then another on a 20-yard pass to Butler on third-and-18. With just 2:11 left and ISU needing one first down to ice the game, the Cyclones threw an incomplete pass on second down. The clock stopped. On third down, Kempt threw it up to soon-to-be NFL receiver Allen Lazard. Lazard appeared to be in position for the catch, and the K-State defender knew it. Instead of defending the ball, he put his arms around Lazard to prevent him from having a shot at it. A yellow flag flew. It was going to be pass interference. Game over.

The referees huddled. *What are they talking about? Why are they taking so long? Surely, they won't change this … OH MY GOSH THEY ARE PICKING UP THE FLAG!*

My future father-in-law was stunned. My text message chain of fellow Cyclone fans was in disarray. And I knew. We were going to lose.

Kansas State got the ball back and had little trouble gaining yards in big chunks. On the final play of the game from the one-yard line, Wildcats quarterback Skylar Thompson scrambled and found a receiver in the back of the endzone. Touchdown. 20-19. No time left.

It was likely the first and one of the few times I've ever cursed in front of my in-laws. For his part, Paige's dad just kept saying, "That never should have happened. The game should have been over."

It could be argued that losing 10 games in a row to Kansas State, some in excruciating fashion, made it even sweeter to finally break through in 2018. And I'd buy that argument. The Cyclones were down by 17 points in the fourth quarter. It was the Saturday after Thanksgiving, and it was cold. A number of fans had already left and I'm sure were thinking, *Same old*

Iowa State. At one point, Iowa State tried a long pass that from my vantage point looked like a completion. I started to cheer, then realized the K–State defender had come up with an interception. The Wildcat fan in front of me, who had stood out all game due to his boisterous cheers in a road venue, turned around and yelled, "YEAHHH!!!" into my face. Talk about adding insult to injury.

Still, Iowa State began to go on a drive early in the fourth quarter. A fan from a few rows behind us, who I did not know, came and sat next to us as a few people had begun to clear out. He sat next to me and we commiserated about the 17-point deficit and how this always seemed to happen against K–State. He then began talking to my new K–State acquaintance. It was a generally happy, lighthearted conversation with questions like, "How do you like Jack Trice Stadium?" The K–State fan's demeanor would slowly begin to change over the coming quarter.

Iowa State scored a touchdown to cut the lead to 10 with just over 10 minutes left, and Kansas State then faced a third-and-six at its own 29-yard line. There was a little life in the crowd. Paige later admitted that she thought about asking if we could go home when the team was down 17 (she was cold), but knew after that play we were in for the long haul. Thompson, still the K–State quarterback, faced a blitz. Before he could react, the ball was loose and the next thing I saw was stud freshman Mike Rose running unabated toward the endzone with that football. It didn't truly dawn on me what was happening until I noticed everyone in the south end zone seats with their hands straight up in the air. Touchdown, Iowa State. A 17-point deficit was now three.

The cell phone flashlights were out. The crowd was hopping as the "Juicy Wiggle" played in the stadium. And I knew. We were going to win.

It seemed like a foregone conclusion when the Cyclones stopped K–State three-and-out, got the ball back, and David Montgomery ran for the game-winning touchdown. It felt like destiny when Iowa State made the final fourth down stop with less than two minutes left and was able to run out the clock. Sweet redemption. I looked down toward the Wildcat fan. He was nowhere to be found.

Proving things are not always linear, the next year was largely a dud as Kansas State (now led by Chris Klieman, who led Football Championship Subdivision team North Dakota State to four national championships in five years) was the more physical team and outplayed the Cyclones in a 27-17 win to end the regular season. It was, in many ways, a reminder to me of what Rhoads had said seven years prior. As the Cyclones were trying to compete with K-State within the Big 12 hierarchy, it felt like a major toe-stub to lose to the Wildcats in a similar style as what Iowa State was trying to perfect. In the time since, I have heard it mentioned that the loss ended up having a positive effect on the program, as it led to a further evaluation of what Iowa State needed to do to truly take the next step from a good team to a championship contender. In 2020, Iowa State beat a depleted Wildcat team 45-0 in another late November game, this time on its way to a Big 12 Championship Game appearance.

Coming into the 2021 game, the Cyclones have finally begun to turn the tide in the series. They have not, however, won at K-State since 2004. That's seven straight losses by the Cyclones at Bill Snyder Family Stadium. Being called "Family Stadium" makes it seem so friendly, but it has been downright cruel to Iowa State. The Cyclones have lost in surprising, gut-wrenching and disheartening ways in Manhattan over that time. A win in 2021 would be sweet.

Like any rivalry game, a win for the Cyclones in Farmageddon stands out beyond the immediate storylines of the season. I want Iowa State to win in part *just because* it's a rivalry game. This year's game takes on added importance. It is a swing game in the season for Iowa State. The Cyclones have gotten off to a 3-2 start, not as good as anyone hoped for. There is still a lot to play for, and a spot in the Big 12 Championship is still very much alive. A win against K-State, and it will feel like the Cyclones have captured that so far-elusive momentum. A loss would unofficially end their conference title hopes.

If it's a swing game for Iowa State, the Wildcats probably feel much the same way. K-State began the season 3-0, which included a big win over Stanford, but then lost back-to-back games to open the conference season. The Wildcats lost to two conference title game contenders in Oklahoma State and Oklahoma. Thompson, who is still K-State's quarterback at 24 years old, was out with an injury against Oklahoma State but threw for 320 yards and three touchdowns in the upset bid against the Sooners.

Iowa State has so far had two opportunities to really grab control of its own destiny to make this the successful season everyone has hoped for. The Cyclones fell short against Iowa and Baylor. This is the third opportunity, and it is critically important.

CHAPTER FOURTEEN

IOWA STATE VS. KANSAS STATE RECAP

A CELEBRATION 17 YEARS IN THE MAKING

Oct. 19, 2021

I couldn't believe what I was seeing. *It can't be real,* I thought. *There's nobody around him!* I was barely even conscious of the fact I had jumped out of my seat.

We had just settled in for the first play of Iowa State's game at Kansas State on Saturday night. My wife, Paige, and I were in the stadium's southeast corner, 35 rows up. Although there were a good number of Iowa State fans in the vicinity, we were surrounded on all sides in our immediate seating area by Kansas State fans: the row in front of us, behind us and to each side. I told myself not to be *that* guy — the loud, possibly obnoxious guy that sits in an away team stadium and tries to outcheer the home fans. One of the first times I had gone to a road game as a non-band member, I had been that guy. I didn't mean to be; I was just excited and cheering. It was only hours after the game, after reflection, I realized I had probably been the annoying person that everyone around me was rolling their eyes at. I didn't really want to do that again.

So on Saturday night in 2021 in Manhattan, Kan., I was trying to mostly take my cue from the fans in my area. I figured I'd cheer a respectable amount when Iowa State had a big play, and other than that try to blend in and be a good guest.

Which is what I was trying to do when Iowa State took the ball to begin the game and lined up for its first play from scrimmage. My adrenaline made me want to stand, but I took my seat as those around me began to sit down and settle in. The next thing I knew, Iowa State running back Breece Hall was seemingly by himself, just beyond the line of scrimmage but yards away from anyone else on the field. There was nothing between him and the endzone. I could barely register what I was seeing, and I yelled, "OH!" Without thinking, I was on my feet cheering for Breece as he booked down the field.

"Go! Go! Go!"

I was vaguely aware that throughout our corner of the stadium, hundreds of other Cyclone fans were having the same reaction. Hall outran the one defender close enough to chase him, scampering away from a diving tackle attempt around the 10-yard line. The last few steps were a relaxing jog into the endzone. It was a 75-yard touchdown run on the game's first play, and Iowa State was up 7-0 after the extra point.

I was standing and clapping, taking in the scene of other Iowa State fans doing the same. Many were high-fiving. About 10 rows in front of us, my longtime friend Jason turned around, locked eyes with me and gave me an air-five. Paige, who does not have quite the same level of irrational passion about sports as I do, had not even been paying attention until she heard Iowa State fans yelling.

"What just happened!?" she asked.

"Breece just scored on the first play!" I yelled.

A few hours later, I didn't need to worry as much about how loud I cheered. Kansas State fans had filed out of the stadium following a convincing Iowa State victory (which, as I'll get to, still had me nervous until nearly the final play). The Iowa State fans had begun to congregate in the seats closest to the field as the teams shook hands after the game. Paige and I, along with Jason and his family, went down to join them. First came Iowa State tight end Charlie Kolar and special teams standout Rory Walling, running toward our corner. Then the rest of the team followed. The Iowa State fans in attendance clapped and yelled as the players waved and high-fived the fans closest to the field.

We had all just witnessed the type of performance many of us expected to see more of going into the season. The Cyclones had controlled the game in a 33-20 victory, winning for the first time in Manhattan since 2004. Seniors such as Kolar and Walling had been on the team during a heartbreaking loss in 2017 and a frustrating loss there in 2019. Fans had experienced even more heartburn in prior trips. This night, it had all come together.

It felt like Iowa State was hitting its stride. Brocktober was in full swing. The Cyclones had a rivalry win and a conference road win, which set up an even bigger game the following week.

I clapped and cheered with fellow fans and took a selfie with Paige. I wanted to remember this night for a long time.

—

The bye week on the Saturday before Iowa State played Kansas State set up to be a fun weekend of college football. The Red River Showdown between Texas and Oklahoma kicked things off, followed by a top five matchup between Iowa and Penn State, and a number of other games worth keeping an eye on. It was the kind of day I could have sat and watched football for 10 hours or more.

In another year, maybe I would have done that. Given my journey of going to 12 games in 13 weeks (at least) and traveling to four different time zones within this same time span, it seemed like a good day to spend with family in my hometown of Pella. My brother and his wife, big Hawkeye fans, were on their way to Kinnick Stadium to watch the Iowa vs. Penn State game, and my dad was going with them. My mom was taking care of my niece, so I decided to keep them company and make a visit to my great aunt and great uncle's house in the process.

While Texas was jumping out to a big lead over Oklahoma, I was eating lunch and catching up with my great aunt and uncle. When Oklahoma was making an improbable comeback with its backup quarterback, followed by Penn State jumping out to a lead over Iowa, I was watching The Addams Family 2 with my mom and niece at the movie theater. While Iowa was making its comeback, I was catching up with my mom. It was a compelling day of college football, and I didn't watch a minute of it. But I couldn't help but check scores often. Two of the biggest games of the day directly or indirectly affected Iowa State. If the Cyclones were to stay in the Big 12 title race, the Red River Showdown would very likely have an impact on tiebreaker scenarios. I didn't have a strong preference who won, but had a feeling Iowa State would ultimately be better off if Oklahoma beat Texas, which is what happened in a thrilling game.

As for the Hawkeyes, I was feeling some complicated emotions. I bet a lot of Cyclone fans could relate. Iowa defeated Penn State to go 6-0 and would be solidly in the College Football Playoff conversation, with six very winnable games to end the regular season. The Hawkeyes and their fans were living the season we dreamed of just four weeks prior. I couldn't help but feel impressed at what the Hawkeyes had accomplished, happy for my brother getting to see a big win, and yes, a little jealous. It was another reminder that no matter what you think will happen going into a season, you really can't predict everything.

I again had to remind myself to enjoy the journey. Quit worrying about a rival winning and again start focusing on the experience of following my team. My working assumption from that point on was that Iowa was in the driver's seat for a playoff spot. It felt like an almost foregone conclusion, so I figured I might as well stop thinking about it.

It became easier to put on the backburner as we got into the K-State game week. The Wildcats were rivals to Iowa State in their own right.

The Iowa State vs. Iowa rivalry is a big deal in large part because the fans can't avoid each other. Everyone is related to, friends with or works with fans from the opposite fanbase. For anything I do in the Greater Des Moines area, for example, I'm almost guaranteed to see both Iowa State and Iowa fans. The Kansas State rivalry was, in some ways, born out of longevity, necessity and the age of social media. Both schools lost in-conference rivals when Nebraska and Missouri left the Big 12 in the early 2010s. The Cyclones and Wildcats, who have now played more than 100 times in their history, naturally grew their rivalry at that point. Both schools have similar profiles, and there's an aspect of fighting for spots in the conference pecking order. Kansas State, for most of the 1990s, 2000s and 2010s, was the program Iowa State aspired to be in the conference.

And social media has a way of fueling the rivalry. I don't know too many Wildcat fans but doing my normal scrolling through Twitter during Farmageddon game week opened my eyes to the rivalry smack talk that was happening.

On Wednesday, Iowa State announced it would wear cardinal helmets, white jerseys and cardinal pants. A Kansas State fan account photoshopped a spoof graphic of Iowa State announcing it would wear purple jerseys. The joke was that, similarly to how Iowa State wore black jerseys (Iowa's primary color) when it played the Hawkeyes, it would wear purple jerseys (Kansas

State's primary color) when it played the Wildcats. K-State fans pointed out variations of the argument that Iowa State wasn't a legitimate program because it stole Iowa's colors. Yes, it was uniform-related trash talk.

Over the course of the week, I saw Kansas State fans make fun of Iowa State for the 2015 loss (when the team failed to take a knee). I saw Wildcat fans argue that somehow K-State did not commit pass interference on Allen Lazard in 2017 despite the defender literally hugging him. And I saw Wildcat fans express their annoyance that Iowa State fans would dare compare their program to Kansas State, or that we'd dare wish for coach Matt Campbell to be our school's version of the legendary K-State coach Bill Snyder, who built the Wildcats into Big 12 Champions and national title contenders. I even saw one K-State fan express dislike at how "cocky" Iowa State fans had gotten after a little bit of success the last four years. (He must not know the same fans I know.)

Now Twitter, in my opinion, doesn't represent an entire fanbase. My assumption is that only a fraction of fans are on Twitter, only a fraction of those fans are vocal and only a fraction of the fans that are vocal give their opinion in a negative way. It just seems like those are the ones I tend to stop and linger on. It would be foolish of me to put too much stock into what some random Twitter users write, but it at least showed these thoughts were out there. And it built up the rivalry just a little more in my mind. As long as it stays good-natured, which it seemed to, this is part of why I love college football. Rivalries are fun, and a little trash-talking can be fun. There's enough serious stuff to argue about, so why not poke fun at each other over a game?

Since the game was scheduled for a 6:30 p.m. kickoff, Paige and I left Saturday morning and made plans to stay at a hotel in Topeka on Saturday evening after the game. We left a little before 9 a.m., strategically placing us in Kansas City on the way at lunchtime. We stopped for lunch at Jack Stack BBQ, a favorite restaurant of ours. I first ate at Jack Stack before Iowa State's 2014 Big 12 tournament championship win in men's basketball, and had eaten there before each one of the Cyclones' tournament wins in Kansas City in the 2010s. I was used to it being full of Cyclone fans when I was there, and I was used to it being a precursor to a Cyclone win. This time, we were the only Cyclone fans I noticed, but it still led to good vibes.

We arrived in Manhattan a little after 3 p.m. and found a place to park north of the stadium. The tailgate lot was already mostly full. There were enough Iowa State fans scattered about to make us feel at home. We had made plans to meet some friends, who were not arriving until a little later. To kill some time, we decided to walk around the lots and over to the stadium. I grabbed a beer and we began our walk.

Passing through the lot, we interacted with fans on both sides. The common refrain between Iowa State fans was, "Go Cyclones!" For the Kansas State interactions, I wasn't quite sure what to expect, but I found the fans to be exceedingly friendly.

"Try not to beat us too badly today," one fan said, to which I replied, "I'm not *that* confident."

I had seen too many games go awry in that stadium.

Multiple fans and stadium staff went out of their way to say, "Welcome to Kansas State."

The scene felt a little bit like a game in Ames in terms of the layout. There were thousands of parking spots surrounding the stadium, with people setting up tents and grills and playing music. It was a festive atmosphere. It wasn't quite as impressive as Iowa State, in my opinion, but I could be biased.

We walked by the northeast corner of the stadium and saw a handful of Iowa State fans standing outside a stadium entrance.

"I bet this is where the team is coming in," I told Paige.

We walked to the west side of the stadium and heard marching band sounds. The Kansas State band was putting on a mini-pep rally. We stopped to watch as they played a few tunes. They began the fight song and played it a few times in a row. Just as I was questioning why they weren't switching it up, I realized why: The Wildcat team had arrived and were walking into the stadium.

"They are huge," Paige remarked.

We walked back toward where we came from and noticed the Iowa State team's buses had pulled into the parking lot by where the group of Iowa State fans had been. We saw the last of the team filing into the stadium and made our way back to the car. On the way, we passed by a pair of K-State fans.

"Corn sucks," one said. Who doesn't love a little crop-based trash talk?

We got back to the car and relaxed a bit as I caught up on some college football scores. I was surprised to see Oklahoma State, the Cyclones' next opponent after Kansas State, had defeated Texas on the road. This meant the Cowboys would be undefeated coming to Ames the next week. What a big game it could be … if Iowa State could beat Kansas State. I also noticed Iowa, now ranked No. 2 in the country, was losing to unranked Purdue at home.

Our friends arrived a few minutes later. Jason is a former coworker of mine and someone who I have kept in close touch with over the years, usually in some way related to Iowa State sports. When we worked together, I would go out of my way to stop at his office and rehash the latest game until we felt we had successfully analyzed all angles. He had made the drive to Manhattan with his wife and adult children. As we approached their family, I noticed something a little out-of-the-ordinary.

Jason had a mustache.

That mustache, quite frankly, did not do Jason any favors. Although he is a grown man with adult children, the mustache looked about like what you'd expect to find on the face of a teenager trying to grow facial hair for the first time. In Jason's own words later, the 'stache was thin and wispy. I knew he wasn't trying to make a fashion statement.

"Did you lose a bet or something?" I asked.

He explained the story. After Iowa State lost to Baylor, he said he wasn't going to shave his mustache until Iowa State won another game. Since the Cyclones played Kansas the following week, one of the worst teams in the entire country, he was confident Iowa State would win and he'd only need to keep the 'stache for a week. Iowa State did, of course, defeat Kansas handily. But it couldn't be that easy.

During home games, Jason sits next to a fan who brings a helmet to every game, and has earned the affectionate nickname Helmet Guy. During big plays, people take turns banging the helmet on the bleachers to create more noise. Helmet Guy is a diehard fan, and apparently wasn't about to leave anything to chance.

Toward the end of the Kansas game, he told Jason, "You *cannot* shave this mustache until Iowa State loses."

So there we were, two weeks later, and Jason still had that ugly mustache. I began hoping the 'stache would last for a long time!

We caught up, each enjoyed a drink, and watched much of the fourth quarter of the Iowa game on my phone, as Purdue shockingly pulled off an unexpected upset. Those complicated feelings I had earlier about Iowa's success turned into complicated feelings about seeing Iowa lose. I legitimately felt bad for the Hawkeye fans I am close to; I know how I would have felt in their shoes. And yet, I'd be lying if I said we weren't a little bit relieved that our rivals were no longer undefeated. (I'm sure some ISU fans had stronger emotions than relief.)

That said, we still had our own game to play, and nothing else would matter if Iowa State lost to Kansas State.

We began our walk back to the stadium.

"Go State!" I said to one fan, before Paige reminded me that both teams today were "State."

"OK fine, go Cyclones!" I corrected myself.

Standing in line to get into the stadium, I was again struck by just how friendly the Kansas State fans were. Everyone was jovial. We were joking with each other. It was a rivalry, but a friendly rivalry.

Paige and I said goodbye to Jason and his family and found our seats a few rows up from them. I had purposely tried to purchase tickets that would be near other Iowa State fans. I had an idea of where the visitors section would be but was not completely sure exactly how many Iowa State fans would be there and how close we would be to other Cyclones. As the stadium began to fill in, I noticed a good number of Cyclone fans in our section. Two sections over, right behind the goalposts, there was a block of about 10 to 15 rows of Cyclone fans. The seats immediately surrounding us, however, were occupied by Kansas State fans.

The atmosphere began to ramp up in the stadium as the band came on the field and played its fight songs and the national anthem. Kansas State also has one of my favorite college football traditions. The band plays the song "Wabash Cannonball" and the fans sway back and forth to the beat. It's especially impressive when you watch the student section do it.

The crowd was ready to go for kickoff. K-State fans were loud. Bill Snyder Family Stadium holds the sound in well, and Kansas State fans know how to create it. Iowa State took the kickoff and lined up for its first play. The fans around me yelled, "OHHHHHHHH." And then Hall silenced everyone not wearing Iowa State gear with his 75-yard run. A few rows behind us, a group of Iowa State fans had lifted one of their friends up and were doing pushups with him as they counted to seven.

The run set the tone for the entire game. I later read in Cyclone Fanatic's recap that even though coach Matt Campbell usually chooses to kick off first when given the choice, this game he decided to give his team the ball first. Campbell saw it as an opportunity to seize momentum. It worked. Iowa State had all the momentum.

The decision to take the ball first also meant Iowa State would not risk Kansas State getting a big play right off the bat. Two years ago, K-State's

Joshua Youngblood returned the opening kickoff 92 yards for a touchdown, putting Iowa State behind the eight-ball early. In 2021, Kansas State again had a strong kick returner. Malik Knowles had returned a kickoff for a touchdown in each of Kansas State's last two games. Iowa State had already given up a touchdown return in 2021. It was the kind of storyline that made Iowa State fans more than a little uneasy, which is why when the kickoff following Hall's touchdown was fielded by Knowles at the three-yard line I cursed under my breath. I then held my breath as he took it 32 yards before finally being brought down.

Over the course of the first quarter, we got to know a few of the people around us. Paige struck up a conversation with the fans to our right. I conversed with one fan who was to my left in the row behind me. He told me how he had been to Ames for the Iowa State vs. Kansas State game in 2014. He was so impressed with then-ISU coach Paul Rhoads that he wrote a letter to Rhoads asking for an autograph, which Rhoads actually sent him.

"That's so cool," I told him.

"I just loved how you guys would fight so hard every game, even when you were underdogs," he said. I agreed.

"I also think you guys have a special coach in Matt Campbell. He seems to really have things rolling," he said.

"We love him," I replied.

A little while later, the video board showed scores from around the Big 12, including Texas' loss to Oklahoma State. I turned to the Kansas State fan and said "Horns down! That's something we can all agree on!"

Over the course of the game, I heard him refer to the 2017 game between the two teams and how exciting it was when Kansas State caught a pass in the back of the endzone on the game's final play to pull off the improbable comeback. I just stared straight ahead. It was still too painful. At another point, the conversation turned to Rhoads' last game against K-State in 2015. I couldn't help but turn around.

"All we had to do was take a knee!" I said. Six years later, we could all laugh about it.

On the field, Iowa State forced K-State quarterback Skylar Thompson into an interception and capitalized with a 44-yard field goal by Andrew Mevis to go up 10-0. The group behind us had picked another person to lift up this time, pushing him into the air 10 times. On the ensuing kickoff, Mevis again kicked it short, setting up Knowles for a 30-yard return. Iowa State again avoided the really big play, but K–State used the good field position to score its first touchdown, a 40-yard pass from Thompson to Phillip Brooks to make it 10-7. Iowa State went three-and-out and was forced to punt, and the Wildcats again began to drive as the first quarter came to a close.

Given Hall's big run, an interception and a 10-0 lead to begin the game, I was a little shellshocked that K–State had the ball with a chance to take the lead. It looked like that was going to happen when one of Thompson's passes was scooped up for a big gain inside the 10-yard line. However, a replay review clearly showed the ball hit the ground before the receiver could catch it, negating the play. Iowa State held the Wildcats to a 43-yard field goal attempt. I knew the kick was no good when I saw the Cyclone fans behind the endzone cheering. Iowa State had held onto the lead.

The Cyclones capitalized with an impressive drive of their own. Iowa State converted three third downs, ran 13 plays in just more than seven minutes and scored on a one-yard run by Hall to go up 17-7. (Followed by 17 air pushups by the Iowa State fans behind us.)

Mevis' kickoff went into the endzone to force a touchback this time, prompting many Iowa State fans to give him a standing ovation. I saw Jason leading the cheers a few rows down.

"Are you guys serious with that cheer," a fan behind me asked.

I had to explain the general lack of confidence a lot of fans had in the kickoff game, coupled with the propensity for Knowles to return kicks for touchdowns.

"A couple weeks ago we gave up a kick return touchdown against Baylor," I said.

"Yeah, I saw that," he responded.

Iowa State held K–State to a three-and-out and got the ball back for another seven-play drive to end the half with a Mevis 41-yard field goal. I was feeling good as Iowa State took a 20-7 lead to halftime.

I went to the concourse to try to find some dinner, but the lines were packed. I decided it wasn't worth the wait as I didn't want to miss any of the game, and figured I'd grab food at some point in the third quarter after the rush subsided. My decision paid off as Iowa State forced a punt on Kansas State's first possession of the second half. A Wildcat punt was downed at the seven-yard line, setting up Iowa State in poor field position. If Kansas State was going to flip momentum, this was the time to do it.

The Cyclones had other ideas.

My brother Kent and I cheer for the same NFL team but have always been on opposite sides of the Iowa State vs. Iowa rivalry.

I am back in my element with Chris, Kaci, James and Derek as we enjoy the first tailgate of the season. I have no idea what we are laughing about but I'm sure it was as hilarious as it looks.

Paige and I finally back in Jack Trice Stadium for the first game of the 2021 season after nearly two years away. Look at me, full of opening day optimism!

There were plenty of signs and flags during ESPN's "College GameDay" before the Iowa State vs. Iowa game.

Chris, Kaci, James and I take in the sights and sounds in Las Vegas before Iowa State's game at UNLV.

Cyclone fans make their way towards the stadium prior to Iowa State's game at UNLV.

The moment I had been daydreaming about for a year-and-a-half happened in real life when Brock Purdy threw a touchdown pass to Charlie Kolar during the second half of the UNLV game.

The "Zombie Cyclones" leave Allegiant Stadium by the thousands after Iowa State's win at UNLV. The words of "Sweet Caroline" rang in the air.

DFW tailgate attendees wave as the team buses drive by on their way to the stadium in Waco.

I cheered along as Jeff Johnson led cheers before Iowa State's game at Baylor.

I felt as connected as ever to the team as they huddled before the first true road game of the season at Baylor.

My dad and I enjoy our Jack Trice Club seats during the Kansas game.

ne Cyclone Marching Band during its pregame show
efore the Kansas game.

Paige and I enjoy celebrating with the players and
Cyclone fans after the win over Kansas State. A win in
Manhattan had been a long time coming!

My friend Jason, with his temporary winning streak-
related mustache, flips pizza rolls on the grill before
ne Oklahoma State game.

Paige and I snapped a photo with thousands of people
rushing the field in celebration of Iowa State's win over
previously undefeated Oklahoma State. These are the
types of moments I envisioned when I began this journey.

Our seats for Iowa State's game at West Virginia. It was
tough day with cold, rainy weather, a less-than-full
rowd and a maddening Cyclone loss.

Adam, me and Charles in the stands at Texas Tech
while Iowa State was making a furious comeback.

Texas Tech has just hit a 62-yard field goal to win. In this moment I'm pretty sure I was thinking, "Why the heck am I doing this?"

Our seats in Oklahoma's historic stadium.

Seniors and their parents line the field before Iowa State's final home game. I had to be in the stadium for this!

I snapped a panoramic photo of the stadium as the team huddled moments before the TCU game kicked off.

After waiting for 21 months between the last home game in 2019 and the first home game in 2021, the final game at Jack Trice Stadium was over, just like that.

One of my lasting memories from the bowl trip: Iowa State fans dancing to "Juicy Wiggle."

Iowa State began the possession with a six-yard run by Hall. Quarterback Brock Purdy then found tight end Chase Allen for 12 yards and a first down at the 25. *Phew, at least we are out of our own end,* I thought. The next two plays went nowhere, setting up a third-and-11 and getting the crowd to its feet. Purdy's pass was broken up, but Kansas State was called for a penalty for having too many players on the field. Iowa State had another shot, and this time converted a third-and-six with a seven-yard pass from Purdy to running back Jirehl Brock.

A couple plays later, Iowa State again faced a third down, this time third-and-four. Purdy scrambled for seven yards to the Iowa State 49 and another first down. *Even if we don't score here, it's still exactly the drive we needed to flip field position,* I thought. *This is what veteran teams do.* They weren't done. Iowa State again faced a third down, this time third-and-one, and Hall broke through for five yards. By this point, I was deeply impressed with the drive Iowa State was putting together, and also noticed the game was now past the halfway point of the third quarter. The more the clock ticked when Iowa State had a two-score lead, the better. Kansas State fans seemed to notice too. The noise level had dropped considerably since the first third-down play of the drive.

Purdy found Kolar for 13 yards and a first down before facing another third down on the next sequence. Iowa State needed five, and Purdy found Kolar for six. First down Cyclones. Finally, Iowa State faced a third-and-eight from the 11-yard line. With the third quarter clock now below three minutes, Purdy threw a strike to Sean Shaw Jr. near the sideline in the endzone. Shaw was covered well, but Purdy placed the ball away from the defender and into an area where only Shaw could find it. Shaw turned his body away from the defender and made a spectacular catch as the defender tried helplessly to stop him. Touchdown, Iowa State. The Cyclones had taken a commanding 27-7 lead.

It was perhaps the most impressive drive I had ever seen a Cyclone football team complete. Eighteen plays, 93 yards, more than 10 minutes of game time. For Iowa State fans, it was a thing of beauty, the kind of drive that future drives will get compared with. For Kansas State fans, it had to be deflating. Iowa State had taken the air out of the stadium. Except for, of course, the Iowa State fans behind us lifting their friend in the air for 27 pushups.

By this point, I was really wanting some food. Remembering how I had left the stands right when Baylor returned a kickoff for a touchdown just a few weeks prior, I decided to wait until after the kickoff. This time it was a touchback.

"Don't let them score," I told Paige.

I walked up to the concourse and noticed quite a few Kansas State fans making their way out of the stadium. They believed the game was over. I felt comfortable, but had seen too many improbable K-State comebacks in this series to count it as a win just yet.

As I waited in line for a sandwich, I watched the in-stadium video feed and listened to the crowd cheer as Kansas State picked up first downs on five straight plays as the third quarter ended. I got my sandwich and watched from the concourse as Kansas State scored a touchdown five plays into the fourth quarter. K-State missed the extra point, keeping it a full two-touchdown lead for Iowa State at 27-13. When I got back to my seat, I looked at Paige.

"I told you not to let them score!" I said jokingly.

"I know! At least they missed the extra point," she said.

Still, with more than 12 minutes left, the comfortable victory I was envisioning was hanging in the balance. Hall made another monster play to begin the next drive, this time taking it 43 yards to the Kansas State 32-yard line. A few plays later, Mevis knocked in a 41-yard field goal to give Iowa State a 30-13 lead. The Cyclone fans in the endzone cheered as the kick sailed through. I breathed a little easier. Behind me, the Iowa State fans did 30 pushups.

K-State wasn't going to make this easy for the Cyclones, again driving down the field. This time, Iowa State's defense made it tougher, forcing a third-and-11 and then a third-and-two. Kansas State converted both and drove inside the 10-yard line. Iowa State forced a fourth-and-eight from the nine. *A stop here would end it.* Thompson threw it to the endzone, where Iowa State's T.J. Tampa was waiting. *He's going to intercept it,* I thought. The play took place in the opposite endzone, and I lost sight of it but began to cheer as I thought I saw Tampa make the catch. I saw the K-State student section on that end of the field start cheering and realized something had gone wrong.

"What? How did they score?" I wondered out loud.

The replay showed it. Somehow the ball got past Tampa into the hands of Knowles, who was able to hold on for the touchdown. Kansas State cut the deficit to 30-20. Behind us, some Kansas State fans had copied the Iowa State fans, but instead of lifting a full-grown adult into the air 20 times in honor of the Wildcats' 20 points, they were lifting a toddler into the air. As they reached 20, I joined others in clapping for them.

Despite this lighthearted moment, my anxiety was spiking. I thought back to 2014, 2015 and 2017. I thought back to Iowa State's own comeback in 2018. Crazy things tend to happen when Iowa State plays against Kansas State. *If we somehow lose this game,* I thought, *it might be the most painful loss of all of them.* My friend Chris, watching from home, texted, "Any other team right now ... and I wouldn't feel even a twinge of worry. But this team ..."

Yep.

Kansas State attempted an onside kick to try to get the ball back with just more than five minutes to play. The ball was a slow roller, executed well. It gave time for K-State's kicking team to catch up to it. Right as it reached the required 10-yard mark, an Iowa State player tried to jump on it ... and it bounced away. *This is how it happens,* I thought. *They are going to recover this.* The Kansas State fans that were still in attendance cheered in hopeful anticipation. Players piled on top of players. It was impossible to tell who had the football. Iowa State players were claiming their team recovered it, but so was at least one Kansas State player. After what felt like 10 minutes, the referee signaled Iowa State ball as a Cyclone player came out of the pile holding the football. The Cyclone fans cheered appreciatively as I breathed a literal sigh of relief.

Iowa State was able to convert another 40-yard field goal with 1:23 to play to grab a 33-20 lead, and I could finally relax just a little bit. The fan behind me, the Paul Rhoads fan, told me goodbye.

"It was nice to meet you," I said.

The clock ran out as Kansas State tried to score one more time, and I stood with the other Iowa State fans — now with most of the K-State fans having left — and cheered as the clock hit 0:00. Iowa State had finally won in Manhattan.

We headed down a few rows to catch up with Jason. "We are going to go down and cheer on the team," I said.

"Yeah, we'll come too," he said.

It had been 17 years since a Cyclone win in this stadium. Now was the time to enjoy the moment.

Following the celebration, we began our walk back to the car.

"I can't imagine being more nervous during what felt like such a dominating victory," I remarked to the laugh of another fan filing out.

Jason and I shared stories of our interaction with fans during the game and remarked how friendly they were. One Wildcat fan walked by us and said, "Good luck the rest of the season."

Speaking of the rest of the season, we began to look ahead to the next game — a home game against undefeated Oklahoma State. The win over Kansas State ensured there would be extra anticipation for the Oklahoma State matchup. For Jason, the mustache would last for at least one more week.

Iowa State was now halfway through the regular season at 4-2, and more importantly 2-1 in the Big 12. We had finally seen the Cyclones line up against a major conference opponent not named Kansas and win, and do so convincingly, in the style we had enjoyed watching during the historic 2020 run. Farmageddon 2021 belonged to Iowa State.

CHAPTER FIFTEEN

IOWA STATE VS. OKLAHOMA STATE PREVIEW

SOMETHING SPECIAL IN THE AIR

Oct. 21, 2021

An undefeated Oklahoma State team will enter Jack Trice Stadium on Saturday afternoon. We've seen this movie before, more than once in fact. And we've also seen a lot of other crazy things happen.

The Iowa State vs. Oklahoma State series over the last 10 years leading into 2021 has been possibly the most memorable series the Cyclones have played. It's not a full-fledged rivalry, but it has elements that have made it compelling since 2011.

The Cyclones are just 2-8 in that timeframe, which has coincided with the last round of conference realignment that resulted in the teams playing every year rather than two of every four years. The series has been anything but ordinary. It has featured thrilling wins on both sides, blown leads, plenty of controversy, one moment that changed the course of ISU football history and one game that changed the course of college football history.

It's only fitting we start with that last one.

Even the most casual of Iowa State fans remember the warm November evening in 2011 when Oklahoma State came to Jack Trice Stadium undefeated and No. 2 in the country. It was a rare Friday night game, scheduled that way to fit into ESPN's television schedule. Chris, Kaci and I drove up from Des Moines early in the afternoon after getting off work early. On the way, as we tend to do, we talked about the game.

"Do we actually have a chance?" seemed to be the topic of conversation.

The Cyclones were 27.5-point underdogs. I'm a sucker for trying to talk myself into believing Iowa State has a chance in any game it plays. In my heart of hearts, did I really believe the Cyclones could win that game?

No. I had literally never seen anything like it.

I still tried to talk myself into it, and I remember listening to a talk radio show during the drive. The hosts were talking about the game, and similarly to me were making the case for why Iowa State could win. I don't remember what my arguments were, or what their arguments were. It doesn't matter.

The seed was planted for me to have just a twinge of hope.

We arrived at the tailgate, and as I recall, most of the rest of the group had been there since around Noon. We were a few hours behind. No matter. Collectively, we — shall I say — hit it hard. If the Cyclones really were going to lose by four touchdowns, this was going to be the highlight of the day.

Normally, especially at that point just a few years removed from being in the band, my goal was to be in the stadium by the time the band took the field for its pregame show. As we were packing up, I heard the first notes. We weren't going to make it!

By the time we finished putting our stuff back in the car, walking to the stadium, going through the ticketing area, likely using the restroom and finally finding our way to our seats in the pre-renovation south endzone, the game was underway. I looked around. The stadium was almost entirely full, a rarity in those days for a November game. Fans had yellow towels, also something that I never remembered happening before. I took in the scene of fans standing, waving their towels and yelling to encourage the defense. I had sat through my share of games at that point where the atmosphere in the stadium said, "We don't expect to win." This crowd was different from the get-go. It felt like a big-time atmosphere, and it felt like a crowd that believed our team belonged.

It just felt different.

Iowa State's head coach that evening, Paul Rhoads, was in his third year at the helm and had pulled off a few unexpected upsets and near-upsets. I can only imagine that fed into the crowd. *Maybe tonight. Just maybe.*

Oklahoma State's typically high-powered offense struggled with turn-overs that evening and had a tough time getting into its normal rhythm. The

Cowboys still jumped out to a 17-7 lead at half. Conventional wisdom said Iowa State probably was not coming back from that, but it was close enough to still have hope. When the Cowboys scored early in the third quarter to go up 24-7, it felt like Oklahoma State was about to pull away.

Good effort, Cyclones. You kept it close for a while.

I have sat through a good number of games that the crowd stops believing, and fans begin filing toward the exits in the third quarter, slowly but surely emptying out during every timeout or possession change until only a few thousand (including me) remain when the clock hits triple zeroes. I was convinced this was about to happen … until Jarvis West took the ensuing kickoff 50 yards.

OK, we'll stick around for this drive, people seemed to think. Six plays later, James White ran 32 yards to the endzone to cut the lead to 24-14.

One of the things Iowa State fans loved about the early years of Rhoads' tenure is that he would take chances other coaches would shy away from. That's exactly what he did as he sent kicker Grant Mahoney onto the field for a surprise onside kick, recovered by Iowa State. It was one of those moments where the world seems to be in slow motion, as I watched the ball float in the air toward the Iowa State player. I was simultaneously shocked and yet I knew exactly what was about to happen. As he came down with the football, the crowd erupted. For the first time that evening, I really believed the Cyclones could win this game, and the onside kick was a signal to me that *they* believed they could win this game.

A lot of the rest of the game was a blur. From that moment on, I somehow knew Iowa State was going to come back and tie it. Which they did, 24-24 in the fourth quarter.

On the broadcast, ESPN announcer Joe Tessitore remarked, "Something special is in the air here."

The fans were standing and waving their towels every time Oklahoma State's offense had the ball. Proving this was a game where there was something special in the air, OSU kicker Quinn Sharp lined up to attempt a 37-yard field goal with 1:21 remaining. As the kick sailed toward the uprights, my friend Chris yelled, "Oh, it's no good!"

Sure enough, the refs signaled no good as the ISU players celebrated and ran off the field, the crowd around them waving towels and sharing looks of disbelief. It was a questionable call as the kick sailed right over the goalposts, and I do not blame any OSU fan for being sour about it. For as much as bad calls and missed kicks are part of Iowa State football lore, it felt fitting that it went in our favor that evening.

A little while later in the second overtime, Cyclone Ter'Ran Benton intercepted a pass to stop Oklahoma State's scoring chance. All Iowa State needed to do was score any points on its possession in the second overtime to win. Running back Jeff Woody, a crowd favorite whose name would, after this night, always be remembered by Cyclone fans, took the ball three straight times, and on the third powered his way into the endzone to secure the win.

"Come on, let's get on the field!" I yelled to Chris and Kaci.

We headed down toward the gate separating the south endzone stands from the field, which was already open, and joined thousands of others from all corners in rushing the field in celebration. I momentarily let all my emotions out as I ran full speed, screaming "YEEEEAAAAHHHHHH!!!!!" at the top of my lungs. I looked around, and in the crowd I seemed to have lost my friends.

"Kyle!" Chris yelled from a little way away. *Oh, thank goodness.*

A little while later, after belting "Sweet Caroline," we headed up through the concourse. In some of the suite seats, ESPN was on the televisions showing live scenes from our field. Iowa State football was the story of the evening in the sports world. It felt shocking.

On the way home, we needed food, so we stopped at a Perkins in Ankeny. I remember seeing some Oklahoma State fans sitting in a booth, and I almost wanted to go console them about their championship season being ruined. When I arrived back at my apartment in Des Moines, I turned on ESPN and they were showing a replay of the game. I quickly called Chris.

"Hey, ESPN is showing a replay. Do you want to come watch?"

No hesitation. "Yes, I'll be there in a minute."

It's tough to say at what point on that Saturday morning I finally went to sleep.

The game was so unexpected that it was nominated for an ESPY Award in the category of Best Upset. It is often credited as being the game that shifted the college football postseason to a four-team playoff. I believe it forever changed the atmosphere in Jack Trice Stadium into a crowd that believed our team could win on any given gameday. Even though Iowa State could never quite capitalize on that game for future seasons during Rhoads' tenure as coach, I still think it changed the course of Cyclone football long-term in addition to the sport of college football.

It was also the first in what has been a series of bizarre games between these teams.

OSU won comfortably the next two years, but in 2014 an upset-minded Iowa State team entered Stillwater needing a win. Iowa State was 1-3, Oklahoma State was ranked No. 21 in the country. In Rhoads' last three seasons, all of which resulted in significantly more losses than wins, the silver lining was that the Cyclones often played with a chip on their shoulder that helped them keep an upset-bid alive. Such was the case on this early October day. The Cyclones played to a first-half 6-6 draw until the Cowboys lined up near the goal-line on the last play of the half. On the play, it was ruled that OSU's running back was stopped short. Cyclone players celebrated. As is custom, replay officials decided to review the play just to make sure. Watching it over and over on television, I was convinced the outcome was in our favor. I was talking with Chris on the phone, describing what happened.

"Yeah, they are reviewing it, but it was definitely a stop. What a big way to get out of the half ... OH MY GOODNESS ARE YOU KIDDING ME??"

Somehow, the replay officials felt they had conclusive evidence to overturn the play and give the Cowboys a touchdown. It was made even more deflating when Oklahoma State took the second half kickoff 97 yards for a touchdown, effectively burying Iowa State.

In 2015, another upset-minded Iowa State team jumped out to a 24-7 lead over another undefeated Cowboys team in November. It started to feel like déjà vu all over again. *Could we really ruin their national championship aspirations?* Turns out, this wasn't the Iowa State of 2011. Oklahoma State fought back for a 35-31 win.

In 2016, during coach Matt Campbell's first year, Iowa State lost another big lead. Iowa State grabbed a 31-14 lead late in the third quarter, but another Oklahoma State rally knocked off the Cyclones.

In 2017, the tide started to turn in Iowa State's football program, but heartbreaking losses to Oklahoma State were still en vogue. Iowa State entered the game with a 6-3 record, having already defeated highly ranked Oklahoma and TCU. By winning out, the Cyclones could still have secured a spot in the Big 12 Championship Game.

I remember a little extra emotion in the stands that day. It was Senior Day, and the first year in a while Iowa State was good enough to reach a bowl game. There was plenty to cheer about as Iowa State's offense racked up 491 yards and 30 first downs. For each first down, the PA announcer said, "That's another Cyclone …" and fans answered, "FIRST DOWN!" as we extended our arm to mimic the signal that referees give to signal a first down. We got to do that 30 times. After a while, it was almost not fun anymore. Almost.

The problem was Iowa State's typically stout defense seemed to have no answer for Oklahoma State's high-powered offense. A back-and-forth game started to feel special again in the fourth quarter. Joel Lanning, who played as quarterback in a number of games for the Cyclones, transformed himself into a linebacker during his senior year of 2017. A really good linebacker who could also still play quarterback when needed. Lanning's specialty when he had the ball in his hands — particularly his senior year — was to follow his blockers and use his linebacker-style physique to bulldoze through defenders and try to pick up extra yards. So when they put him in the game on second-and-four, conventional wisdom said it was a running play. Instead, Lanning faked a handoff, dropped back and threw it up to a single-covered Allen Lazard, also a senior, in the endzone. Lazard was well-covered, but the pass was in the right spot. He tipped the ball with his left hand, then let it fall gently into his right hand. All while fighting off the defender and getting his feet down in bounds before giving up his balance and falling backwards to the ground, ball safely clutched in his grasp.

The crowd erupted.

The touchdown gave Iowa State a 35-31 lead, and a touchdown on the Cyclones' next drive turned it into a 42-34. It felt like our day until OSU scored two touchdowns in succession to regain the lead 49-42 (truly a wild game). Iowa State had one more chance, driving down deep into OSU territory before facing a fourth-and-13 play. As quarterback Zeb Noland threw it to running back David Montgomery short of the first down, I thought, *Game over.* There was a defender there, ready to make the play, until … Montgomery made him miss and picked up the first down, making it all the way to the three-yard line. The crowd was buzzing again.

We had new life.

Then came a play we still talk about every time the two teams get together.

On second-and-goal, Noland threw it up to Marchie Murdock, who came down with the ball firmly in his grasp. That is, if you ignored the Oklahoma State defender who was literally between Murdock and the ball. Murdock pinned the ball with his right hand against the defender's chest, who after a second realized the ball was in his grasp. They came to the ground simultaneously. We were sitting in our usual seats in the third row of the upper deck behind the endzone in the southwest corner of the stadium. From my view, which would have to be considered just about the best view in the stadium on that particular play, it was a catch. I threw my hands in the air, thinking it was a touchdown. So did a number of other fans. Our joy turned to confusion as I looked around. Nobody was sure what to make of what we just saw. The ref signaled nothing. After a few seconds of pause that felt like a few hours, the referees talked it over and signaled that it was an interception. An audible groan passed through the crowd. *Surely, they'll overturn this on replay review,* I thought. No such luck. Game over. After I got home that day, I watched every replay, scoured Twitter and read through each opinion on the Cyclone Fanatic message board, trying to come to terms with what I witnessed. To this day, I still believe it was a touchdown. I'm pretty sure Murdock does as well.

In 2018, it was a much better memory. As I watched 1-3 Iowa State take the field in Stillwater, I had a bad feeling. After such a positive 2017 season, I could feel this one slipping away. At the time, my wife Paige was my fiancée, and she went wedding dress shopping while I hung out with my dad and her dad to watch the game at her uncle's house. The day started off as bad as I feared. Noland, still the quarterback, was sacked on the first play. Iowa State had to punt after a three-and-out possession. Oklahoma State went 70 yards in five plays to take a 7-0 lead. Iowa State went three-and-out again before punting.

I mentally prepared myself for a blowout. *Just be calm,* I told myself. *You can't make an idiot out of yourself in front of your future in-laws.* The Iowa State defense stepped up and forced a sack of their own back to the seven-yard line, and then recorded a safety on a botched punt attempt. Then came perhaps the most defining moment in recent Cyclone history.

On the first Saturday of October in 2018, freshman Brock Purdy made his first appearance at quarterback. Purdy immediately led Iowa State 75 yards in less than three minutes, capped by a 21-yard pass to Hakeem Butler. On the next possession, he capped a 62-yard drive with a 29-yard touchdown run. It's easy to write now, knowing how it turned out, but I think I also knew it at the time: We were seeing something special. There was something different about this kid. This was the start of something.

Purdy led Iowa State to a win that day and has been the starting quarterback since.

I'd love to end this preview right there, but the 2019 and 2020 games are perfect examples of what worries me about 2021. The 2019 game was at Jack

Trice Stadium. Before our game kicked off, we saw Oklahoma had lost to Kansas State. This opened up the Big 12 race, and Iowa State could be in the driver's seat with a win. Iowa State was undefeated in the last two seasons in October and had also won its first three October games of 2019. This was our time to seize control.

Something just never felt right in the game. Iowa State felt out of synch. The crowd felt out of synch. Oklahoma State jumped out to a 21-10 lead with touchdowns of 71, 50 and 65 yards. It was a very un-Cyclone-like performance on defense, and fear seeped into the Jack Trice Stadium crowd. It was not the script we had grown accustomed to. Iowa State did fight back to tie the game 27-27 before Purdy threw an interception that was returned for a touchdown midway through the fourth quarter to give OSU a 34-27 lead. Purdy then threw interceptions on two of Iowa State's final three possessions to help Oklahoma State seal the win, in what has likely been the most forgettable game of his tenure.

Last year's game was the one blip in an otherwise perfect regular season in the conference. It wasn't a bad loss, but it didn't leave a good taste in my mouth. As weird as it sounds, I felt somewhat fortunate that Iowa State didn't have to play Oklahoma State again in the Big 12 Championship. Since the 2011 upset, other than Purdy's coming out party, Oklahoma State has either had Iowa State's number or found bizarre ways to win games.

This year's game is an enigma in its own right. Oklahoma State is 6-0 and No. 8 in the country. And yet, Iowa State is favored to win. Advanced analytics seem to love the Cyclones going forward, and the game being at Jack Trice Stadium plays into Iowa State's favor. It reminds me of a few games Georges Niang and Monte Morris played for the Iowa State men's basketball team. Top-ranked teams would come into Hilton Coliseum, but I still believed Iowa State was going to win, and it almost always did.

The game has major Big 12 Championship race implications. Iowa State has very little margin for error after losing its conference opener to Baylor. I still think the Cyclones could make the championship game with another Big 12 loss, but a loss to Oklahoma State would make that significantly less likely. This is a game Iowa State has to win for tiebreaker purposes.

That said, Saturday will be fun beyond the Big 12 title race. It is homecoming in Ames. The tailgate lots will be rocking. The air will be crisp. The stadium will be full. This is setting up to be the type of day that made me into a college football fan to begin with.

To borrow the words of ESPN's announcer Joe Tessitore in 2011, there has been something special in the air almost every time these two teams have played since. I am always waiting for something out of the ordinary, or just plain weird, to happen. I get the feeling this year is destined to be the same. In 2011, I — along with everyone else — was shocked at the outcome of a Cyclone win. An Iowa State win this year wouldn't surprise me in the least.

CHAPTER SIXTEEN

IOWA STATE VS. OKLAHOMA STATE RECAP

SPECIAL INDEED

Oct. 26, 2021

There was something in the air on Saturday afternoon as Iowa State played the first half of its homecoming game against Oklahoma State. It was not something special, though, to borrow the words of ESPN's Joe Tessitore from 2011. No, it was something else. Something like anxiety. Something like consternation. Something like frustration.

There were some good moments, but overall, it just didn't feel right inside Jack Trice Stadium as Oklahoma State built up a 14-7 halftime lead. It felt too similar to the games I had watched OSU win the last two years, where it just didn't look quite like the Iowa State football team we expected to see. And after losing to Iowa at home and losing the first Big 12 game to take away almost all margin for error in the conference title race, it felt troublesome.

That feeling changed in one moment in the second half.

I have written before that Cyclone Fans vs. The Refs could be its own chapter. We are so used to weird calls going against us in big moments. We are so used to those calls killing our momentum and making us say, "What if?"

In an Oklahoma State series that has resulted in some of the most bizarre games and plays I have ever witnessed, this one would rank near the top.

On Iowa State's first drive of the second quarter, quarterback Brock Purdy found receiver Xavier Hutchinson on a slant route, and Hutchinson broke free for what should have been a 54-yard touchdown as the crowd roared. Chris pointed out there was a flag on the field near the endzone.

"You have to be kidding me, they are going to call him for taunting!"

Toward the end of the play, Hutchinson turned his head to look behind him. When he saw nobody was around, he semi-high-stepped his last couple steps into the endzone in celebration. Or at least that's what I thought I saw.

The referee saw what he perceived as taunting. My best guess (the referees don't have to answer for their calls after the game, so we don't know for sure) is the referee thought Hutchinson's look back was a form of trash talk … or something. The resulting call was a 15-yard penalty from the spot of the foul, meaning Iowa State's touchdown was wiped off the board.

As tens of thousands of fans booed, I stared in disbelief. *They can't really have called that. I must be missing something.* They really did call it. Instead of a 14-14 tie, it was still 14-7 Oklahoma State. After I finally mentally comprehended what happened, I joined in the boos.

"Worst call I've ever seen," I wrote in my group text chain.

I didn't say that lightly, and I wasn't the only person saying it. National college football personality Brett McMurphy tweeted, "I just witnessed the worst call in [the] history of college football."

On the radio broadcast, play-by-play announcer John Walters yelled, "That is HORRIBLE!" Color commentator Eric Heft said, "This is like the worst call in NCAA history."

On the Fox television broadcast, rules analyst Mike Pereira said, "I really don't like that call."

It was the type of call that could ultimately cost a team a game, and we had seen this play out before. These Cyclones, as I continued to learn, are different under coach Matt Campbell's leadership.

The Cyclones lined up at the 18-yard line and completed a six-yard pass play. (Immediately after the play more boos reigned down.) Purdy then ran for three yards. (More boos.) On third-and-one, Purdy threw it to the endzone to — who else? — Hutchinson. He caught it for a touchdown as the crowd again cheered loudly. Iowa State had overcome the adversity to tie the game.

After the extra point was good, Campbell appeared to chew out the referee near the sideline in animated fashion. Hutchinson looked toward the fans behind the bench and encouraged them to cheer louder. Some fans did cheer, but many more continued to boo. "Juicy Wiggle" came on the loudspeakers, which got fans clapping and dancing, but there were a few more boos after the ensuing kickoff.

Now, there was something special in the air. It wasn't the shocking feeling of seeing a Cyclone team that was a heavy underdog compete with Oklahoma State back in 2011. It was an entire attitude shift. The crowd now had a chip on its collective shoulder; there was some anger in the air. More importantly, there was a feeling of unity. These were *our* Cyclones. This was *our* stadium. This was *our* game to win.

It was Cyclones vs. The World. The team had overcome a bad call to tie the game. And we the fans weren't going to let our Cyclones lose.

—

When your football team is coming off an impressive road win and welcoming a top 10 team to its home stadium, you would think the conversation would revolve around football. Instead, for the first part of the week, the conversation was all about the school's athletic logo.

On Tuesday, the Iowa State University Book Store released a line of merchandise with the school logo that got phased out beginning in 2008. The half bird, half tornado, or as some of us in the band called it, bird-in-a-blender. In the same time period, navy blue had worked its way into the logo and athletic uniforms and merchandise (which many Cyclone fans lovingly, or not-so-lovingly, refer to as tertiary blue), a trend that was phased out heavily with the logo change (to eventually be replaced by Campbell's seemingly favorite color, black). Tertiary blue was back with the Book Store's merchandise. It had become nearly impossible to find merchandise with that logo, or any gear with tertiary blue, in recent years. It was, in my opinion, the perfect time to bring it back; someone like me is just old enough to have gotten rid of nearly all my old logo merchandise and clothing and would have feelings of nostalgia. Someone in college today may not have ever even owned any gear with the old logo or color scheme. It did make me feel a little bit old to have the logo from when I was a student now be referred to as vintage.

It got Cyclone fans on Twitter abuzz. It was a topic on Cyclone-related podcasts. It was a dominant topic on my text message chain. It set off a friendly debate.

"What is the best logo in school history?" "Is the Tornado Cy (or bird-in-a-blender) logo attractive or ugly?" and "Do we love or hate tertiary blue?"

I remember the first few years after the logo and color scheme changed. I would cringe just a little when I saw people wear gear with the old logo. I wanted Iowa State to have a strong, united brand and having the outdated logo out there seemed counterintuitive to that. When the Book Store released its new vintage merchandise, however, I was ultimately all for it. It was the logo I grew up wearing and the logo that was on the front of my marching band uniform. I was just nostalgic enough. I even eyed purchasing a tertiary blue sweatshirt with the logo, a purchase that — as of writing this — I have not pulled the trigger on yet.

Oh, and for my money, the best logo in school history is the Walking Cy logo, of which I happily purchased a t-shirt at Saturday's game.

I think my favorite part of the entire discussion was that it was another reminder how much people who care about Cyclone football (and other sports, and the university in general) have emotional attachments to elements as basic as the logo. On homecoming week, it was the perfect flashpoint of a conversation to make many of us reminisce. It was totally fitting when Paige found the one piece of clothing I had with the old Tornado Cy logo on it that I could wear to the game (no tertiary blue in this one, though).

Eventually, the conversation turned to game week. It was set to be a classic fall day in Ames. Chilly in the morning with temperatures in the 30s, reaching the 50s by gametime, with sunshine. My friend Charles was coming from Minneapolis for the game. Chris and Kaci were bringing their nearly two-year-old son to his first game. The regular tailgating crew was going to be out in full force. And my friend Jason was hosting a reunion tailgate for his old fraternity, Theta Xi, which despite not being a part of, I still wanted to check out. It was shaping up to be a wonderful day of tailgating.

Charles and I decided to go up early to meet the larger tailgating group. Since the parking lots would open six hours before the 2:30 p.m. game kickoff, we made plans to arrive before 8:30 a.m. My wife, Paige, would ride up with Chris and Kaci later in the morning.

Charles and I arrived, met up with the group and caravanned into the grass lot together. I was bundled up with a long sleeve t-shirt, my Welcome to Brocktober t-shirt for good luck to support quarterback Brock Purdy, my Iowa State sweatshirt with the Tornado Cy and a gray zip-up sweatshirt with an I-State logo, in addition to my Walking Cy hat and gloves. As we set up, I poured myself some coffee with cream liqueur, a favorite drink for a fall morning tailgate. Chris, meanwhile, texted us highlights from the 2011 ISU upset of OSU, later telling us he watched the entire game that morning. It seemed to make him feel good vibes.

After catching up, playing a game and enjoying the company, I made my way up to Jason's tailgate. It was the first time this season I had walked from the south side of the stadium to the north during a gameday. Tailgaters were already filling the lots. It was a festive atmosphere all around. Team flags flew everywhere, music blared, people had grills set up and spreads of food. The sun shone brightly. *What a wonderful day.*

I arrived at Jason's tailgate. Generations of Theta Xi members were there. Both of Jason's sons were in Theta Xi, one a recent graduate and one a current student, meaning the tailgate was a confluence of past and present members. Jason was still sporting the mustache, forced to keep it after Iowa State's win at Kansas State. Upon my arrival, Jason was excited to show me how he had adapted a time-honored tradition from my normal tailgate crew: grilling pizza rolls. Except he did it a little differently than us. Instead of dumping the entire bag onto the grill, I watched as Jason neatly laid out each individual pizza roll one by one, in straight rows and columns on the grill. A few minutes later, he flipped each one by one. He brought a higher level of sophistication to the entire process.

Jason also put some homemade habanero peppers stuffed with pork on the grill.

"Do you like spicy?" he asked.

"Just a little bit. Maybe I'll just eat a couple of those ones," I replied.

He laughed and let me know I probably wouldn't be able to handle that. A few minutes later, he handed them out to a number of people. I ate mine; after chewing and swallowing, my tongue began to burn. The burn picked up in intensity, and just sat there painfully. I began to take sips of beer and hold them in my mouth as long as I could to try to take the sting off. I watched others going through the same experience. One unfortunate person had accidentally touched his eye after touching the pepper; tears were streaming down his face. I made a mental note to wash my hands before touching my face. A few minutes later, I ran into my friends Dave and Tyler, frequent visitors of my normal tailgate crew who had also stopped by to say hello to Jason. Dave let me know his mouth was burning. So was mine, 10 minutes after eating the snack.

I headed back to my normal tailgate, where Paige had arrived along with Chris and Kaci and their son. The anticipation of gameday was building. We ate a few snacks, finished our drinks and headed into the stadium. We arrived in time to see the band begin to make their way to the field. The Iowa State University Alumni Band was also in attendance for the homecoming game.

I always get a little extra nostalgic about the band during homecoming. If you ever want to get just a little bit of a taste of what it's like to be a rock star, join a college marching band.

Sure, you may not think playing a sousaphone is all that glamorous, but for 15 minutes or so before kickoff at a Cyclone home game, you are the star of the show.

I thought back to my time in the band. The memory of each game runs together, but I can still remember the overall experience vividly.

About 30 minutes before the game, we would take our spot on the sidelines. The football teams would still be finishing their warmups on the field. Around us, the stands would begin to fill up as people filed in. The student section was already full. There was a buzz in the stadium; even though the game hadn't started yet, I had to talk loudly to the people around me. The public address announcer continued to read ad spots and other general information. All around, my eyes and ears were flooded with the business of gameday; cheerleaders finding their spots, the student section decked out in cardinal and gold, the sound of pads on the field, gameday staff taking care of various tasks.

As the players on either team ended their warmups, they huddled up as a team, then jogged into the locker room. When the Cyclone players headed toward their locker room, the student section and others already in the stadium stood and applauded. The buzz of pleasant conversation around the stadium turned into the first semi-deafening cheer of the day.

I picked up my sousaphone as they came off the field. It was our turn. For the big games, the crowd knew it too. Students slowly began cheering. Those moments signified to the fans in the stadium that the show — our routine, the pregame video, the players' walk to the field and then the game itself — was about to begin. For thousands that were still in the parking lot, our first notes indicated it was time for them to pack up the tailgate and head in.

For the more heavily anticipated games, such as CyHawk gameday, most people were already in the stadium at this point and they were ready for us. Chants of, "I-S-U! I-S-U!" reverberated. Or, "Let's go State!"

The drumline would begin to march on the field in formation. The student section, if they weren't already standing, came to its feet. Our PA announcer began his introductions. "Now entering the field, the pride of Iowa State. It's the Iowa State University Cyclone Football Varsityyyyyyyyyy Marching Band!"

The drum major blew their whistle. ★TWEEEEEEEET Tweet Tweet★ and I answered, "Go State!" as the drumline began its cadence. *And we're off.*

To enter the field, we would do a type of march we called "X-ing." Basically, we lifted our leg to a 45-degree angle with our toe pointed straight down. We performed this motion in rapid succession to the beat of the drumline. It was like the marching version of running. It got your blood flowing, and seemed to match the energy and intensity of the crowd. We would "X" in circles a number of times (I'll be honest, I never actually counted) as the drumline played its cadence. We were moving too fast to say anything. It was too loud to hear the person next to you. Everyone around me looked the same wearing their uniforms. For me, even though I was surrounded by people in my circle, even though there were tens of thousands of fans in the stadium, this was the moment of the day that I felt most alone, in a good way. I would be totally in the zone.

Then, the drum major blew their whistle and it was time to line up in our formation. As the drumline wrapped up its cadence, the PA announcer wrapped up his introduction:

"It's the Iowa State University Cyclone Football Varsityyyyyyyyyy Marching Band!"

Although the routine changed a bit over the years, during my time in the band we would go straight from the cadence into our first song, a processional of sorts, meant to build energy. We were stationary, and although I was watching the drum major, I was also taking in the site of a two-deck Big 12 stadium full of people in the background. It was a surreal feeling to think about, for some games, 50,000 people were watching me (and the other 300-or-so people on the field). We were on stage. We were the stars.

Everyone in the stadium knew what was about to happen next: the fight song. As we played the first notes of the fight song, we began our high-step marching. The fans stood and clapped in unison. We lined up in our classic ISU formation and marched in unison down the field. For the sousaphones, we would form two diagonal lines at the top of the formation that would meet in the middle. My senior year, I was the top point of that line. It wasn't quite "Dotting the I" at Ohio State, but it made it much easier to tell my friends and family where they could find me.

Marching down the field, playing the fight song, 50,000 fans clapping in unison. My middle school and high school self would have thought it was the coolest thing in the world. My college self knew it was the coolest thing in my world.

The first time I watched a game from the stands during my post-band days was truly one of the most emotional experiences I've ever had. Watching the band do all the things I had been a part of just nine months or so ago. I'm not ashamed to admit a few tears streamed down my face as I heard ★TWEEEEEEET Tweet Tweet★ followed by, "Go State!"

Because I knew everything that led up to that moment. The week of camp before school started, with our own version of two-a-day practices. That there were freshmen who, like me before, had arrived on campus just a few weeks ago, nervous about embarking on college life during their first time away from home, who spent the first day on campus going to band practice. Odds were they would meet at least one lifelong friend, just as I met a few (one of whom, Charles, had ridden to the game with me on Saturday). They would sweat their body weight in water learning the drills. Now, they were on the field in front of 50,000 fans, and me, as I was coming to terms with the fact that I would never be in their shoes again.

During the homecoming game each year, there are a number of alumni who do get to relive some of those old memories in the Alumni Marching Band. It's a chance for people to get back on campus, catch up, meet some of the current band members and march on the field again at Jack Trice Stadium.

As I write this, 13 years removed from my last year in college, I haven't yet participated. There are a few reasons for this. For one, I still tailgate with a group I became friends with mostly through the band. For another, I am usually too intense about the game itself to necessarily want to focus on playing an instrument. Perhaps most importantly, I unfortunately haven't played the instrument since I graduated.

For many people, the Alumni Band is one of their major connections back to the university, back to their college days, back to their friends. They participate year after year. Band is such a big part of not only your life, but your identity as a college student, and I think there's something beautiful about the fact the Alumni Band gives people a true tie back to their Cyclone roots. We should all be so lucky to have that kind of bond with something from our younger years. Each year, I watch them and the varsity band with a little bit of nostalgia.

During Saturday's pregame show before the 2021 Oklahoma State game, I clapped along with everyone else as the band played the fight song and cheered as they led the crowd in the "Cyclone! Power!" chant. The Cyclone Weather Alert played, "Cowboy fans in the warned area should seek immediate cover," and the team began its walk to the field. A sellout crowd at Jack Trice Stadium welcomed them. The student section had been handed white towels, which they waved with enthusiasm, providing an eye-catching scene.

Iowa State received the ball first. Last week, the Cyclones had opened the game with a 75-yard touchdown run by Breece Hall. I imagined they would give it to Hall again for the first carry, but instead Purdy rolled out to pass and found a wide-open Charlie Kolar, who caught the ball with space to run. It was a 34-yard gain, and the crowd was alive. Unfortunately, it didn't last. Iowa State faced a fourth-and-one from the Cowboy 32-yard line. Campbell elected to go for the first down. I figured it would be a handoff to Hall, but instead Purdy faked the handoff and pitched the ball forward to Kolar, who was met at the line of scrimmage and dropped. It was a turnover on downs. From the stands, I had no idea what happened. I couldn't tell who had the ball, and never even realized until re-watching later what actually happened. None-the-less, I could feel the excitement in the stadium dissipate a bit.

Oklahoma State was forced to punt on its first possession but downed the ball at the seven-yard line of Iowa State, pinning the Cyclones near their endzone. Iowa State went three-and-out and was forced to punt it back. OSU ended up starting its possession in Iowa State territory at the 48-yard line as clips of the Iowa game the prior month played in my mind. Oklahoma State took advantage of the short field to march down for a touchdown, with quarterback Spencer Sanders finding Brennan Presley to make it 7-0.

Iowa State got the ball back and had its drive immediately blown up as Purdy was sacked at the 10-yard line on first down. On fourth-and-seven from its own 25, Iowa State lined up the punt, but didn't get the play off in time. The delay of game penalty pushed Iowa State back five yards, and the crowd groaned.

"I just don't understand!" I yelled in frustration.

It was a little thing, but with a shaky punt unit and a game where field position would be a big deal, it was extra frustrating. Iowa State had already given up a touchdown on a short field, and now Oklahoma State would have another opportunity to shorten the field. Andrew Mavis, Iowa State's placekicker who got his first call to handle punting duties against Oklahoma

State, made up for it by booting the ball 50 yards. My frustration level still remained high, and I could feel it in the crowd as well.

Oklahoma State again moved the ball as the first quarter ended. Iowa State held Oklahoma State to a field goal attempt. I let out a cheer as the referee called the kick no good. It was wide right, and the crowd had a little bit of life.

Iowa State's offense responded with its first long drive of the game. In the prior week's win over Kansas State, the Cyclones went on an 18-play drive that took more than 10 minutes of gametime off the clock. During that drive, I was hyper-aware of how impressive it was. I didn't fully realize until after the game how impressive Iowa State's first touchdown drive against the Cowboys was. The Cyclones held the ball for 15 plays, with more than nine-and-a-half minutes of possession, converting three third downs. It was almost all for not, though, as the Cyclones were unable to push it in on second-and-goal or third-and-goal from the one-yard line. From the stands, much of the crowd, myself included, thought Iowa State crossed the goal line on a first down run and second down run, but the referees disagreed with us. On fourth down, Purdy rolled out and found Hutchinson a yard into the endzone for a spectacular diving catch to score its first touchdown of the day to make it 7-7. In the ensuing timeout, Paige and I bobbed up and down as a dance beat thumped over the stadium's loudspeakers. *Finally, some momentum!* (I also found myself wishing I knew the name of the song I was dancing to; it was rather catchy. It would be another week before I learned it was "Freaks" by Timmy Trumpet.)

Iowa State forced a three-and-out to get the ball back with just over two minutes before halftime, starting the drive at its own 40.

"If we can go score here, it would be huge," I said.

After trailing most of the half, I was excited to see Iowa State have the chance to grab the lead before halftime. It wasn't meant to be as Purdy was sacked on third down and Iowa State was forced to punt. Oklahoma State then grabbed the momentum back, first with a 25-yard pass from Sanders to Tay Martin, and then with a 42-yard heave to the endzone. The pass was intended for Presley, but both Isheem Young and Greg Eisworth for Iowa State had him well-covered.

"C'mon!" I yelled, hoping for an interception.

"Unbelievable!" I yelled again as Presley somehow got over both defenders to make a highlight-worthy catch for a touchdown. It was 14-7 Oklahoma State and the momentum had turned back.

Between the failed fourth down, the delay of game penalty, the short-field touchdown, the difficulty Iowa State had in scoring from the one-yard line and the unlikely catch for OSU's second touchdown, there was a weird feeling in the air as the first half ended.

We watched the Cyclone Marching Band and Alumni Band play their halftime shows, and the Iowa State defense immediately held OSU to a three-and-out after halftime to get the ball back to the offense. That's when Hutchinson's electric should-have-been touchdown was called back. Iowa State scored a few plays later, and the stadium's vibe had changed. It was now personal for Iowa State fans. I didn't fully realize it at first, but Charles (and other fans) pointed out after that game that it felt like the Jack Trice Stadium crowd needed something like that call to galvanize us. It worked. I feel it's an overused cliché (probably by me as well) to say an atmosphere was electric, but the atmosphere *was* electric from that point on. There's no better way to say it.

Oklahoma State answered with a quick drive down the field, but the ISU crowd got on its feet for a third-and-five play from the 19-yard line. Iowa State stopped running back Jaylen Warren after a gain of four, making it fourth down. Oklahoma State again lined up for a field goal. The kick sailed toward the goal posts. We gave an abbreviated cheer as we *thought* we saw the kick go wide right, and then let loose after the referees signaled no good. It was OSU's second missed field goal of the day, and there was something special in the air.

Iowa State put together another good drive before settling for a field goal attempt of its own, a 29-yarder by Mevis that went through to give the Cyclones their first lead of the day at 17-14. The crowd was electric again as Oklahoma State faced a third-and-14 on its next possession. I later learned it was so loud the television cameras on the Fox broadcast appeared to shake. Sanders faced pressure, rolled out and threw an incomplete pass. Iowa State began another drive as the third quarter ended and the fourth quarter began. The Cyclones faced a fourth-and-two from the Oklahoma State 42-yard line, and Campbell made what felt like an aggressive play call (for him) to go for it. I'll admit I did not have a good feeling about the decision and said so in the stands.

"I hope they prove me wrong," I said.

Purdy took the ball and ran for no gain, giving Oklahoma State great field position. It was a high-risk, high-reward play, and Iowa State did not get the reward. Chris liked the decision; I wasn't as big of a fan.

After the game Campbell told reporters, "Should we have punted the ball over there and played defense? Maybe." Sometimes there is no clear right or wrong decision in game management.

Unfortunately, Oklahoma State did take advantage of the good field position to score on five plays in just more than two minutes, giving the Cowboys the lead again at 21-17 with just more than eight-and-a-half minutes to play.

I had a feeling that however the next drive went could ultimately define Iowa State's season. Down four, the Cyclones would need to score a touchdown to win, and a failure to do so on that drive would squarely put the game in Oklahoma State's favor.

Campbell said a few weeks prior that A-players needed to make A-plays for Iowa State to be successful. Purdy, the senior quarterback, and Hall, the star running back would do just that. Purdy found Hall for a short pass in space that he turned into a 30-yard gain near midfield. The crowd was back into it. Purdy found Hutchinson for 13 yards, and then found Tarique Milton, a redshirt senior who had battled through an injury-filled 2020 season, for a 33-yard gain to the Oklahoma State four-yard line. Hall then took it the final four yards for a touchdown and a 24-21 Cyclone lead. There was again something special in the air.

Oklahoma State got the ball back with five-and-a-half minutes left. Every now and again, maybe once per season if I'm lucky, I get a moment at Jack Trice Stadium where I forget where I am, where I forget anything else in the world, really. I jump up and down, pump my fists in the air and yell as loud as I possibly can while everyone around me does basically the same thing. These are the kind of moments that you dream of as a sports fan.

That moment happened on second down. Sanders went back to pass but fumbled the snap before picking it up, and Will McDonald, who will almost certainly be playing for an NFL team in 2022, finally broke through and got to an off-balance Sanders for a sack and eight yard loss. (Editor's note: Much to my pleasant surprise, McDonald announced his intention after the season to play another year at Iowa State.) The stadium may have generated on the Richter Scale the next play, on third-and-18, as the crowd roared for the Cyclone defense to make a stop, and McDonald broke through for *another* sack. Ten years prior, when Iowa State was in the process of pulling off the big upset over the Cowboys in 2011, Chris would excitedly smack me across the chest (lightly, of course) in excitement after seemingly every big play. After McDonald's second sack in 2021, he did it again. I returned the gesture.

The defense had come up with its biggest stop of the day with less than five minutes remaining. I had begun to lose my voice.

Iowa State was unable to pick up a first down and had to punt the ball away, meaning the defense had to come up with one more stop with just over two minutes remaining. Oklahoma State gained some traction this time, picking up a pair of first downs to get to midfield and close in on field goal range. A key false start penalty made it first-and-15. Sanders completed a pass to Tay Martin for 10 yards to set up second-and-five, before an incomplete pass set up third-and-five. Warren ran for three yards to make it fourth-and-two. The game was on the line, and I was using what was left of my voice to yell as loud as I could.

Sanders threw a quick out pass to Presley, who looked like he had a chance at the first down before being met by Young and Kym-Mani King right at the first down line. The referees spotted the ball, but it was too close to call. Both teams were trying to claim it was their ball. It was going to come down to a measurement.

It is always a little crazy to me how with all the technology that exists in a football broadcast, they still use a chain to measure for a first down. As the chain crew walked onto the field, the tension was palpable. The chain was extended, and … it was just beyond the length of the football, meaning Oklahoma State was short of the first down. It was Iowa State's football. The crowd celebrated. I looked at the stands. It looked like the crowd was bouncing.

Watching the replay later, I noticed the Fox cameras again shook. "Are the cameras strapped down?" play-by-play announcer Aaron Goldsmith asked.

The upper deck of the student section began to fill into the lower deck. "See that?" I pointed out to Paige. "They're getting ready to rush the field."

There was one more hurdle. The referee crew needed to review it. We were ready to party. I just couldn't imagine, in my celebratory state, how they could possibly overturn the play. And then I remembered how often it felt like these calls went against Iowa State. *They can't overturn this one. They just can't.*

The referee came on the microphone.

"After further review, the ruling on the field stands."

Pandemonium. Iowa State had won. We were high-fiving, hugging, yelling.

Purdy, the senior who led Iowa State to its last top 10 win in this stadium as a then-freshman in his first career start in 2018, took the snap and took a knee. *This is why we call it Brocktober.* As we awaited the final snap, I joined everyone around me in yelling "Let's go State! Let's go State!" Yeah, I knew they were both "State," but in this case I was pretty sure there could have been no confusion as to which team we were cheering for. Purdy took the final snap and knee, and I threw my fist in the air as the students (and others) came onto the field in celebration.

How could you not love college football?

"Sweet Caroline" came on the loudspeaker. I swayed back and forth.

"Sweeeeet Caroline!"

"Bah! Bah! Bah!"

"Good times never seemed so good …"

"SO GOOD! SO GOOD! SO GOOD!"

I had a crystalizing moment as I watched the field fill with Cyclone fans. In the big wins in 2020, we hadn't gotten to experience this together. It was the kind of moment I wanted to imprint in my mind forever. It was the kind of moment I hoped never to take for granted again.

Chris and Kaci took a photo with their son. It was his first game. He wouldn't understand the significance at that moment, of course, but I felt sure his parents would tell the story often in years to come. I imagined Chris would sit down at some point with him, perhaps when he was a little older, and watch it with him. Paige and I took a photo as well with the crowd on the field in the background.

I didn't want to leave the stands. I could have stood there for an hour. After a few minutes, Charles and our friends James and Derek joined us (their seats were a few rows above us). We began our walk back to the car. It was one of the happiest walks I've had in a while.

Some games, I wait until the next day to read too much about it. Saturday evening, I read every Des Moines Register article, every Cyclone Fanatic article and what felt like every tweet about the game. Likewise, I almost never go back and watch the game broadcast until months after the season, but Sunday I watched a number of the highlights. I was struck by just how loud Jack Trice Stadium sounded on television. It was a great showcase for Iowa State football.

It would be easy to compare this win to the win 10 years ago. An undefeated Oklahoma State team came into Jack Trice Stadium and lost to an unranked Iowa State team. In so many ways, it was nothing alike. Iowa State was a massive underdog in 2011. In 2021, the people who set the betting lines favored Iowa State. In 2011, we were in shock that Iowa State was somehow even staying in the game with Oklahoma State. In 2021, we expected a close game, and most of us probably expected a Cyclone win. Most importantly, in 2011, the win made the team bowl eligible, and was the kind of game that made the rest of the season feel like a success. Iowa State didn't win any of its last three games that season after the OSU upset. In 2021, it felt like another step in a journey that was far from complete.

When I left that game 10 years ago, I knew to-date it was my favorite Iowa State football game of all time. The 2021 game ranks right up there, but its importance could still take weeks to fully appreciate, depending on how the rest of the season plays out. On top of that, with Iowa State sitting at 5-2 and 3-1 in the conference, there could be games down the road *this season* that end up being more memorable. Only time will tell.

I do know this: Iowa State vs. Oklahoma State in 2021 was one of the best football games I have ever witnessed. It was one of the most passionate, and most intense football games I have ever witnessed. It, like so many games between these two teams over the years, had its share of weird and controversial plays. Both teams clearly wanted it so much, and the fans in the stadium did too. It was college football perfection.

There was something special in the air. To borrow from Tessitore one more time, it was special, indeed.

CHAPTER SEVENTEEN

IOWA STATE VS. WEST VIRGINIA PREVIEW

MEMORIES FROM AN "UNPROFESSIONAL FAN"

Oct. 28, 2021

Let's just get this out of the way. I don't much care for West Virginia football. And that's what makes me love this series.

Iowa State and West Virginia became conference foes in 2012 thanks to multiple years of conference realignment dominoes that resulted in longtime conference members leaving for what they felt were greener pastures, and the Big 12 snatching up TCU and West Virginia to stay relevant.

From the get-go, West Virginia felt like an outlier. Morgantown is a 13-and-a-half-hour drive from Ames, which is its closest in-conference destination. (The University of Cincinnati is set to join the Big 12, which will become the closest Big 12 school to West Virginia.)

In a weird way, the Mountaineers became a natural rival to Iowa State. The Cyclones were the northern-most school in the conference, somewhat an outlier themselves geographically (along with the Kansas schools) after Missouri and Nebraska left. The weekend after Thanksgiving is often reserved for rivalry games, and for the first few years the Big 12 elected to match up Iowa State and West Virginia that weekend. Perhaps my favorite coincidence of this new series was that Jack Trice Stadium and West Virginia's Milan Puskar Stadium were copies of each other. Recent renovations to both have made them look a little different, but I remember watching a West

Virginia game in the mid-2000s and thinking the stadium looked exactly like Iowa State's stadium.

It seemed to me that we might as well embrace West Virginia as a makeshift rival, and it seemed the teams embraced that as well. According to an article in the Des Moines Register, in their first-ever matchup in 2012 at Jack Trice Stadium, the story goes that West Virginia star Geno Smith shoved then-Iowa State defensive coordinator Wally Burnham. Wally's son, Shane, came to his dad's defense, and Cyclone linebacker Jake Knott tweeted after the game that Smith's actions were "classless." Unfortunately, West Virginia gained the upper hand in the series with a 31-24 win.

Further fueling this burgeoning rivalry was the fact that West Virginia was led by Dana Holgorsen at the time. I think most Iowa State fans would agree Holgorsen, an Iowa native himself, was easy to dislike. There was just something about him.

In 2013, things got weird again. I watched the game with my great aunt and great uncle, again during the weekend after Thanksgiving. Iowa State had struggled through a 2-9 season so far. West Virginia was 4-7. Neither team was going to a bowl game; both were just playing for pride. One could have been forgiven for thinking Iowa State had no pride left when West Virginia jumped out to a 31-7 lead in the second quarter. Almost nobody would have given the Cyclones much of a chance to win at that point. Except my great uncle who repeatedly said, "I think they can come back."

Having watched the Cyclones all season, I did not agree with him. But they did begin a comeback, cutting the lead to 31-21 early in the fourth quarter. On the first play of the next possession, West Virginia's Clint Trickett connected on a 76-yard touchdown pass to Mario Alford to give the Mountaineers a 38-21 lead and break my spirit.

That's it, I thought.

My great uncle wasn't ready to give up, and neither were the Cyclones. ISU quarterback Grant Rohach led Iowa State on a 72-yard drive to cut the lead to 38-28. Iowa State forced a fumble and a Cole Netten field goal with just more than four minutes left made it 38-31. I was now starting to believe just a little bit.

"I think they can win," my great uncle said.

On the next possession, Iowa State forced a third-and-10 play, during which Trickett threw an interception to Iowa State's Jacques Washington.

"YES!" I yelled, truly excited about this game for the first time all day.

The Cyclones took only five plays to tie the game at 38-38. Somehow, this game was headed for overtime.

Iowa State got the ball first in overtime and was forced to kick a field goal after only three plays. Netten nailed the kick from 40 yards out, but I was worried. Conventional wisdom says it is a win for the defense to force a field goal attempt in overtime. A West Virginia touchdown would win it. Instead, Iowa State only allowed the Mountaineers to gain one yard and forced West Virginia to kick a field goal to tie it.

In the second overtime, West Virginia started with the ball and immediately gained a first down but was forced to settle for a 26-yard field goal. This was a victory for Iowa State's defense, until … the Cyclones faced fourth-and-three from the eight-yard line. Netten lined up for a 26-yard kick, a kick he should have been expected to easily make. I, however, had seen Iowa State lose like this before, and I wasn't quite confident. I was wrong again. Netten made the kick to tie the game at 44 and bring it to a third overtime.

Finally, one team was able to break into the endzone, and luckily that team was Iowa State. Rohach found Justin Coleman for a 25-yard touchdown pass on the first play to take the lead, and then found E.J. Bibbs for a two-point conversion attempt to put Iowa State ahead 52-44. West Virginia would need to answer to keep the game going.

It looked like they would do just that after the Mountaineers set themselves up for a first-and-goal from the three-yard line. Iowa State stopped a run, broke up a pass and stopped another run to force fourth down. Trickett threw it toward the endzone, where it looked like a sure Iowa State interception … until it was tipped in the air (I held my breath) and it was caught by a West Virginia receiver (I still held my breath) who was immediately tackled at the two-yard line by Deon Broomfield (★Exhale★). An unpredictable game deserved an unpredictable ending. Iowa State had improbably completed a 24-point comeback to win in three overtimes. The television feed showed head coach Paul Rhoads jumping up and down with his fist in the air as the team ran onto the field in celebration.

"You were right," I told my great uncle.

Rhoads had become well-known for his passionate locker room speeches, the two most famous being at Nebraska in 2009 when he said he was "so proud" to be the team's coach, and after the biggest upset in school history over Oklahoma State in 2011. This one against West Virginia got posted to social media, and I could feel the same passion. It was an essentially meaningless game to end a 3-9 season, but it meant something to Rhoads and it still means something to me.

The games from 2014 through 2016 did not move the needle much as Iowa State was struggling in a stretch of losing seasons. The 2017 game was the first in which now-Iowa State coach Matt Campbell really got things turned around, but the Cyclones lost a close game at West Virginia.

2018 gave us the defining moment in the new rivalry (at least from an Iowa State perspective), one of the great moments of Campbell's tenure as coach and one of the most fun games I have ever witnessed in person. And it took my dislike to another level.

The game was no longer Thanksgiving weekend, but instead took place in early October. West Virginia entered undefeated at 5-0 and ranked No. 6 in the country. It was led by senior quarterback Will Grier, a Heisman Trophy candidate. Iowa State was 2-3 on the season. It had been a weird start for the Cyclones. Their first game against South Dakota State was cancelled due to lightning around the stadium. That was the only time I could remember an Iowa State game being cancelled due to weather, and that includes the 2005 Colorado game when a tornado touched down in Ames before kickoff. Iowa State had lost to Iowa and Oklahoma to begin the season as it tried to find its footing, and then started 1-3 after a loss at TCU. Quarterback Brock Purdy got into game five against Oklahoma State and led the Cyclones to an upset road win the week before facing West Virginia. There was some excitement among the fans that we had our quarterback of the future and that the team was going to hit its stride just in time to challenge the Mountaineers.

The game was scheduled for a nice October evening. The day felt a little different than normal because the grass tailgate lots we normally parked in were closed due to too much rain in the days before. We instead went to Welch Ave. Station in Ames' Campustown area and ordered pitchers and pizza while we took in other games during the day.

The stadium that night also felt a little bit different. There was anticipation in the air in addition to a slight fall chill. The crowd believed the team could pull an upset. The crowd wanted the upset. We had a sense that this could be a memorable evening.

On Iowa State's second possession, Purdy, making his first official start, threw an interception. West Virginia scored four plays later to take a 7-0 lead. *Oh no,* I thought. *We are losing early and the freshman quarterback made a critical mistake. This could be ugly.* Instead, Purdy and Iowa State running back David

Montgomery took the Cyclones down the field in just six plays, capped by a touchdown pass to Hakeem Butler to tie the game at 7-7, and then scored again near the end of the first quarter to go up 13-7. The extra point was no good but, on that night, it wouldn't be a problem.

On West Virginia's next possession, I began to notice a trend. Grier was sacked for a loss of 12 yards. It was Iowa State's third sack of the game on Grier, and the star quarterback seemed flustered. Iowa State got the ball back and scored again to go up 20-7, then sacked Grier for the fourth time on the next possession. The crowd definitely believed in Iowa State's upset possibility now.

Shortly before halftime, West Virginia blocked an Iowa State field goal attempt and returned it for a touchdown to make it 20-14. Some days this would have been backbreaking to Iowa State, but not that night.

Nobody scored in the third quarter. (Iowa State missed a field goal, which, quite honestly, I had forgotten how much actually went wrong that could have lost Iowa State the game.) On Iowa State's first drive of the fourth quarter, Purdy, Montgomery and Butler again got Iowa State into scoring range, where Purdy found Deshaunte Jones for a 32-yard touchdown pass. The ensuing two-point conversion made it 28-14.

Back in the Kansas game recap, I described the "Juicy Wiggle" song and how it came to life this night. The crowd began to dance with cell phone lights flashing. It was one of the coolest things I had ever witnessed. The two-touchdown lead, and the good vibes from "Juicy Wiggle," made it feel like our night. On West Virginia's next possession, Grier was sacked by Marcel Spears Jr. on second down (the sixth of what would be seven sacks of Grier on the night). At this point I was jumping up and down, yelling uncontrollably (not unlike during last week's Oklahoma State game when Will McDonald forced back-to-back sacks). Everyone in the stadium seemed to have a similar reaction. The next play, with the crowd roaring, Grier threw an interception to D'Andre Payne. Every few years it seems there is a moment at Jack Trice Stadium where the defense makes a play, the crowd cheers them off the field, and it truly feels like we are one. They are playing for us, and we are cheering like crazy for them. This was one of those moments. (Again, similar to last week's win over Oklahoma State.)

For good measure, Iowa State forced Grier into a safety on West Virginia's next possession to wrap up a 30-14 win.

As time was winding down, I turned to Paige, my now-wife, then-fiancée.

"Do you want to go on the field?" I asked.

I had been part of field rushes a couple times after big wins. The year prior, in the 2017 win against TCU that elicited a field rush by the fans, I decided to watch from the upper deck. On this night against West Virginia, I was content either way. Paige, however, had never gotten to go on the field, so we decided to make our way down.

The final seconds ticked off, and the two of us joined thousands of others entering the field to celebrate. College sports provide a unique opportunity for fans and students to celebrate with players after a big win in a way that just doesn't happen in the pros (and many colleges and conferences are now trying to limit it). It was a magical moment, singing our victory song, Neil Diamond's "Sweet Caroline" and basking in an upset win. (I need to clarify for a moment: I wrote most of this chapter well before Iowa State's 2021 game against Oklahoma State, but the feelings from both games at Jack Trice Stadium were very comparable. I didn't plan for it to work out this way — how could I? — but it worked out just right.)

One person, however, did not think the field rush of 2018 was so great. The ever-unlikable (in our eyes, at least) Dana Holgorsen was still feeling sour two days later, when he told reporters, "It was unprofessional." He said the players felt unsafe with so many fans streaming onto their playing surface. (Campbell, for his part, didn't seem to feel that way, according to a story in the Des Moines Register.)

I found the statement a bit ridiculous. *What does it even mean to be an unprofessional fan? Are there professional fans? How do I get that job?* College football fans have celebrated on the field with their teams countless times in the history of the game, and rarely did anyone, particularly an opposing coach, seem to complain all that much. The Big 12, however, agreed with Holgorsen's assessment and fined Iowa State University $25,000. I'm pretty sure more than 25,000 Iowa State fans would have donated a dollar each to cover the cost. Cyclone Fanatic had a little fun with the situation, printing t-shirts that said, "Unprofessional Fan" and "Publicly Reprimanded."

Although I didn't purchase a shirt, I'll still wear the label of being an unprofessional fan. (Which begs another question: Does writing a book about being a fan of a team make me a professional fan? Such a conundrum.)

Part of me was sad to see Holgorsen leave West Virginia after the season. The dislike between the programs seemed to dissipate a bit. The Cyclones took advantage of West Virginia rebuilding in 2019 and 2020 and dispatched of the Mountaineers rather easily both years. The lasting memory of the 2019 game was Cyclone running back Breece Hall breaking out for the first time, rushing for 132 yards and three touchdowns, and earning his spot as the Cyclones' starter ever since. In 2020, Iowa State wrapped up an 8-1 conference season in what would have been a celebratory atmosphere at Jack Trice Stadium, if only social distancing protocols weren't in effect.

At the beginning of this section, I wrote that I didn't much care for West Virginia football, and that's true. At the same time, I love that it's a game that gets my blood boiling just a little bit. I want Iowa State to beat them, and I'm a little more upset with a loss to West Virginia than most other teams on the schedule. Coincidentally, the same is true for the series in men's basketball, which has developed into a nice little rivalry of its own. This is part of what makes sports fun.

Besides, I'm able to compartmentalize it. I'll generally cheer for the Mountaineers when they play nonconference games and bowl games. I have also heard that a game at Milan Puskar Stadium is a lot of fun. The fans are passionate (not sure if they're professional, but I'll find out), and also friendly to away fans. It sounds like a tremendous atmosphere in which to take in a college football game.

This year, it's Iowa State that will be on upset alert. The Cyclones are back in the top 25 after the important win over Oklahoma State. West Virginia has been up and down to begin the season. The Mountaineers pulled off a dramatic upset of then-No. 15 Virginia Tech in September, making a goal line stop to seal the victory at home. (In the time since, Virginia Tech has struggled.) The next week, West Virginia took Oklahoma down to the wire in Norman before losing 16-13, leading me to believe maybe West Virginia had a team capable of competing for a spot in the conference championship game. Instead, the Mountaineers then had a disappointing stretch, losing at home to Texas Tech and getting blown out by Baylor on the road. Last week, however, West Virginia got a somewhat surprising road win at TCU.

The Mountaineers are now 3-4, but I'm guessing they see Saturday as an opportunity to pull off an upset and turn their season around.

For Iowa State, this has the potential to be a trap game. The Cyclones are coming off an emotional win and have another much-anticipated game at Jack Trice Stadium next time out against Texas. It can be human nature to have a tough time getting ready for this type of game. Saturday's weather calls for rain, which sometimes has a way of evening out the game not to mention dampening spirits. I'm sure the crowd will be loud, which will provide a challenge to Iowa State after last week's boisterous home crowd that carried the Cyclones to the win.

For these reasons, this is actually the most worried I have felt going into a game all season.

On the flip side, Iowa State is somewhat built to win this type of game. From a mental standpoint, Campbell's "win in the dark" and "trust the process" mantras should carry over to a game like this. Iowa State's senior quarterback Purdy is playing the best football of his career and Iowa State proved at Kansas State that it can take the air out of an opposing team's stadium with solid defense and consistent offense that picks up third down conversions.

Heading into the Baylor game, I wrote that Iowa State needed to win that type of game if it was going to have the special season it (and really, I) was hoping for. I had underestimated how good Baylor was at the time; it turned out to be an understandable loss that Iowa State could overcome in the conference title race. We now have the benefit of having seen more games, and I feel confident in saying this West Virginia game is the type of game Iowa State needs to win if it is going to have a special season and compete for a conference championship.

I'm nervous but, as I've reminded myself before, I also need to enjoy the journey. That's what unprofessional fans do.

CHAPTER EIGHTEEN

IOWA STATE VS. WEST VIRGINIA RECAP

AFTER FURTHER REVIEW ...

Nov. 2, 2021

I stood in Milan Puskar Stadium in West Virginia in the fourth quarter, watching the replay on the video board.

"Touchdown!" I yelled and put my hands in the air.

Iowa State was losing 38-31 against West Virginia but had just appeared to score a touchdown as Breece Hall powered his way through to the goal line. I hadn't even seen the play as I was watching the replay from the play before: A 23-yard scramble by quarterback Brock Purdy to push the ball down to the two-yard line. I was admiring Purdy's vision, toughness and resiliency as he put Iowa State in position to score the game-tying touchdown as the clock ticked toward six minutes left.

Then I looked away from the video board and watched in confusion as two West Virginia players were running toward the other end of the field, one with the football. As everyone was trying to figure out what happened, the referee's voice came over the loudspeakers to inform us the ruling on the field was a fumble recovered by West Virginia for a touchback, and the play would be reviewed.

Having not even seen the play, at first I thought that somehow Purdy had fumbled it, which didn't seem right based on the replay I had just watched. Then I saw the video board as it showed the actual play in question: Hall trying to fight his way into the endzone. It seemed pretty clear to me: Hall's elbow was down, the ball was in it and it appeared to be across the goal line. It was a touchdown for Iowa State. We were near the majority of other Iowa State fans in the stadium, most of whom cheered appreciatively after seeing the replay. This was clearly going to go our way.

The replay took what felt like forever, and in fact the stadium sound system played two full songs while the play continued to be reviewed, meaning the review took at least five or six minutes. The video board kept showing the few seconds of the play that showed Hall's elbow hitting the turf with the ball secured in his arm. I sensed even West Virginia fans thought it was a sure thing this play would get overturned.

"It's either a touchdown or he was down, but it wasn't a fumble," I said confidently to my wife, Paige.

As the replay review dragged on, I began to wonder what the holdup was. *Surely, they are just trying to decide if he scored a touchdown or was down before crossing the goal line,* I thought. Either way, it was going to be a good outcome for Iowa State. On a day when defending Big 12 Defensive Player of the Year Mike Rose was out with an injury, and perhaps as a result the defense had its worst performance in years, Iowa State was going to be tied late in the fourth quarter with a shot to win. *This is what it takes to be a championship football team,* I thought.

Finally, the referee came back on the sound system. I fully expected him to let us know, after further review, it would be a touchdown for Iowa State (or maybe, *maybe* Iowa State's ball inside the one).

Instead, I heard these words: "After further review, the ruling on the field stands."

I yelled at the field. It was inconceivable.

Earlier in the quarter, I had turned off my phone. I was getting discouraged about the game and reading too many negative reactions via text message and Twitter. I needed to put myself back in the moment and enjoy the game. As soon as I did that, Iowa State drove down the field to seemingly score the touchdown. After the review, I turned my phone back on.

I later described to Paige's sister, who was with us at the game, about 75% of the time when I am *just sure* a call went against us in the stadium, I see the replay later after the game and determine that I was wrong. This was not one of those times. My friends on my text message chain were confirming for me they saw the same thing I did. I turned my phone off again. I couldn't take it.

We were sitting in a mostly empty area of the stands, but a little way away from us were a couple West Virginia fans.

"I can't believe they called that a fumble," one of them told me.

It was the third questionable call that had gone against Iowa State on the afternoon; all three had resulted in either a West Virginia touchdown or had taken an Iowa State touchdown off the board. It was a potential 21-point swing. No matter how well a team plays (and the Cyclones didn't play their best game), it is very difficult to overcome that in a Big 12 road game.

The Cyclones could not overcome it on Saturday in Morgantown.

I have written multiple times there could be an entire chapter in this book on Cyclone Fans vs. The Refs, and Saturday's game brought back all those helpless feelings of bad calls of yesteryear. It reminded me of seeing Tony Yelk's potential game-winning field goal called no good in the 2001 Independence Bowl. It reminded me of seeing Seneca Wallace called out at the one-yard line against Florida State ("Seneca was in!" as most Cyclone fans will still tell you). It reminded me of seeing Kansas' men's basketball team hit a three-pointer *while Iowa State was at the free throw line* for a two-shot foul at Allen Fieldhouse, and benefiting from questionable calls at the end of a 2013 showdown in Hilton Coliseum (more on that next chapter). It reminded me of Texas somehow not getting called for a fumble during a 2013 game at Iowa State that would have sealed the victory for the Cyclones (more on that in the next chapter as well). It reminded me of the Oklahoma State and Kansas State games in 2017.

These moments, and many (many) more, have been engrained in me to the point I almost expect them. But they still hurt every time.

Iowa State could have played better on Saturday. As Cyclone coach Matt Campbell said after the game, the Cyclones should have put themselves in a position not to let the referees control the outcome.

For me, though, I'll pretty much never be able to think about the game without some level of wondering, *what if*, due to the officiating.

After each West Virginia win at home, the loudspeakers play John Denver's "Take Me Home, Country Roads" as Mountaineer fans sing and sway. I've seen videos of this and knew it would be impressive to see in person. I also knew that if I saw it, it would signify an Iowa State loss. I tried to tell myself before the game that if they played "Country Roads," I would try to put my disappointment aside and enjoy it.

As the final play ended and West Virginia players and fans celebrated a 38-31 win, I knew it was coming. After further review, I just didn't have it in me to stick around.

—

There was one more massive storyline to Saturday's game that I felt somehow went under the radar in the postgame discussion. Rose, Iowa State's star senior linebacker, a first team All-American and Player of the Year in the Big 12 in 2020, was injured. The storyline really began during the Oklahoma State game at Jack Trice Stadium the week prior. Rose had been down on the field during Oklahoma State's final possession, to an audible gasp from the crowd. We were able to push it to the back of our brains as Iowa State pulled off the win and we celebrated.

During the week, Campbell seemed confident in telling reporters that he expected Rose to play. That was good enough for me to stop worrying about it.

Other than Rose's status, I could feel a letdown game within the fan base. There did not seem to be as much chatter on Twitter about the upcoming game as normal (and I have no way of actually measuring that). My text message chain wasn't nearly as active in talking about Iowa State as it was the week prior. There was no logo or color scheme news to get us talking.

Personally, the day after the Oklahoma State game was miserable in some ways. My mood tends to be more affected by weather than I'd like it to be, and it poured rain all day Sunday. I felt like I was taking a cold shower each time I took my dog for a walk. And what made it even worse was I had looked ahead to the upcoming Saturday's forecast in Morgantown and saw a rainy day on the horizon. It just *felt* like the kind of day that could lead to a depressing loss. In Iowa, the rain came back on Wednesday and Thursday; it was a tough week to keep my energy level up, coupled with a tough game to get truly excited about as a Cyclone fan.

Still, I had plenty to look forward to. Paige's sister, Gwen, lived in West Virginia about 20 minutes from WVU's campus with her husband and three children. They were in the process of moving closer to Paige's childhood home in Colorado, but at that time Gwen and the children were still in West Virginia. It worked out perfectly so that we could spend the weekend with them and attend the game together. We made plans to dress up for Halloween on Sunday and trick-or-treat with the kids.

Our flight out of Des Moines was on Friday evening. We boarded the airplane in Des Moines and sat right in front of some Iowa State fans who also informed us they were going to the game. As we got to talking, I learned their son played for the team and they had gone to more than 30 straight games. (As I wrote this, I had gone to eight straight games; it was highly doubtful I would make it to 30.) They reminded me there was a Cyclone Alumni Association gathering before the game at a bar called Mountain Mama's within walking distance of the stadium. One of the somewhat unexpected perks of making out-of-the-way Big 12 road trips was the opportunity for chance encounters like that one, all of which made me feel even more emotionally connected to this team.

We flew into Pittsburgh, where Gwen picked us up for the drive to Morgantown. By the time we got to their home and talked for a while, it was already well past midnight Eastern Time. It was gameday! (Sort of.)

All week, I had watched the weather trying to figure out what would be happening during gametime. On Saturday morning, it looked to me like the rain was likely to hold off until near the fourth quarter. As I was thinking that, it began to rain very lightly outside. We decided to make a stop at a sporting goods store to search for raincoats. This proved to be a helpful decision. At the store we saw a few people wearing West Virginia gear.

"I hope you have a great trip until the end of the game," one man told us.

We decided to check out Mountain Mama's for the Iowa State gathering. We quickly discovered we were in the right place as we saw a bar packed full of Cyclone fans. The tailgate had been provided on behalf of the ISU Alumni of Cincinnati, Indianapolis and Washington, D.C., which all had members make the trip. I almost immediately ran into one fan I had talked to in Waco who was also attending every game. After a brief conversation, Paige, Gwen, the kids and I ordered food and found a spot outside under a covered area where the kids could have more room to run around.

A little while later, I walked inside just as Iowa State University Alumni Association President and CEO Jeff Johnson was leading the fans in cheers including "Cyclone! Power!" As the fight song played in the background, he told us we should feel at home in the stadium, which was designed by the same architect that designed Jack Trice Stadium. He also encouraged us to represent Iowa State well.

The rain continued outside and I checked the forecast again. It was now calling for rain throughout the game.

At about 1 p.m., an hour before kickoff, we put on our extra layers and began the walk to the stadium. Gwen and Paige took turns carrying my nearly two-year-old niece. (She was still scared of me as this trip was the first time we had met.)

On the way, I heard one West Virginia fan tell an Iowa State fan, "I hope you guys hear 'Country Roads' today."

We arrived at the gate where they let us know we weren't allowed to take umbrellas into the stadium. Gwen offered to take our three umbrellas back to the car as we headed into the stadium, the rain still coming down. The raincoats had come in handy, for sure.

It felt just like walking into Jack Trice Stadium as we entered and immediately began the trek up the hill behind the bleachers. We had entered on the north side, but our seats were in the southeast corner. As we went through the tunnel into the stands, I looked around. It was remarkably similar to Iowa State's home stadium.

It was a slow-arriving crowd, and the stadium never did fill up. Even though West Virginia was coming off a win at TCU, I suspected the 0-3 conference start before that coupled with the dreary and wet weather forecast had kept many fans from coming out to this one. There was a solid showing for Iowa State. We took our seats behind the south endzone with the booming video board right behind us. It was loud, and given the hundreds of empty seats in the sections around us, we decided to move a section over and be closer to Iowa State fans and further away from the speakers.

The game kicked off, and West Virginia got the ball first. The Mountaineers picked up a first down but were then forced to punt. On Iowa State's third offensive play, it felt like a replay from the Kansas State game a couple of weeks prior: Hall broke through and was running free as Cyclone fans cheered; nobody would catch him as he completed a 70-yard run into the endzone to give Iowa State a 7-0 lead.

West Virginia got the ball back, and my nephews needed to use the restroom so I took them. In what is seeming to become a trend this season, as I was away from my seat the Mountaineers were moving the ball down the field. I checked my phone and got a message that would quickly change my outlook on the day. My friend James had informed us that Rose was not playing.

I later saw on Twitter that Rose had apparently warmed up with the team before the game, and then had changed into street clothes. It looked to me like the defense was missing Rose from more than just a talent or X's and O's standpoint. Rose was also the leader of the defense and played a position that is in many ways the equivalent as what a quarterback brings to the offense. If the starting quarterback of any team is injured, especially one who was conference player of the year a year ago, I think most fans would expect the offense to struggle. In the case of the Iowa State defense, it struggled as much as it had in recent memory. Whether that was directly tied to Rose's absence, I would need someone who understands the intricacies of the game better than I do to make that judgement. But my gut told me Iowa State was disproportionately affected by not having the Big 12 Player of the Year on the field, which was probably made worse by the fact that it was seemingly a game-time decision.

Of course, anyone watching on the ESPN+ broadcast could have been forgiven for not realizing Rose was out. The text messages I was getting from my friends James, Chris and Charles let me know the broadcast announcers were, in their opinion, not doing a very good job in general and had failed to mention that key fact.

We got back up the stands in time to see West Virginia complete its drive. By this time, Gwen had arrived and luckily it had stopped raining. The good vibes were squelched when West Virginia's Leddie Brown tied the game at 7-7 with a two-yard touchdown run.

The teams traded punts, and on Iowa State's third possession Purdy went back for a pass to begin the drive. He stepped up to throw and I saw Tarique Milton running down the field wide open. Purdy calmly delivered the ball into his hands and Milton ran into the endzone for a 68-yard touchdown.

With Iowa State up 14-7, I was starting to feel like the Cyclones could take control of the game. Instead, the Mountaineers methodically marched down the field as the West Virginia fans became more and more excited. The drive ended with a pass by Jarret Doege to Bryce Ford-Wheaton in the corner of the endzone for a touchdown. Iowa State was in a game at 14-14 and the defense was not performing to its usual standards.

Iowa State went three-and-out its next possession, and West Virginia gained the lead with a field goal to go up 17-14. West Virginia's energy level seemed a step above Iowa State's. My hopes for Iowa State pulling away like it did in the Kansas State game seemed dim. I realized at this point it was everything I had feared before the game. The Cyclones had seemed to come out flat. However, I didn't know before the game Rose would be out, which worried me even more. Iowa State's defense had many times over the past few years given up a good amount of yards and points in the first half before tightening things up. *Will they be able to do that today without their leader?*

Iowa State's offense failed to produce on either of its next two drives, but the defense did stop a promising West Virginia drive with a tipped interception by Craig McDonald and thwarted another drive before it started by forcing a three-and-out inside the Mountaineers' 15-yard line. The Cyclones took the ball with just more than a minute left in the first half and converted a 34-yard field goal by Andrew Mevis. The game was tied at 17-17 at halftime. I felt OK. The Cyclones had weathered the storm and would have a chance to take control when the second half began.

Unfortunately, Iowa State went three-and-out to start the half. That's when the first controversial call of the day happened, this one in favor of Iowa State. WVU quarterback Doege threw it deep to Ford-Wheaton. From my view in the southeast corner of the stadium, looking toward the northeast corner of the field, I saw what I thought was a pretty clear shove in the back by Ford-Wheaton on Iowa State's Kym-Mani King. I yelled for the flag as King fell down and Ford-Wheaton caught the pass. West Virginia fans' cheers turned to boos as a flag came down. I clapped appreciatively. Later on, I saw some Iowa State fans saying they didn't think it was a penalty. Since the game was on ESPN+, I didn't have it recorded and never was able to find a good replay to see for myself.

On the next play, Iowa State's Jake Hummel jumped the passing route to make an interception and return it 24 yards to the endzone as I jumped up in celebration. *This is the break we needed!*

For the third time, West Virginia answered an Iowa State touchdown with one of its own. On a third-and-six play, Doege found Winston Wright Jr. for 35-yards to the Iowa State 23-yard line. On the next play, Doege threw to the back of the endzone, where Ford-Wheaton jumped up to make an incredible catch for a touchdown. *That was close to being out of bounds*, I thought. Sure enough, the officiating crew chose to review the play.

A few weeks before when it was announced the game would be on the internet-based ESPN+, a lot of Cyclone fans complained. The 1 p.m. Central Time Zone kickoff was a weird time in and of itself, and it felt like to some that we were being relegated to second-class status by not having the game on ABC, ESPN or one of the Fox channels. At the time, I didn't worry too much, knowing, for one thing, I would be at the game, and for another I figured more and more games would eventually be broadcast on internet-based channels in the future (which is already true in men's and women's college basketball, for example). The more I read my text messages, the more I realized that not only was the game not on a regular television channel, but ESPN+ had seemed to have used the B-team on everything from the camera crew to announcers. Sure, it was annoying, but then it became worse: It started to have a potential impact on the game.

As they showed replay reviews of the touchdown catch in question, there was no conclusive evidence to show whether Ford-Wheaton got a foot down in bounds. Since it was inconclusive, after further review, the ruling on the field stood as a touchdown. A lot of Iowa State fans, and some impartial observers, disagreed on Twitter. When I watched replays later, I couldn't tell for sure. If I had to guess, I would have said no catch. It made me wonder if a better broadcast would have had a better camera angle. Regardless, in the minds of Iowa State fans, it felt like a questionable way to give up seven points.

Iowa State responded with a touchdown of its own after Hall broke free for a 53-yard run to the West Virginia four-yard line and Purdy completed the drive with a one-yard touchdown run. Iowa State was back up 31-24. West Virginia again answered Iowa State's fourth touchdown of the day with its own touchdown drive. The Mountaineers took 12 plays and converted two third-downs before facing fourth-and-three from the 22. Doege found Wright over the middle for a touchdown. After further review, as my text message friends pointed out, the play clock had hit zeros well before the ball was snapped. The play should have resulted in a five-yard penalty, which would have made it fourth-and-eight, a much tougher play to convert. That didn't excuse the Iowa State defense for giving up a touchdown, but it again stoked the feeling of having gotten a bad break from the people in stripes. It was now 31-31, and 14 of West Virginia's points had come in controversial fashion.

The fans were now fully in the game. "Let's go!" chanted the east side of the stadium. "Mountaineers!" the west side answered. It was similar to Iowa State's "Cyclone! Power!" chant, except it went on for what felt like three minutes. I noticed one of my nephews, who had no affiliation to either team, getting into the chant. Even though I was upset about the game itself, I couldn't help but appreciate the pull that college football has on people. (I also had to give my nephew major props. At one point the loudspeakers played the same song I had fallen in love with at Jack Trice Stadium, and I said, "I wish I knew what this song was." He let me know it was the song "Freaks" by Timmy Trumpet.)

Iowa State was forced to punt on its next possession, and West Virginia had no trouble marching down the field for 85 yards in six plays. The key play was a 45-yard pass from Doege to Ford-Wheaton.

"My gosh. They have just picked apart our secondary all day," I said to Paige.

On second-and-goal from the six, Iowa State's T.J. Tampa got called on a pass interference penalty in the back of the endzone. It was the kind of play I would have loved to see a replay of, but I didn't get it. Brown scored on the next play to give West Virginia a 38-31 lead.

At this point, I shut off my phone. There was too much negative energy coming from it, which was matching my energy as a light rain had returned and the Cyclones were losing.

With just more than nine minutes left, Iowa State answered with an important drive. The Cyclones moved the ball to midfield with gains of seven, nine, eight and eight again. Purdy, facing pressure, then scrambled for a 22-yard gain, and two plays later ran for 23 yards down to the West Virginia two. I was still admiring his run as they showed the replay on the video board when the now-infamous fumble by Hall gave the ball back to West Virginia. Earlier, I wondered about whether the lack of good camera angles had hurt Iowa State. This time, I'm not sure what angle the referees needed to see to overturn the play. It seemed like a pretty clear touchdown to me, and seemingly everyone else watching. In one of the biggest moments of the season, a crucial call had gone against the Cyclones. I felt sick as I thought of the post-game conversation if West Virginia was to hold on for the win.

The Cyclones would get one more chance at it, taking the ball on their own 16 with 3:42 remaining. *In a few minutes, I will either hear "Country Roads" or be celebrating a memorable comeback,* I thought. I wanted the comeback badly.

Iowa State again moved the ball, but time ticked down. Hall extended the game with a run of eight yards on fourth-and-one.

Maybe this is going to be a special drive!

A couple plays later, Purdy was sacked to bring up a third-and-15. On the next play, he again scrambled and appeared to be very close to the first down. The referee marked him a yard short (after further review, I thought the officials should have reviewed the play and judging by Campbell's reaction on the sideline, so did he), and in the ensuing seconds the clock continued to tick as Iowa State lined up for another fourth-and-one play. Instead, a Cyclone lineman moved early for a false start. In addition to losing five yards, 10 seconds were taken off the clock. There were now only four seconds left, meaning Iowa State would have one more play to score from the 30. Had they reviewed the play, the clock would have stopped with around 40 seconds left and allowed Iowa State plenty of time to run its normal offense and try to score. Instead, it would now take something miraculous.

West Virginia took a timeout as I stood nervously.

The best games are the most unexpected, I thought hopefully.

Just maybe the Cyclones could find a way to score.

Purdy took the snap and waited for his receivers to get to the endzone before heaving a Hail Mary pass. The play was in the opposite endzone from the one we were sitting behind, and I couldn't tell what happened. All I knew was the roar I heard from West Virginia fans as their team ran onto the field in celebration.

The Mountaineers had pulled the upset.

As we walked out, listening to "Country Roads" in the background, one fan saw my red stocking cap and said, "Good game."

We made our way toward the exits and I finally turned my phone back on. I had a message from my friend Jason, who had shaved his mustache after Iowa State's loss. I had a message from my friend Adam who lives in Waco. I had several messages from my normal text chain. I asked them all whether the fumble call was as bad as I thought. They all assured me it was.

Right outside the stadium, some tailgaters were playing "Sweet Caroline." *This does feel like home.* Except in the part where we'd normally sing, "Bah! Bah! Bah!" West Virginia fans answered with less appropriate insult toward their rivals to the north: "Eat ★★★★, Pitt!"

"I think they dislike Pitt more than we dislike Iowa," I said to Paige.

Throughout the evening, my text message chain discussed the ramifications of the game. My friend Chris compared it to Iowa State's loss to UAB in men's basketball in the 2015 NCAA tournament. At first blush, that may seem dramatic, but in the context of a college football season and a team fighting for a conference championship, there are some similarities. For one, I felt like Iowa State would have won each of those games 80% of the time, but in a one-game scenario the 20% option happened. The days surrounding both games felt similar: the 2015 game was one of the first games in the entire tournament to tip off and there was a sleepy atmosphere that I could feel even through the television. Similarly, the football game against West Virginia was a rainy and overcast early afternoon game on an obscure television feed (ESPN+) in a stadium that was a little over half full; it was a sleepy atmosphere in its own right (at least until the WVU fans realized their team had a chance to win).

More importantly, each game was critical for the Cyclones to win in order to reach their goals (or at least the goals most fans had for the teams). For the basketball team, the dream of reaching the Final Four was gone. For the football team, the dream to reaching the Big 12 Championship Game was all but gone. And both happened not in a high-profile matchup, but in upset fashion. They were both games where nobody even seemed to consider the possibility of the Cyclones losing.

Except, there's one big difference.

After further review, at 5-3 overall and 3-2 in the conference, Iowa State's Big 12 title hopes in the 2021 football season are not completely out the window. If the Cyclones win out, they will very likely be in the championship game (assuming tie-breaker scenarios work out correctly). Iowa State will need to win four games in a row, including a game at top five-ranked Oklahoma, to make it a reality. The odds are against the Cyclones, but there's still a chance. Oddly, I still like this team's chances to pull off something special.

Even if it doesn't happen, the Cyclones still have the opportunity to end the season on a high note. There are still big games left to play and big wins on the table. After further review, there are still memories to be made.

CHAPTER NINETEEN

IOWA STATE VS. TEXAS PREVIEW

WE SHOULD BEAT TEXAS PROBABLY

Nov. 4, 2021

Texas is, quite frankly, a natural villain to pretty much everyone else in the Big 12. It seems like every year there is some version of controversy over opposing fans (and sometimes players) using the horns down hand symbol to mock the Longhorns. (If you are unfamiliar, Texas's signature hand-signal includes putting a person's index finger and pinkie in the air to make the hand look like it has horns.) Everything is bigger in Texas, including the whining.

Texas has the money, resources and recruiting base to make a lot of other schools jealous. Texas is a national brand name and is perceived to get the benefit of the doubt in most situations because of it. For example, in 2014 TCU and Baylor both finished 11-1 in the regular season, and both missed the College Football Playoff. There's little doubt in my mind an 11-1 Texas team would have been in.

During the offseason leading up to 2021, Texas and Oklahoma decided to join the SEC Conference and leave their Big 12 brethren in a poor spot. While there was definitely ill-will toward Oklahoma for the decision, the majority of vitriol was aimed at Texas. For years it had seemed Texas got what Texas wanted. When the Longhorns had threatened to leave in prior years, others in the conference did whatever they could to keep Texas around (including allowing Texas to show games on its own television network). After all that, Texas still decided to chase more dollars at the expense of schools like Iowa State.

Perception matters in college football, more than any other sport in the country. Those who are perceived to be good get ranked higher. Programs that are perceived to be prestigious tend to draw the better coaches (and often have higher budgets to pay those coaches' salaries). Programs that are perceived to be better have an easier time in recruiting. By design, the rich have an easier path to getting richer. Schools like Iowa State, Iowa, Wisconsin and Kansas State have shown it is possible to have various levels of success without being a "blue blood," but schools like Texas, Oklahoma, Ohio State, Michigan, Alabama, USC, Notre Dame and others consistently have a leg-up if they are able to capitalize on it.

Texas has lived off perception. The Longhorns have not won a Big 12 Championship since 2009 and have not won a national championship since the 2005 season. Texas has only played in one New Year's Six bowl game since the 2009 season and has been a mediocre program for much of that time period especially compared to most of the other schools I listed above. The on-field performance has not matched the program expectations, but when it comes to television time slots and conference realignment, the Longhorns are still the darlings.

I'm sure Texas fans do not appreciate how often the Longhorns have lost to teams like Iowa State in the last decade-plus.

It wasn't always this way. Iowa State started off 0-7 in its history vs. Texas. I remember in my junior year of college in 2007, as a member of the Cyclone Marching Band, Iowa State hosted Texas in a midseason game. The Cyclones were 1-5 entering the game under first-year head coach Gene Chizik, who had joined the Cyclones after working as an assistant coach at Texas. For some reason, I talked myself into thinking the Cyclones would have a chance. *Chizik knows the players and coaches on the other side,* I thought. *That must give him an advantage.*

I quickly gave up any hope of that notion being true when Texas star quarterback Colt McCoy found Jordan Shipley on a 58-yard touchdown pass on the Longhorns' first play from scrimmage to make it 7-0. Texas led 28-3 at halftime and poured it on even more in the second half in a 56-3 victory. I sometimes tell people that part of the marching band experience is that I had to stay until the very end of the game, no matter how bad it was. Usually when I say that I'm thinking of that Texas game. It wouldn't surprise me if the stadium was 80% empty in the second half that day.

The day my perception of Texas began to change was in 2010.

Heading into the game, I thought Iowa State had no chance. The Cyclones were 3-4 and coming off a noncompetitive 52-0 loss at Oklahoma. Their reward was to play at Texas. The Longhorns were 4-2 but had just come off a win on the road at No. 5 Nebraska and the year before had played in the national championship game. There was still a mystique about the Longhorns, a feeling that the Cyclones could not possibly compete with them.

I was not amped up for this game. I watched by myself in my apartment in Des Moines, expecting it to go south quickly.

I was pleasantly surprised when Iowa State quarterback Austen Arnaud found Darius Reynolds for an 18-yard touchdown midway through the first quarter to give Iowa State a 7-0 lead, and started to feel a little bit of shock when Alexander Robinson rushed for a one-yard touchdown in the second quarter to give Iowa State a 14-3 lead. Iowa State held off a potential Texas touchdown drive when Michael O'Connell intercepted a pass in the endzone, and Texas missed a field goal late in the second quarter.

Maybe this could be our day.

Still, I didn't think Iowa State was going to win. Not really. I expected Texas to make a few halftime adjustments and impose their will in the third quarter.

Instead, Arnaud and Robinson led Iowa State on an 89-yard touchdown drive midway through the third quarter, capped by a pass to Josh Lenz in the back of the endzone to make the score 21-6. Now I was starting to change my mind. Iowa State was controlling the game. Texas' next drive ended with an interception by Iowa State's Jeremy Reeves, and a little while later Iowa State's Jacob Lattimer recovered a fumble at the Texas 40-yard line.

I'm pretty sure at this point, I was audibly cheering even though I was all by myself. I know that when Robinson broke free for a 20-yard touchdown run early in the fourth quarter that I was jumping up and down pumping my fist. Iowa State was up 28-6, and it had turned into a blowout.

It couldn't be easy. Texas marched down the field for an 80-yard touchdown drive to make it 28-14. Iowa State ended another threat when Leonard Johnson intercepted the ball at the seven-yard line. With just more than three minutes to go in the game, Texas scored again to make it 28-21. The Longhorns were finally making the run that I had feared all day.

When they got the ball back with just more than a minute left, I was a ball of nerves. Lattimer forced a big sack on first down, and Texas eventually faced a fourth-and-15 from its own five-yard line. *If any team could still find a way to lose this, it would be Iowa State,* I couldn't help but think. Instead, the Cyclones forced an incomplete pass to wrap up the win.

I called my friend Chris. "I can't believe it!!"

For Iowa State, it was regarded as one of the biggest wins in school history. After the game, word spread there would be a welcome party for the team in Ames when their flight arrived home. Of course I was going to be there for that! I drove to Ames and joined hundreds of other Cyclone fans for what turned into a mini-pep rally. Rhoads spoke, players spoke and fans cheered. Some people thought it was overkill, perhaps even a sign that Iowa State was not a big-time program. At the time, I didn't care. I thought it was a sign of how strong our fanbase was that we would show up for an event like that. Our fanbase experience was intimate enough to warrant it. Even though the program has had a lot more success since then, and even though I can't imagine a pep rally like that happening today, the elements that led to that celebration are the same elements that make it special to be an Iowa State fan even in the bad years. We care — a lot — and we'll go out of our way to show our support.

If you are wondering how Texas felt about the loss: "It's bad for the program," one player said after the game, in a quote dripping with arrogance. "They beat us today, but we just shouldn't lose to certain teams here at Texas."

I've never forgotten that quote. It says everything about the place each of these programs have, or are perceived to have, in the hierarchy of college football.

A few years later, it was Rhoads' turn to have postgame comments I will never forget.

In 2013, after Iowa State got off to its first poor start of the Rhoads era, the Cyclones welcomed Texas to Jack Trice Stadium for a Thursday evening matchup. Iowa State was 1-2, and Texas was 2-2 entering the game. I know Iowa State's fanbase was antsy about the poor start to the season, and I imagine Texas fans were more than a little upset. The Cyclones came out and went toe-to-toe with Texas in a back-and-forth game. I remember feeling like, *If we can just win, Rhoads will have turned this season around,* just as he had done so successfully in multiple seasons in the past.

The Jack Trice crowd was electric after Sam Richardson found Quenton Bundrage for a 97-yard touchdown pass midway through the third quarter to give the Cyclones a 20-17 lead. Early in the fourth, Aaron Wimberly broke through for a 20-yard run to give Iowa State a 27-24 lead. My seat at the time was in the south endzone, and it felt like Wimberly was running right at me as he broke the goal line for the score. I yelled as loud as I could and threw my hands in the air.

Iowa State had a chance to put the game away as the clock ticked under four minutes, making it all the way to the Texas four-yard line. Iowa State instead had to settle for a field goal and 30-24 lead, setting up Texas for one more chance to score a touchdown and win.

The crowd got antsy as the Longhorns marched down the field. Texas lined up for a second-and-goal play from the one-yard line with less than a minute to play. Just as I and probably most other fans in the stadium had given up hope, Texas ran the ball, got stuffed and Iowa State's Jeremiah George emerged from the pile with the football. The crowd went from quiet and dejected to a feeling of pandemonium.

We just won!!

Slowly we started to realize that the referee had blown the play dead and ruled that Texas would maintain possession. As officials reviewed the play, we watched the replay on the video board. It looked clearly to be Iowa State's football. The referees didn't see it that way. The play stood for Texas.

Earlier in 2013 was the angriest I have ever experienced a stadium when the Iowa State men's basketball team lost an overtime game to the Kansas Jayhawks. ISU's Georges Niang had appeared to take a charge in the final seconds that would have given Iowa State the win. Instead, there was no call and a few seconds later Niang was called for a questionable foul himself. Hilton Coliseum went to a negative place that night. The second-angriest stadium I have ever experienced was that Thursday night in 2013 in Jack Trice Stadium. (Third place was probably the Oklahoma State game in 2021 after Xavier Hutchinson's touchdown was wiped off the board, but since Iowa State ultimately won the anger was muted.)

The crowd booed and booed some more as Texas scored to take a 31-30 lead. After Iowa State threw an interception to end the game, I'm pretty sure there were more boos. It seemed like these calls always went against Iowa State, and it seemed like teams like Texas would get all the breaks. (How eerily similar this game was to Iowa State's 2021 game between Iowa State and West Virginia. *Sigh.*)

After the game, Rhoads didn't hold back in his postgame press conference.

"To make a play on the one-yard line with our backs against the wall ... and have it taken away from them, that's hard to express. You don't just put an arm around a guy and tell him it's OK when that happens to him," he told reporters. As he talked, his voice got louder. It was part of an impassioned speech that made national headlines and provided plenty of fodder for local talk radio.

Rhoads stood up for his team. He expressed the anger that Cyclone fans were feeling. A lot of coaches (including current head coach Matt Campbell) shy away from blaming officials for a loss. Rhoads embraced it. At the time, I loved it.

Two years later, he again made some memorable postgame remarks. Iowa State beat a 3-4 Texas team 24-0 in 2015, in a game that at the time felt like it could be a turning point for Rhoads to save his job at Iowa State.

According to the Des Moines Register, after the game Rhoads told reporters, "I don't know how this comes across. But I'll say this anyway. We shouldn't beat Texas probably. We shouldn't beat Texas probably. Every kid that they recruit, if I go recruit them, I'm not going to get them. I'm not going to get them. OK? But we did and we have twice because the program's moving in the right direction."

Again, at the time I agreed with him. I appreciated Iowa State taking on the bully and winning. I appreciated Iowa State doing more with less.

Looking back, I firmly believe that I limited myself in the idea of what Iowa State football could be. I was happy just to see the team get a win against a poor Longhorn team. I was happy conceding Iowa State shouldn't be able to compete with Texas.

I still appreciate the wins in 2010 and 2015, but I no longer believe Iowa State's ceiling is as low as I thought it was at those points. And I no longer believe Iowa State shouldn't beat Texas.

It took coach Matt Campbell awhile to prove that Iowa State *could* beat Texas when he got hired. 2016 was a lost year in terms of wins and losses for the Cyclones, so a loss at Texas was more-or-less expected. In 2017, Texas came to Jack Trice Stadium for an early-season Thursday night showdown. Iowa State was 2-1 with an overtime loss to Iowa, and I was still trying to decide if I believed this Cyclone team could compete for a bowl game. I felt worse after Texas controlled the game in a frustrating 17-7 win for the Longhorns. Looking back, it's the last time I did not feel confident in Iowa State's trajectory under Campbell; the Cyclones upset Oklahoma the next week en route to an 8-5 season.

In 2018, Iowa State played one of the most anticipated games in school history in a late-season trip to Austin. The winner of the game would essentially earn a spot in the Big 12 Championship Game two weeks later, something Iowa State's program had never done at the time. I watched with Paige and Chris as West Virginia lost in the final minute against Oklahoma State, which was the one domino the Cyclones needed to clear their path to the title game.

If they could beat Texas, of course.

Star running back David Montgomery was suspended for the first half after throwing a punch at a Baylor defender the week before (after getting illegally driven into the bench several yards out of bounds). It was a blow to Iowa State, as Montgomery was a key part of the Cyclones' offense. The game just never felt right. The Cyclone offense could never seem to get into a rhythm, and that night Texas did look like the big bad bully that it expects to be. Iowa State scored a touchdown late to make what was a 24-3 deficit look more respectable at 24-10. However, that night Rhoads' words seemed to ring true, "We shouldn't beat Texas probably." It was one of the more disheartening games I had ever watched. It felt like Iowa State was still a long way away.

Ironically, in 2019, the Cyclones' Big 12 title hopes had been dashed the week before in a close loss at Oklahoma when Iowa State hosted Texas in November. This time, though, Iowa State looked every bit like it belonged on the same field, taking control of the game early. If anything, it was frustrating when the Cyclones couldn't put the Longhorns away and somehow found themselves trailing 21-20 late.

Iowa State needed a field goal to win when they took the ball at their own 18-yard line with three minutes remaining. Purdy got things going with a 15-yard pass to Deshaunte Jones followed by a 22-yard pass to La'Michael Pettway. A pass interference penalty moved the ball to the Texas 30. Iowa State was moving in on field goal range.

The Cyclones faced a fourth-and-five from the 25. With just over two minutes left, even a made field goal would give Texas the ball back with a chance to win. Until … a Longhorn defender jumped offsides to give Iowa State the first down. Cyclone players pumped their fists in celebration. The game was now in Iowa State's hands. Iowa State ran three more plays, took the clock down to 0:04, and sent Connor Assalley out for a field goal attempt.

Assalley lined up for the kick. I felt a little bit sick as I thought about how many times I had seen the Cyclones lose this type of game or miss a big field goal in an important moment. For most seats in the stadium, it's difficult to tell whether a kick is good until the referee makes a signal. It may be long enough, but it's nearly impossible to tell whether the kick split the uprights or was pushed to one side or the other. This time, I knew it was good as soon as I saw the fans in the Sukup End Zone Club begin to put their hands in the air. The referees followed by signaling that the kick was good, and I cheered as the Iowa State team ran on the field to celebrate. "Sweet Caroline" blasted on the stadium speakers, followed by the "Juicy Wiggle."

Some people around me had begun to file out, but I stood there trying to soak in every moment, jumping up and down with my fist in the air as "Juicy Wiggle" played.

"I've seen Iowa State lose this game enough times that I'm going to enjoy this!" I declared to some of my seatmates who were also sticking around. (Looking back, it feels a little bit like I was predicting the future, but little did I know we were about to face a pandemic that would limit moments like this the next season.)

The 2020 game set up to be a lot like the 2018 game. The winner would essentially earn its spot in the Big 12 Championship Game. It was fitting in many ways that Iowa State had to overcome mighty Texas to take this next step as a program.

The game was the day after Thanksgiving on Black Friday. Normally for a game of this magnitude I would have watched with Chris or my dad or gone to a sports bar. Given the ongoing pandemic, I watched at home with Paige.

Texas jumped out to a 10-0 lead before Iowa State scored on a 35-yard pass from Brock Purdy to Sean Shaw Jr. to make it 10-7. Texas added a field goal to go up 13-7 before Iowa State put together a 15-play drive that at one point took the Cyclones all the way to the two-yard line. Unfortunately, they had to settle for a field goal to make it 13-10. It felt like a missed opportunity. Adding to my stress level in the game, during the second quarter we had a pest control person come to our house. I had the game recorded and paused it for about 30 minutes. This meant I had to totally ignore my phone as my text message chain continued to converse. I was feeling highly anxious knowing that everyone else in my texting group was ahead of me. *What do they know that I don't yet know???*

It was an intense game that stayed in the Longhorns' favor most of the way. Texas scored on its first drive of the second half to go up 20-10. Iowa

State then drove all the way to the Texas five-yard line before again being forced to settle for a field goal to make it 20-13, followed by a kickoff return to midfield for Texas.

"We're doing everything we can't do if we want to win this game," I lamented. Paige was too stressed to watch; she decided to take a nap.

The Cyclones forced a stop after the long kickoff return, and then caught a break when Texas tried to fake the punt, which was stopped three yards short of the first down line. *Finally, some momentum!* Purdy connected on a 44-yard pass to Charlie Kolar to the Texas 13-yard line, before a holding penalty derailed the drive and forced another Assalley field goal to make it 20-16.

Early in the fourth quarter, after fast-forwarding through halftime and commercials, I finally caught up and checked my messages.

"Is Kyle OK?" one of them had asked. I assured them I was.

Texas put together a 13-play drive to begin the fourth and decided to go for a fourth-and-two from the 13 rather than kicking a field goal. Texas quarterback Sam Ehlinger was stuffed for no gain. Iowa State had dodged another potential scoring drive.

The Cyclones took the ball back and faced a fourth-and-three from their own 42-yard line. With less than five minutes left and down by four points, I was (silently, in my head) yelling at them to go for it. I'm pretty sure I was not the only person who felt that way, but Campbell sent out the punting unit. He decided to "trust the process," and apparently the process called for a punt in that situation. He looked like a genius a few minutes later.

Iowa State forced a three-and-out to get the ball back. I felt an odd sense of calm as Iowa State took the ball back with just more than three minutes left. Hall began the drive with an 18-yard run. Purdy found Dylan Soehner for 22 yards, and then Kolar for 17 yards. Hall ran for nine, and then with just 1:25 to play took it the final three yards into the endzone for a touchdown. For the first time all day, Iowa State held the lead at 23-20.

Still, there was enough time left for Texas to get the game to overtime. Texas began to move down the field, converting a third-and-11 and then completing passes of 13 and nine yards before Ehlinger ran for seven more. Texas was at the Iowa State 36, in range for a field goal attempt. On a big play, ISU defender Latrell Bankston sacked Ehlinger for a loss of four yards, forcing a field goal attempt from the 40. Those extra four yards would loom large.

With 0:03 left, Texas' kicker lined up for the kick. Since I was watching on television, this time I could tell exactly where the ball was in relation to the goal posts. The kick sailed toward the uprights. *It's going to be good.* At the last second, it began to veer to the left and ... NO GOOD!

"YES!!" I yelled, waking up Paige in startling fashion. "We just won!" I told her as my voice cracked.

Iowa State was going to the Big 12 Championship Game.

In rewatching the highlight later, I noticed a smattering of cheering as the kick went wide left. In the pandemic-limited crowd, there had still been a few Cyclone fans there to cheer. Wide Right and Natty Light, a Cyclone fan site, put together a compilation of fan-submitted videos showing people cheering (and tearing up) at home as they watched the kick miss. It was an all-timer of a moment to be a Cyclone fan.

Heading into the 2021 game, this isn't quite the game we thought it was going to be when the schedule came out. Iowa State is coming off a disappointing loss at West Virginia. Texas is 4-4 in head coach Steve Sarkisian's first year. Still, this was a game fans circled since Texas announced it was leaving the conference.

When Kansas comes to Hilton Coliseum to play a men's basketball game, there's a little bit of dislike in the air. A little something extra. The feeling of trying to beat the program that is one of the most storied in the country. There is a similar feeling when Texas comes to Jack Trice Stadium for football. There will be some anger in the air on Saturday. Texas is always the enemy, but even more so now that it is defecting from the Big 12. This may be the final time we ever see the Longhorns at Jack Trice Stadium. The crowd will be charged. The "horns down" hand symbol will be prominent.

For Iowa State, every game at this point is a de facto elimination game in terms of making it to the Big 12 Championship. The Cyclones need to win to keep that dream alive.

The beauty of college football is that some games are exciting no matter the records, no matter how the season finishes. Some games, because of their own circumstances and storylines, live on in fans' minds. This game has the potential to do that. We really want to send Texas away with a loss.

It may have been true before that Iowa State shouldn't beat Texas. On Saturday, we'll see if there is still any truth to it.

CHAPTER TWENTY

IOWA STATE VS. TEXAS RECAP

FIVE-STAR CULTURE WINS OUT

Nov. 9, 2021

Breece Hall ran toward me. Well, at least in the direction of my seats in the southwest corner at Jack Trice Stadium.

I temporarily forgot everything else as I ecstatically joined 60,000-plus fellow Iowa State fans in yelling as loud as I could. I turned to my friends around me and gave high-fives. One of them hugged me in celebration.

On Iowa State's first possession of the second half, Hall had broken free. He zigged and zagged, making Texas defenders miss, and then ran all the way across the field to outpace defenders and sneak across the pylon on the goal line for a touchdown. It was a 47-yard run for Hall to give Iowa State the lead. After the extra point made it 10-7, "Juicy Wiggle" came on the loudspeakers, and we danced. Thousands of fans shined their cell phone lights. I jumped up and down and waved mine.

I didn't know it quite yet, but the route was on.

As that route was nearing its completion awhile later, "S-E-C! S-E-C! S-E-C!" chants filled the air. I joined in as the cheers rained down in a mocking fashion as the clock ticked toward 0:00 in the fourth quarter. After years of being made to believe that our team didn't belong on the same field as mighty Texas, and months of uncertainty caused by the Longhorns' decision to leave the conference for what they perceived to be the greener pastures of the SEC, the crowd at Jack Trice Stadium was in a celebratory mood.

Iowa State had beaten up on the Longhorns to a tune of 27-0 during the second half. The final seconds were ticking away on a 30-7 win. All week, I had felt like this was the most likely scenario. The Longhorns came in at 4-4. Their fans, coaches and players expect better, and there were rumblings of turmoil within the program. Texas likely had more talent, sure, but I thought the game would come down to who wanted it more. I couldn't imagine Texas was actually going to want it more.

The crowd had a point to prove from the get-go. We didn't like Texas. We wanted our team to beat Texas. In what was likely the last time Texas would play at Jack Trice Stadium as a conference foe, we wanted to humiliate Texas.

The second half was like a dream. Touchdown after touchdown, defensive stop after defensive stop. The "Juicy Wiggle" and "S-E-C" chants. It was exactly what we wanted it to be.

As fans, we had put a lot of emotion into this game. It was circled on our calendars from the day rumors began to leak that Texas was leaving. For me, it was like a shining beacon on the horizon; no matter how good or bad Iowa State's season had gone, I knew the first weekend in November would be an emotional standalone game.

Iowa State delivered the blow we were all hoping for.

After the 2020 game, ISU running back Breece Hall famously told the Des Moines Register's Travis Hines that while Texas had five-star players (referring to the highest level used to measure player talent in recruiting rankings), Iowa State had a five-star culture.

Hall, who himself was a three-or-four-star recruit depending on the rating system, was talking about the team, but I think the same thing also applies to fans. I know very few Texas fans, so it's tough for me to make a definitive judgement. My perception has always been that cheering for the Longhorns has a lot of similarities with cheering for the New York Yankees; it's easy to cheer for a traditional winner. As Iowa State fans, we cheer for a team that has had more bad seasons than good seasons for most fans' lifetimes, but our investment makes us appreciate the good seasons even more.

In the 2021 game, we cheered as Iowa State players ran off the field and booed as the Longhorn players sang with their band at the end of the game. I thought about how Texas was now off to the SEC, widely considered the best conference in college football, and how the Longhorns were poised to have a losing record in the Big 12 in 2021. Iowa State was competing for a spot in the conference championship game in November for the fifth year in a row. If the SEC was choosing schools based on results of the past five years (which it was not), Iowa State would be picked over Texas.

What a time to be an Iowa State fan, I thought.

—

If I was writing a sitcom, I don't think I could have even tried to come up with the storyline that led off the week between Iowa State and Texas. On Halloween night six days before the game, rumors surfaced that a child was bitten by a monkey at the home of a Texas assistant coach. The story got more bizarre as more details came out about the coach's wife. This is a family book, so I won't get into it more than that, but a Google search of "Texas assistant coach monkey" should get you all the info you'd want if you aren't already aware of the story.

Regardless, some fans in Ames made plans to bring monkey dolls and wear monkey masks, adding a little extra layer to the hype surrounding the game. Texas coach Steve Sarkisian was also asked about it by reporters, and he assured them it wouldn't be a distraction for the team. Most of the time when a coach says something isn't a distraction, well, it's probably a distraction.

On Wednesday, word came out that a Texas player had gotten into an altercation with Sarkisian during practice. It seemed Texas was a little bit in disarray. *If Iowa State can just take away their will early*, I thought, *it could be a blowout.*

Saturday arrived. I began the day by texting my brother "Gameday!" and texting my friends some "horns down" GIFs. It had shaped up to be about as nice of weather as anyone could ask for on a November Saturday afternoon. Highs were in the 60s and there was bright sunshine. It felt like a night and day difference from the week before at West Virginia. (One thing that I realized after the season is that for the first few games, when the weather is warm, I am a lot more superstitious about what I wear. For November games, it becomes less about the content on the clothing and more about wearing the appropriate layers, almost all of which have some sort of Iowa State logo on them. All that to say… I couldn't actually remember what I wore to this game.)

We had a few extra tickets for the game, so I had invited my friend Joe to join. Joe is an Iowa State graduate who got a little more into football while watching a few games with Chris and me during the 2020 season. He was eager to go to a game with us and see us in our element. Chris, Joe and I headed up a little closer to gametime than normal due to some family obligations but got there in time to enjoy an abbreviated tailgate. We met up with others in our group, including my friends Charles, James and Derek. Also joining us was Charles' wife, a Texas fan. We gave her a few good-natured "horns down" hand gestures.

Since we had gotten to the tailgate late, we had to park further away than normal. At around 6 p.m., we started to walk back to the car to pack up our coolers and head into the stadium for the 6:30 kickoff. The walk took a little longer than expected. We got to our seating area just as the team was taking the field. I often get to the game early enough to see the stands fill up. On Saturday, I walked in to a nearly full stadium, with cellphone lights flashing and the crowd cheering. It was sensory overload in the best way.

Iowa State was wearing black helmets, jerseys and pants, a departure from what the team had announced earlier in the week. Iowa State hadn't worn its black jerseys since the loss to Iowa. It had become somewhat of a tradition that the Cyclones would wear the black uniforms during night games at home, but they didn't do that during the Kansas game, and I had begun to wonder if they were retired for the year. The fact they surprised fans with it against Texas made the game feel a little more like a special occasion.

We took our seats and I surveyed the scene. I expected a packed stadium and a loud crowd. I had wondered if the loss the week before had dampened spirits at all. That thought was quickly put to rest. The fans were into it and ready to go. It reminded me of the beginning of the Iowa game. We really wanted this game. *I hope the team is ready to capitalize on this emotion,* I thought.

It seemed Iowa State was ready. On the second play from scrimmage, Iowa State's Isheem Young forced a fumble from Texas' star running back Bijan Robinson. Young recovered. After further review, the ruling of a fumble stood and Iowa State was in business. My pregame hopes of Iowa State getting momentum early and destroying Texas' will seemed attainable, especially as Iowa State drove from the 39-yard line down to the 10 in just three plays. Unfortunately, that's where the drive stalled as the Cyclones were forced to settle for a 24-yard field goal by Andrew Mevis. It was a good start, but it could have been so much better.

Still, Iowa State's defense, which featured Mike Rose's return after being held out for injury the week prior, held Texas to four straight punts, three of which were the results of three-and-out series. All it would take was for Iowa State's offense to capitalize, and it just couldn't quite do it.

The Cyclones' second possession ended when quarterback Brock Purdy dove a yard short of the first down on a fourth-down play in Texas territory. *Ughh. Another missed opportunity.* The Cyclones punted on their third possession, and then gave up a turnover after Xavier Hutchinson fumbled after a 24-yard gain. It was another one of those plays that on the stadium video board I thought was the wrong call, but after my own further review watching highlights the next day, I realized was probably the correct call. After another punt a little while later, it was becoming frustrating to see Iowa State let Texas hang around when the Cyclones were outgaining the Longhorns by a lot of yards.

Unfortunately, in the middle of the second quarter, Texas put together what would end up being its only good drive of the day. The Horns completed a 24-yard pass to get things going on third-and-seven, and then got Robinson going with a number of consistent solid runs. After 14 plays, 78 yards and 5:38 taken off the clock, Texas took the lead with a four-yard pass from Hudson Card to Xavier Worthy to make the score 7-3. After how much the Cyclones had seemingly controlled the game, they were now losing.

Our consternation got worse when the Cyclones were forced to punt after a three-and-out. The crowd that was so fired up at kickoff was now sitting on its hands, so-to-speak. The Longhorns had taken us out of the game for the time being.

What I'm about to describe is one of those things that feels so silly knowing what I know now, but losing 7-3 and watching the offense stall put both Chris and me in a negative place. We were frustrated that Iowa State couldn't capitalize on the early turnover for a touchdown. Frustrated that the team couldn't capitalize on the excitement of the crowd. Frustrated that the team was going to be losing at halftime.

"Why do we need to make it so hard on ourselves?" Chris asked.

As fans do, we were overreacting. Like I said, it felt silly just a little while later.

At halftime, Chris went to the restroom and to buy concessions. I watched as the Cyclone Marching Band put on a video game-themed show, complete with people in Pikachu and Poké Ball costumes. My mood began to improve.

Iowa State took the ball to begin the second half. Chris still hadn't gotten back to his seat. Hall ran for six yards and we let out an "Ohhh" as he just missed a much larger gain. On third-and-seven, Purdy found Hutchinson for 10 yards and a first down. On the next play, he threw it deep for Hutchinson, who drew a pass interference penalty to bring the ball to the Texas 47. Iowa State was driving. I looked over and saw Chris near the entrance tunnel.

Hall then ripped off his 47-yard run to give Iowa State the lead at 10-7. Chris came back to his seat to celebrate after the play.

"You missed the touchdown!" someone said. "You aren't allowed to watch anymore."

"I saw it," he remarked. He was lucky. "I'm going to be positive from this point on," he let us know.

"Juicy Wiggle" played, and we danced. Texas got the ball and faced a third-and-four. The crowd came to its feet. This felt like it could be a pivotal play to put momentum squarely on Iowa State's side. Texas quarterback Card was chased out of the pocket, and threw the ball out of bounds. I yelled for a flag for intentional grounding, and the referee must have heard me as he threw it. Iowa State had gotten the stop and forced Texas to punt from its own 12-yard line.

Iowa State got the ball back but was stopped after picking up just one first down. The Cyclones were punting from the Texas 48.

Chris, continuing his quest to be positive, said, "We're going to down it inside the 10."

Sure enough, the ball did bounce inside at the five and died right there as Greg Eisworth took control at the four-yard line. Texas would have to begin the possession inside its own five.

Now it felt like everyone in the stadium was on their feet. I yelled, "Ohhhhhh!" on first down to cheer on the defense. I kept yelling on second-and-seven and third-and-six as Card was chased by Uwazurike and forced to throw the ball away. Texas was called for both holding and for having an ineligible man downfield. It didn't matter. The Longhorns had to punt again. I could tell Chris wanted to say something, but he held back. Iowa State's Jaylin Noel fair caught the Texas punt at the Texas 49-yard line, setting up Iowa State in great field position.

On the next play, my friend Eric pointed out that Tarique Milton was in the game. Milton had made a big catch on Iowa State's go-ahead touchdown drive two weeks prior against Oklahoma State and had caught a bomb from Purdy the week before at West Virginia.

"Good time for a play-action pass to Tarique," I said.

I was close.

Purdy threw the ball behind the line of scrimmage to Hutchinson, and I think we saw what was about to happen before the Texas defense did.

"OH, THEY'VE GOT HIM!" I yelled as I saw Milton streaking down the sideline. As the defenders were trying to pursue Hutchinson, he stopped and threw to a wide-open Milton. It didn't matter that there wasn't much juice on the ball. There was no Longhorn player close enough to even attempt to make a play. The football landed perfectly in Milton's hands and he jogged into the endzone as we jumped around mosh pit style in the stands.

"OK I was wrong. It wasn't play action. But it was basically the same thing!" I yelled.

Iowa State was now up 17-7, and everyone was feeling good.

"See, this is what happens when I'm positive!" Chris exclaimed. "I just about texted myself that we were going to fumble the punt, but I didn't."

I thanked him.

Iowa State kicked off again to Texas, which started its next possession at the 20. We again stood on first down. The crowd sensed the Cyclones were on the verge of blowing out the Longhorns. We roared even louder as Will McDonald picked up a sack on third down, forcing Texas to punt. The crowd was in a frenzy.

Iowa State again took over at the Texas 49-yard line. Campbell likes to talk about playing complimentary football, where the offense, defense and special teams work off each other. It was fitting that the Cyclones had set themselves up in great field position two possessions in a row just as Texas was reeling.

Hall immediately broke through for 21 yards, and Purdy found Charlie Kolar two plays later for 23 yards down to the two-yard line. Hall broke through into the endzone standing up on the next play to give Iowa State a 24-7 lead. This was the outcome I had hoped for. Iowa State was dominating the once-mighty Texas Longhorns.

Chants of "S-E-C! S-E-C!" formed around the stadium as thousands of people made a "horns down" symbol with their hands. We weren't going to let them go down quietly.

Texas picked up a first down on its next possession but was forced to punt again. This time, it was downed at the Iowa State two-yard line.

"That's fine. We'll just have to go 98 yards this time and kill some clock," I remarked.

"That's right, Kyle," positive Chris chimed in.

The Cyclones began their drive by picking up two first downs as the third quarter ended. We stood and cheered appreciatively as the team ran from one end of the field to the other. A 17-point lead for Texas wasn't insurmountable, but it felt like there was no way Iowa State was going to let the Longhorns back in the game.

Iowa State methodically drove down the field all the way to the Texas 12 before settling for a field goal. Mevis knocked through a 29-yarder to put Iowa State up 27-7.

Texas converted a couple third-down conversions on its next drive. On the next first down, as Iowa State defensive lineman Zach Petersen got tackled by two Texas offensive linemen to draw a holding call, Robinson took a short pass nine yards before fumbling. Iowa State's Jake Hummel recovered to again give Iowa State the ball in great field position.

The Cyclones ran nine plays to take five minutes off the clock. Mevis ran out for a field goal attempt of 46 yards, but a false start penalty backed up Iowa State another five yards. I wondered if the Cyclones would decide to punt from the Texas 34, but Mevis and the field goal team stayed on the field. Mevis drilled a 51-yard kick to the appreciative cheers of the crowd.

When it's your night, it's your night, I thought. (Chris later admitted he was scared Texas would somehow block the kick and return it for a touchdown, but in his final act of positivity for the game he decided not to verbalize his thoughts.)

Iowa State was up 30-7 and had outscored Texas 27-0 in the second half. More "S-E-C!" chants filled the air.

Texas ran four plays on its next possession and punted on fourth-and-eight. It's always a little extra satisfying to see the opponent make the decision to punt in the fourth quarter of a blowout. Texas had officially waved the white flag. The Cyclones returned the favor after going three-and-out with a number of backups on the field, and Texas took the ball with just 35 seconds left.

"S-E-C! S-E-C! S-E-C!" we chanted as the Longhorns ran out the clock. We sang "Sweet Caroline" in celebration as Iowa State players gathered near the Cyclone Marching Band in the north endzone and Texas players gathered near their band in the southeast corner.

It was one of the more satisfying wins I could remember walking out of Jack Trice Stadium.

As we walked back to the car, the conversation turned to the future. Iowa State had three games left. Baylor had lost unexpectedly to TCU earlier in the day, further opening things up for Iowa State's path to the conference championship game. Oklahoma, undefeated in the conference (and overall), had three games left against the other three contenders: Iowa State, Baylor and Oklahoma State. We started running the scenarios of what could happen if Oklahoma were to win or lose against Baylor and win or lose against Oklahoma State. The conclusion we ultimately came to was that if Iowa State could win out, it would very likely be in the championship game. The Cyclones didn't quite control their own destiny, but it was close.

It still seemed somewhat surreal that Iowa State had not only defeated Texas for the third straight year, but that it was Iowa State still playing for a conference championship while Texas was just trying to qualify for a bowl and answering questions about a monkey biting a child. The Cyclones had moved to 6-3 and were now officially bowl eligible. For most of my childhood, most of my college years and the first half of the 2010s, becoming bowl eligible was seen as the ultimate sign of a successful season. In 2009, after Iowa State won its sixth game of the season over a sub-.500 Colorado team at Jack Trice Stadium, some fans rushed the field in celebration of a successful season. Since Campbell started his run of success as ISU's coach in the breakthrough 2017 season, win number six wasn't seen as the ultimate milestone anymore.

We were still hoping for more.

CHAPTER TWENTY-ONE

IOWA STATE VS. TEXAS TECH PREVIEW

REMEMBERING "THE RUN" AS IOWA STATE CONTINUES ITS RUN

Nov. 11, 2021

For Iowa State fans, Texas Tech doesn't elicit the same kind of emotions as most other teams in the conference. It's not an old Big Eight Conference rival that goes back 100 years. It's not the big bad Texas Longhorns or Oklahoma Sooners. There haven't been a ton of controversial or memorable games like when Iowa State plays Baylor or Oklahoma State or West Virginia.

In my mind, any memories of playing Texas Tech in the past have to start with the 2002 game when a solid Red Raiders team came to Ames to face the No. 14 Cyclones. Iowa State was coming off an emotional win over Nebraska. Earlier in the season, Iowa State had taken storied Florida State, led by the legendary Bobby Bowden, to the wire in a first-game matchup at Arrowhead Stadium in Kansas City. The Cyclones had also come back from a 24-7 deficit to beat the rival Hawkeyes in Kinnick Stadium. And they were led by Heisman Trophy contender Seneca Wallace at quarterback. I'm in my 25th year of being an Iowa State fan, and up until 2020 this was the most excited I can ever remember being during a season. It felt like Iowa State had a legitimate shot at winning the Big 12 and playing for a national championship.

That excitement would dissipate quickly in the weeks ahead, but not before reaching its peak in the game against Texas Tech. Early in the third quarter, with the game tied at 3-3, one of the most memorable plays in school history occurred.

Wallace went back to pass, faced pressure, ran backwards out of the defender's grasp, turned the corner to tiptoe down the sideline, then cut back inside and ran all the way vertically across the field, picked up a key block from Michael Wagner and walked into the endzone to complete what went into the record books as a 12-yard touchdown run, and became imprinted in our minds as "The Run."

It's hard to believe, but someone in college today would not remember The Run if they had even been alive to see it. It has now been 19 years.

Every Iowa State fan old enough to remember it probably remembers where they were when they watched it. My friend Charles was in the Cyclone Marching Band. At that time, the band stood in the south endzone bleachers during the game. The band was in prime position to see the play develop and cheer as Wallace ran right in its direction as he crossed the goal line.

I remember approximately where I was, and it was not in Jack Trice Stadium, nor was it at home watching on television. No, I was a sophomore in the Pella High School marching band, and we were at a band competition that evening. In those days (I feel so old writing this), we didn't have smartphones. I couldn't check the score or updates on my phone every five minutes like I can now. It's possible the announcer at the marching band competition read the score at some point. I don't remember. It seems likely that I found out somehow that evening the Cyclones had defeated Texas Tech. If not, I would have found out when I looked at the newspaper the next day.

Regardless, I didn't have much comprehension of what The Run was. I seem to recall at some point my brother, who had watched the game, tried to describe it to me, telling me how thrilling it was. I remember as he finished trying to describe it, he said "I can't do it justice. You really just need to see it."

The problem was it wasn't easy to just see it, at that time. The internet wasn't what it is now. There was no ISU Athletics Facebook account. I'm pretty sure you couldn't see highlights on ESPN.com at that point (I remember a few years later watching highlights of sports online and thinking, *Wow, I can't believe this exists!*).

I don't even remember when I first saw the play. I think I saw one angle of it on a college football highlight show at the end of the year (to which I think I remember my brother telling me it wasn't even the best angle).

At some point, when YouTube became a thing, I found the clip. *OK, now I see why they call it "The Run."*

I bet I watched the play 10 times, alternating between Pete Taylor's call and the television broadcast. I imagined how excited Jack Trice Stadium must have been at that moment. Fans were watching a top 25 football team play a prime-time game where the Heisman Trophy candidate made a high-light-worthy play. The Cyclones went on to win the game 31-17 to move to 6-1, further building hype around their national championship hopes. I imagine that moment to be one of the best moments in history to be an Iowa State football fan. Knowing what we know now about how the 2002 season ended, it is probably easy to forget how that moment felt. But the fans in the stadium that night, and watching at home, and reading about the result in the newspaper the next day, had no idea what was to come. Those moments were college football bliss.

The other more recent game that lives in Cyclone lore was the 2016 game at Jack Trice Stadium. It was a cold November day when a 4-6 Texas Tech team took on a 2-8 Iowa State team during Matt Campbell's first year as Iowa State's coach. When we entered the stadium, we went to our regular seats in the upper deck and saw there was barely anyone in the visitors' section in the lower deck below us. We decided to abandon our normal seats and sneak down close to the field. It was not a heavily attended game, and nobody stopped us. Given the fact we weren't really impeding the view of anyone behind us, and to help stay warm, we stood the entire game.

Some guy named Patrick Mahomes was playing quarterback for Texas Tech that day. We had no idea two years later he would be an NFL Most Valuable Player or that he'd lead Kansas City to the Super Bowl win in the 2019 season. Joel Lanning was the quarterback for Iowa State, and he had a day to remember.

Iowa State jumped out to a 7-0 lead as Lanning ran for a 24-yard touch-down. Iowa State grabbed a 14-3 lead a little while later.

I'm trying to decide when I really believed it was going to be a blowout. I don't think I quite felt that way even when Allen Lazard caught a 34-yard touchdown pass, or when Lanning ran for his second touchdown of the day to make it 28-3 early in the second quarter. Iowa State had developed a habit of jumping out to a lead and then trying to hold on (unsuccessfully) as the other team stormed back. Already in 2016, the Cyclones had blown leads of 14 points in the fourth quarter to Baylor and 17 points late in the third quarter to Oklahoma State, and the year prior had lost big leads to Oklahoma State and Kansas State.

It became tougher to doubt the Cyclones as they continued to stop Mahomes and took a 35-3 lead after a 39-yard catch by Hakeem Butler. All doubt was removed when Mahomes had a pass intercepted by Kamari Cotton-Moya and returned 48 yards for a touchdown to make the score 42-3. For good measure, Iowa State added a field goal just before halftime to make it 45-3.

In the second half, Lanning ran for touchdown runs of 19 yards, 35 yards and 10 yards to cap a 66-10 win. It was one of the more satisfying blowouts I had watched the Cyclones play, and a turning point in the Campbell era. Even with all the success the team has had since then, this game still gets brought up fondly by many Cyclone fans.

Campbell has not lost to Texas Tech, and all but one of the victories has been fairly comfortable.

This year, Texas Tech got off to a strong 5-2 start, but after a loss to Kansas State, the Red Raiders decided to part ways with coach Matt Wells with the four toughest teams in the conference still on the schedule. The Red Raiders are now led by interim coach Sonny Cumbie, and just days before the game announced that Joey McGuire would take over as head coach at the end of the season. It's an unusual circumstance to have a coach fired with four games to play, have a new coach waiting, but to still have an interim coach leading the team for the rest of the season.

Texas Tech is coming off a blowout 52-21 loss to Oklahoma in its first game post-Wells. I've been trying to decide if it makes me feel better that Texas Tech has an interim coach, or worse. Sometimes these can be just the type of situations that seem to galvanize a team to pull an upset.

And yet, I feel confident in Iowa State. In fact, it's the most confident I have felt about any of the Big 12 road games Iowa State has played so far. I had major nerves going into the Baylor, Kansas State and West Virginia games. (In fact, the West Virginia game was the least confident I had felt about a game all year, and unfortunately my hunch played out.) Iowa State is rolling after winning four of its last five games, including the win over previously unbeaten Oklahoma State and the dominant wins over Kansas State and Texas. The West Virginia loss feels like a blip.

My gut feeling is that Iowa State will be locked in, ready to go. At 4-2 in the Big 12, Iowa State is still very much alive for the conference championship game.

I have to admit, when the schedule first came out, the trip to Lubbock was at the bottom of my list. Lubbock is off the beaten path, so to speak. It's not a place I likely ever would have chosen to go if not for seeing Iowa State play a football game, and it's not the first road trip I would have chosen for a Cyclone game. This would have been an easy road trip to try to find a way out of.

Now that the game is here, I'm feeling significantly more excited. The Cyclone Club of Dallas/Fort Worth is having a pregame tailgate, I get to meet up with my friends Adam and Nicole — who I met in Waco — and my friend Charles is making the trip from Minneapolis.

I don't know exactly what to expect in terms of the gameday atmosphere. My impression is Texas Tech fans are passionate about their team, and I almost imagine Texas Tech to be the pro team of northwest Texas, similar to how Iowa State fans feel about the Cyclones in Central Iowa. I'm not totally sure whether to expect a raucous crowd excited to see their team try to pull an upset, or a somewhat sleepy crowd given the mid-season coaching change.

Either way, it's another de facto elimination game for the Big 12 Championship. A loss would all but end Iowa State's hopes.

If Iowa State can take care of business, however, it will set up an even bigger game ahead.

CHAPTER TWENTY-TWO

IOWA STATE VS. TEXAS TECH RECAP

62 YARDS

Nov. 16, 2021

The kick was in the air. *It feels too good,* I thought. Texas Tech fans began to buzz in anticipation. *There's no way this can happen.*

A 62-yard game-winning field goal attempt was ripping through the air at Jones AT&T Stadium. There was every reason to believe this kick would be well short of the uprights, or that it would harmlessly zing wide left or right. Honestly, if I wasn't an Iowa State fan, I probably wouldn't have even entertained the idea in my mind that the kick *could* be good.

A few hours earlier, my friend Charles and I had arrived at the tailgate in Lubbock hosted by the Cyclone Club of Dallas/Fort Worth. We had almost immediately started a conversation with an Iowa State fan who lived in Dallas. One of the topics of conversation focused on the heartbreaking ways Iowa State sometimes finds to lose games.

I had sat through some doozies, many of which I have already written about. Missed field goals, a missed extra point, referee decisions going against the team in critical moments, failing to take a knee to run out the clock. The list goes on and any die-hard Cyclone fan could name a handful without blinking.

I did not expect Saturday's game at Texas Tech to be one where we'd experience anything close to heartbreak. I felt confident Iowa State was going to win this game comfortably. It didn't play out that way, but the Cyclones fought back from a poor first half and a 21-point deficit to tie the game with one minute on the clock in the fourth quarter. It was the kind of comeback that happens in dream seasons.

Texas Tech had one more chance to win the game before overtime and moved its way to the Iowa State side of the field. With only a few seconds left on the clock, the Red Raiders decided to line up for a field goal kick on the 44-yard line. It would be an attempt longer than 60 yards. I was almost relieved.

Almost.

No way they make a kick from that distance. Right?

Iowa State's coaches seemed to feel the same way as they sent Jaylin Noel to the back of the endzone for a chance to return the kick if it was short.

In recalling the play later, I was trying to decide at what moment I believed the kick was going in. I think it was a split second before it came down. As the crowd anticipation built, I just knew. We were in the northwest corner of the stadium, behind the endzone. We had a good enough angle at the goalposts to be able to tell exactly where the kick was going to land. I couldn't believe it, and yet I could believe it, as I saw the kick sail over the crossbar. It was a visual that I believe will be etched in my mind for years to come. If there was any doubt at what my eyes were telling me, it was erased as I heard the roar of the crowd. I looked around and saw thousands of Texas Tech fans with their hands in the air.

Iowa State's realistic hopes at a Big 12 Championship Game appearance were gone.

I just stood there, silently, as the Red Raider players ran onto the field in celebration and fans followed. It was a big win for their program; in an up-and-down season, Texas Tech had just clinched bowl-eligibility in dramatic fashion. I imagine it was a game their fans will remember fondly.

As thoughts were forming in my brain, one stood out.

That was such an Iowa State thing to happen.

As Charles and I talked about later, this game will be one we bring up as we reminisce around a summer campfire in some year to come, recalling the good and bad Iowa State memories. I imagine it will be something like, "Can you believe Texas Tech hit a 62-yard field goal to beat us?" Followed by a heavier-than-necessary sip of our drinks.

After the game, we were sitting at a brewery eating dinner in Lubbock. Some Texas Tech fans walked by us.

"62 yards!" one of them said.

How unlikely was the kick? Well, according to Cyclone Fanatic's Rob Gray, the kicker had never even attempted a kick of more than 50 yards in a game. It was the longest field goal made so far all season in the entire Football Bowl Subdivision.

A lot of things can be true at once. Iowa State played poorly enough to dig itself a big hole. Texas Tech seemed to play inspired football. The Cyclones fought back valiantly to tie the game in dramatic fashion. Iowa State likely didn't necessarily *deserve* to win (or lose), and Texas Tech didn't necessarily *deserve* to win (or lose) either. In a game like that, you can look back at any number of plays in the first three quarters and say, "If only the team had been better on this play, it wouldn't have mattered that Texas Tech hit a 62-yard field goal." That's true. It's all true.

But when we sit around the campfire, I won't think about that stuff. I'll think about 62 yards. Sixty-two yards between my favorite team and its chance to play for a spot in the conference championship game. Sixty-two improbable yards.

"62 yards!" will live on, at least in my mind.

———

When the schedule came out way back in February, I knew this stretch would be tiring in terms of the amount of travel. The day after the Texas game, I was supposed to fly to Colorado for a wedding. I was then going to stay in Fort Collins for the week and work remotely in my day job, and fly out of Denver to Lubbock on Friday morning for the Texas Tech game.

Our plans ran into a glitch. My wife, Paige, had flown to Colorado the Tuesday before the Texas game. On Friday evening, she lost her sense of taste and smell. Saturday morning, she took a COVID-19 test and tested positive.

Change of plans.

Luckily, I tested negative. Paige made plans to isolate at her parent's house, and I cancelled my flight to Denver.

Instead, on Thursday I drove to Fort Collins and dropped off our car so she could drive home when she was ready, and got a ride to the airport Friday morning from her mom. I knew when I began this journey that I was going to need to really want it (and get a little lucky) if I was to make all the games. Luckily, Paige never had any strong symptoms, so everything worked out OK.

I got into Lubbock on Friday around Noon. I found the shuttle from the airport to my hotel. Standing outside it was a man wearing a Red Raiders t-shirt. He saw me walk up with my Iowa State sweatshirt.

"There's no room on this shuttle," he said jokingly.

We talked for a bit and he told me he had flown in from Dallas. His two sons went to school at Texas Tech and he had become a Red Raider fan. He and another fan on the shuttle told me they just hoped Texas Tech could cover the spread. He also mentioned the Texas Tech team was staying at the same hotel. Charles and I later joked we should set off the fire alarm in the night. (We wouldn't *actually* have done that.)

Charles arrived from Minneapolis a little after 5:30 p.m. We went out for dinner and then watched the last few minutes of the Iowa State men's basketball game vs. Oregon State on my laptop. The overlap between college football and college basketball season each year is one of the most fun times on the sports calendar, in my opinion. The Cyclones won their first game over major conference competition since February of 2020. The weekend was off to a great start for Cyclone fans.

The next morning, we grabbed breakfast in the hotel. We were among the few Cyclone fans in a room that was full of Tech fans. We saw a couple of ISU fans and gave them a "Go State!" After breakfast, we wandered out to grab drinks and snacks for the day. Behind the hotel, we saw from a distance what appeared to be some players doing some warmup exercises.

Charles and I took an Uber to the DFW tailgate around 11 a.m. for the 2:30 p.m. game. We immediately met up with the president of the DFW club, who offered us burgers and hot dogs. We also talked to a fan from Dallas who told us stories of his days in school in the early 1990s. We lamented how often bad things seem to happen to Cyclone fans. It seemed funny at the time; I did not think the day was going to be a heartbreaker for ISU.

We met up with my friend Adam who I had met in Waco. Adam had graciously offered to have me stay at his house during the Baylor trip, and we had kept in touch since. We hung out, enjoyed a couple of beers and caught up. We kept a close eye on the Baylor vs. Oklahoma game, which had major Big 12 title game implications. After all, at that moment Iowa State still had title game aspirations. We were hoping for an Oklahoma win, as wrong as that felt. It gave Iowa State the best chance to get back to the title game.

A young couple approached our group. They seemed like they were looking for friends. They struck up a conversation with us. We learned that

Drew was a recent ISU grad, and Lauren was a University of Northern Iowa grad. They were living in Midland, Texas, about two hours away from Lubbock, and had taken the opportunity to come and watch the Cyclones.

We took a bus to the stadium about 45 minutes before kickoff. As we walked to the bus, Adam's wife Nicole told me we may not be able to watch games together anymore if the Cyclones lost. After all, we had also witnessed the Baylor loss together. Speaking of Baylor, it had become increasingly clear that the Bears were going to beat Oklahoma, putting a slight damper on our hopes to make the Big 12 title game. Winning out would still put the Cyclones in great position, however.

I had purchased the tickets for Charles and myself separately from Adam, but when we got to our seats we realized we were right next to each other. Perfect. Drew and Lauren were in the same row a little way down.

"If these seats don't fill up, come sit next to us," I told them. They eventually did.

As I went down to the concession stand, I ran into one fan who I also knew was going to every game. I had also seen him at the Baylor and West Virginia games.

"You know, every time I see you, well, I'm not going to say it," I told him. Still, I firmly believed there was no need to worry about a jinx today.

I knew Texas Tech had experienced a weird season so far but was still surprised that the stadium was not fuller as we approached kickoff. The stadium, from what I could tell, was barely more than half full. It was a little eerie. There was very little atmosphere as the teams came out of the locker rooms. Texas Tech took the ball first, and it was almost completely silent as the Red Raiders ran their first offensive drive. Unfortunately, similarly to the West Virginia game, the crowd that was there made more and more noise as the game went on.

It seems unbelievable looking back, but Iowa State forced a third-and-11 play on Texas Tech's first possession. What followed was disaster. Iowa State jumped offside to give Texas five free yards, and Red Raiders quarterback Donovan Smith, a redshirt freshman making his first start, scrambled away from pressure and completed a pass to Myles Price, who had room to run. It was a 36-yard play that gave Texas Tech a first down in Iowa State territory. Four plays later, Tahj Brooks broke a 14-yard run on third-and-one to give Texas Tech a touchdown and a 7-0 lead. Iowa State was forced to punt, but flipped momentum a few plays later with an interception at the Texas Tech

16-yard line. ISU quarterback Brock Purdy found Xavier Hutchinson along the sideline for a nice 15-yard catch, and Breece Hall ran it in from a yard out to tie the game at 7-7. I high-fived Adam and Charles. The Cyclones were in business.

Twice before during the season, we had watched Iowa State's defense uncharacteristically give up yards in chunks and look like it had no answer for the opposing offense. Texas Tech's redshirt freshman quarterback seemed to have the Cyclones' number. His scrambling and running ability kept Cyclone defenders off balance, and he had little trouble finding open receivers down the field. On fourth-and-six from the 39, Smith found a wide open Price for a 39-yard touchdown to make it 14-7. Iowa State put together a promising drive, but it ended with a pass from Purdy being intercepted just before the first quarter came to a close.

My hope, and prediction, before the game was that with Texas Tech's instability within the program, the Cyclones could grab a lead early and take away Tech's will to compete. That's not how it played out. The Red Raiders looked inspired, and a step faster than Iowa State. They put together a 15-play touchdown drive to grab a 21-7 lead. Iowa State was forced to punt after only three plays, and Tech was again rolling. Smith found Price for another deep pass of 29 yards, coupled with a 15-yard roughing the passer penalty. In one play, Texas Tech was at Iowa State's 22-yard line. Two plays later, Smith found Erik Ezukanma for an 18-yard touchdown. It was 28-7 Texas Tech, and a nightmare scenario was happening. I began to wonder why I took a trip all the way to Lubbock.

"We need a touchdown, and we get the ball back at halftime," Adam said optimistically.

The Cyclones caught a break on a third-and-18 play, as Texas Tech was called for a pass interference penalty. Iowa State capitalized with a 17-yard run by Hall to make it a 28-14 game with just 1:11 left before halftime.

"We needed that," I said.

In one of many signs that it just wasn't Iowa State's day, the Cyclones forced the Red Raiders to a third-and-eight before running back SaRodorick Thompson ran up the middle for nine yards.

"They were conceding to go to halftime, and we just gave up a first down!" I said in frustration.

Instead, they were going to try to score, and inexplicably put themselves in position to do so with pass completions of 17 yards and 20 yards to set up a 45-yard field goal. The entire sequence, in hindsight, seemed to foreshadow what would happen at the end of the game. The kick was good to make the score 31-14 at halftime.

I still felt a sense of calm. I just felt like the Cyclones had a comeback in them.

"The most memorable games are the comebacks," I said.

I was right, though not for the reason I wanted to be.

It didn't look good to start the half as Purdy threw his second interception of the day, and Texas Tech answered with a drive to the Iowa State 11. On fourth-and-one, instead of taking a field goal, Texas Tech went for the first down, and Smith got stuffed for no gain. *Crisis averted, for now.* Iowa State was immediately forced to punt, and Texas Tech again went for it on fourth-and-three from the 23. Iowa State again stuffed Smith, this time for a loss, and avoided another Red Raiders scoring chance.

Finally, Iowa State put together a much-needed drive. Hall broke a 21-yard run, and Purdy found Charlie Kolar and Hutchinson for a pair of 19-yard gains. The Cyclones capped the drive when Purdy connected with Kolar in the back of the endzone. Iowa State had cut the lead to 31-21.

"Time to force that big turnover!" I said.

Not quite, but Iowa State did force a three-and-out to get the ball back. Now the offense was rolling. Purdy threw to Hutchinson for 22 yards. Tight end Chase Allen caught a pass in space and hurdled over a defender, drawing extra cheers from the Iowa State fans. As the third quarter switched to the fourth, Hall took a pass from Purdy for 15, and Hutchinson caught a nine-yard pass for a first down. Kolar adjusted to make a heavily guarded catch in the endzone to bring Iowa State within 31-28.

The couple hundred-or-so Cyclone fans in the stadium were now into it. We believed our team could win.

Unfortunately, the defense continued to be an issue, immediately giving up chunks of yardage, capped by a Smith pass to Price for 28 yards on a third-and-10 play. Thompson ran for a 13-yard touchdown, and Texas Tech had regained a 38-28 lead. A "Raider! Power!" chant rang through the stadium.

With just more than 10 minutes left, Iowa State still had time. The offense was now rolling. Purdy threw to freshman Jaylin Noel for a big 43-yard gain down to the nine-yard line.

Then things got weird.

Purdy's pass intended for Kolar was off target. Texas Tech's defender dove and appeared to make an interception.

"No …" I said dejectedly. With 7:30 left, it felt like game over.

The Texas Tech sideline erupted. I saw coaches giving giant fist pumps. A number of players ran all the way to the opposite endzone in celebration, drawing a penalty flag. As the referee announced the penalty, he also announced the previous play was under review.

There was only one video board in the stadium, and we were sitting behind it, so we could not see the replay. The play had happened on the opposite end of the field, so I hadn't seen a good angle live. I thought surely the call would stand.

After a few minutes of review, the officials actually changed the call. The ball had apparently hit the ground before the defender gained possession. Shocked, the Iowa State fans let out an immediate and massive cheer.

"Let's go!" Adam said.

Tech fans let out their loudest "Boooo!" of the afternoon.

"Bring it!" Adam yelled, to nobody in particular.

Iowa State lined up at the four-yard line with new life and was immediately called for a false start. Everyone stood around for a bit in seeming confusion.

"What is going on?" I asked, as though Charles, Adam, Drew or Lauren would have any more idea than I did.

After a few more seconds of standing around, ISU coach Matt Campbell called his players back to the sideline. In one of the more bizarre scenes I have witnessed at a game, the public address announcer asked all the fans in two sections to leave the stadium or move. Through text messages and Twitter, we began to get the full picture. Fans near the goal line in the student section had been throwing objects onto the field. Later, on the television replay, I could see that a water bottle had landed on the field a few yards away from Iowa State players right before the false start was called. We all watched as the majority of the fans in the two sections in question moved to different sections closer to where Iowa State players were standing on the sidelines. It wasn't exactly the most effective crowd management.

I don't usually tweet during games, but I was feeling it.

"This place just got weird and I'm here for it. Let's go State!!" I tweeted.

For some reason, despite a water bottle being thrown onto the field, the false start penalty was upheld. After all the commotion, it was first-and-goal from the nine-yard line. The crowd had come to life, but I still felt confident. Hall ran for no gain on first down. Iowa State was called on another false start to move the ball back to the 14. Purdy threw to Hall, who made a nifty spin-move at the 10-yard line and found the space to outrun Texas Tech defenders and find the endzone.

"YES!!!" I yelled, high-fiving everyone around me. With 6:20 left, it was a 38-35 game. Iowa State was going to have a chance to win this thing!

The Iowa State cheerleaders down on the field yelled toward our section, "Cyclone!" We answered, "Power!"

Texas Tech took the ball back, and we were now standing to cheer on the defense. Iowa State responded by forcing a three-and-out. The Cyclones were going to get the ball back with a chance to tie or take the lead!

This is going to be the time the Cyclones finally put together the game-winning drive, I thought, recalling attempts at Baylor and West Virginia to tie the game that fell just short.

The Cyclones were able to methodically run their offense now. On third-and-three, Hall threw to Kolar for six yards. Purdy scrambled for 18 yards into Texas Tech territory as I yelled "GO BABY GO!" On third-and-10, Purdy threw to Kolar for 11 to move the sticks, and on the next series, he threw to Kolar for three yards on a third-and-two. Iowa State had first-and-10 at the 18. Hall ran for two yards and forced Texas Tech to call its final timeout. Purdy threw an incomplete pass in the direction of Jared Rus on second down. On third down, Purdy scrambled to the outside and couldn't quite get to the corner before being forced out of bounds. Had the clock kept running, it likely wouldn't have left Texas Tech enough time later to get a kick off, but as it was the clock stopped. Iowa State sent out kicker Andrew Mevis to try to tie the game.

As Mevis lined up for the kick, we were nervous. We had seen Cyclone kickers miss these kinds of kicks before.

"Don't do this to me," Adam said.

We breathed a sigh of relief as the kick went through. The Cyclones had come all the way back to tie it.

With one minute left on the clock, it seemed like overtime was coming.

With no timeouts, we wondered aloud if Texas Tech would try to score or play for overtime.

"Maybe they will go for it and we can force a turnover," I said hopefully.

Iowa State's defense had been poor all day, and that was also in my mind. All it would take was one big play to put Texas Tech in field goal range.

Instead, the Red Raiders moved slowly down the field. Iowa State's defense seemed content to concede small chunks of yardage to avoid giving up a big play.

The strategy worked. Almost.

Texas Tech was on the Iowa State 46-yard line with 0:08 left, and then gained just two yards on its final play before the field goal attempt. Would the two extra yards have prevented the Red Raiders from even attempting the field goal? I don't know. Either way, I felt confident the defense had done its job. Most teams don't even attempt a field goal that long, and even fewer make it.

I don't think I'll be able to ever forget what it felt like to watch the kick go through.

I couldn't help but think about how just a few weeks ago our fans had rushed the field after the win against Oklahoma State. It had been so much fun. It stung realizing we had given another team it's biggest win of the season.

I was totally numb. I knew I had just watched a historically great play. For a Texas Tech fan, it was memorable in the best way. If I had watched that ending happen in a game I didn't care about, I would have probably thought, *Hey, you've just got to tip your cap to the kicker.* As an Iowa State fan, it felt so unfair.

That could only happen to Iowa State.

We walked out and said our goodbyes to Adam. The walk back to our hotel was about a mile, and it was painful. Jubilant Texas Tech fans streamed out and we ended up in their midst, forced to listen to them talk about how much fun the game was. We avoided conversation. About a block from the hotel, one fan struck up a conversation with us.

"I can't believe that kick went in," he said.

Neither could we.

I told him, "I know this is such a cool moment for you guys, but I've got to tell you, from our end it is painful."

He seemed to understand.

A few minutes later, Charles and I headed out to find dinner at a local brewery. I checked my text messages and saw I had a message from my friend Eric.

"I'm sorry you had to live that," he wrote.

"I really don't have the words," I replied.

My mom had also texted me words of encouragement. I realize it may sound like I take games too seriously, and I probably do. But, quite frankly, when I had decided to take on this journey, a 6-4 record was about the worst-case scenario. It really did hurt. It effectively ended the chance that my book would chronicle a championship season. It made me question everything.

Why am I doing this?

We sat on a patio on a nice night and ordered a couple beers and some food. We rehashed the game. We just kept coming back to, *How could that happen?*

"Look at the bright side," I said sarcastically. "Years later we will be two of like 200 Iowa State fans to be able to say we were here for this."

A few Texas Tech fans walked by. One remarked "62 yards! I thought there was one-tenth of 1% of a chance that was going in."

Throughout the rest of the weekend, we saw random Iowa State fans here and there, including one at a restaurant on Sunday afternoon, and one at the airport on the way home.

"Go State," we would say to them, somewhat sheepishly. In each instance, we just kind of looked at each other and shook our heads, silently sharing in the same thought: *I can't believe that game.*

The headline in the print edition of Sunday's Lubbock Avalanche-Journal was "WHAT A KICK."

I felt that on multiple levels.

WHO-TV's SoundOFF show dubbed it "a kick in the guts."

I read some of the stories after the game. I read in the Des Moines Register how distraught Purdy and others were in post-game interviews. So many of these seniors could have moved on with their life or football career but had chosen to come back. A 6-4 record and losing a shot at the Big 12 Championship was not what they had in mind, either. It really just made me sad to think about.

There were a lot of stories and Twitter discussions about Iowa State underachieving. The Cyclones were a preseason top 10 team, and a favorite for the conference title. It would be easy to label this team as a failure.

The nature of college football is it sometimes does not provide a lot of room for nuance. Teams get 12 games to prove themselves. If a few games don't go their way, things feel a lot different. In other sports, a close regular season loss doesn't hurt nearly as much in most cases, or affect a team's long-term goals nearly as much.

Iowa State had experienced three of the more painful losses that I could remember. A two-point loss at Baylor that was punctuated by Cyclone special team mistakes. A seven-point loss at West Virginia that sticks out for multiple officiating decisions going against the Cyclones. A three-point loss at Texas Tech that ended on one of the most improbable plays I've ever seen.

Critics will rightfully point out that a team with as many returning veteran players as this team had should win more games. Maybe the Cyclones shouldn't even have been in position to lose the three conference games they have lost. Relative to the lofty preseason expectations, Iowa State had not performed up to its standards. I'd imagine most players and coaches would feel that way at least a little bit, as do nearly all fans.

This was supposed to be our year.

There's another way to look at it, which I believe is just as true. There could be an alternate reality where two plays in each Big 12 loss go differently, and Iowa State would be 7-0 in conference. We'd all feel like, *Hey, this team hasn't made it easy, but what a ride!*

I thought about that scenario a lot while trying to gain perspective that the results I so badly wanted didn't come to fruition. Winning a championship is difficult. Other teams want to win too. They have Division I athletes. They have professional coaches. Sometimes things just don't go your way.

Again, I think two things can be true at once. The season had been disappointing, and it had also been tantalizingly close to being the season we all desired, even though it didn't feel like it in the moments after the Texas Tech loss. This team wasn't able to match last year's success, but it still has a chance to be better than 99% of teams in school history.

I'm reminded of the importance of focusing on the journey. Saturday was a fun time in Lubbock overall. I met some nice people and enjoyed time with good friends. In its next game, Iowa State plays Oklahoma. It's not for a trip to the championship like we hoped, but it could still be a major win, a giant step forward for the program and a day we'd never forget in a good way.

For now, though, there's no getting around it. Saturday hurt. It hurt bad.

I wrote at the beginning of this that you never know what will happen in a college football season. In going on this journey, I took a chance that this would be the best season in school history. "62 yards!" ended any hopes of that.

I would say I've gained a lot more than I've lost on this journey. Any comforting feelings from that perspective will have to come later.

CHAPTER TWENTY-THREE

IOWA STATE VS. OKLAHOMA PREVIEW

NOT THE SEASON WE WANTED, BUT STILL A BIG GAME

Nov. 18, 2021

I'm an optimist by nature, but it's time to be honest for a second. The 2021 matchup with Oklahoma is not what I wanted it to be. It's not what anyone hoped for at the beginning of the season. I had imagined, in the absolute best-case scenario, a 10-0 Cyclone team competing with a 10-0 Sooner team in the game of the year in college football. In lesser scenarios, I imagined Iowa State still having some shot at the College Football Playoff, and at least having a chance to get to the Big 12 Championship Game. For all intents and purposes, those hopes slowly evaporated throughout the season, punctuated by the kick in the guts by Texas Tech just a week ago.

It's not the meaningful game we hoped for. It's not the season we hoped for.

Winning at Oklahoma would still be a big, big step for the program.

The nature of being a fan of a historical underdog is that every now and again, there are situations that remind you your team doesn't seem to belong. In Iowa State's football history, no series has better epitomized that than Iowa State vs. Oklahoma. The Sooners are 77-7-2 against Iowa State all time. It is difficult to imagine a more lopsided record between two longtime conference opponents.

The game in my mind that really sums up the Oklahoma series in the era prior to the most recent five-year stretch is the 2002 game. Coming in, Iowa

State was on top of the world. The 6-1 Cyclones were in the top 10 in the country and had a Heisman Trophy contender in Seneca Wallace. Iowa State had just defeated Texas Tech and made national headlines with "The Run" by Wallace. Next up was a trip to Oklahoma, led by coach Bob Stoops and just two years removed from a national championship.

I was a sophomore in high school. We had a marching band competition that day. I had high hopes Iowa State could pull off a win and keep its national championship trajectory. I couldn't watch the game, but someone on the bus to wherever we were going seemed to know the score. First it was 7-0. Then 14-0 Oklahoma.

This team is good enough to come back, I told myself.

I'm pretty sure that wherever our competition was, they announced an update at the stadium. It had turned into a full-blown blowout.

The Hawkeye fans in our high school band seemed a little extra smug.

Iowa State went on to lose 49-3. The dream season was over. The Cyclones started the 2002 season 6-1 and ended the season 7-7 with a bowl loss.

That game was a microcosm of how Oklahoma had always made me feel as an Iowa State fan. The Sooners were the haves. We were the have nots. Most years, OU could name the score. In my years in the Cyclone Marching Band, I saw one of the closest (and most surprising) games in the series in 2007. A 1-6 Iowa State team grabbed a 7-0 lead and held on for dear life in front of a stunned Jack Trice Stadium crowd. Oklahoma finally pulled away for a 17-7 win in the second half.

In 2010, thanks to conference realignment, the teams began to play each other every year. For a while, this meant you could basically pencil in a loss every season. If Iowa State was going to get to the magical six-win mark and bowl eligibility, it would need to find those wins within the other 11 games on the schedule. Scores in that timeframe included 52-0, 48-10, 59-14 and 52-16.

In 2016, in Campbell's first year as coach, we began to notice signs of change in a Thursday evening matchup.

The previous night, the Chicago Cubs had won Game 7 of the World Series. If the Cyclones are my No. 1 true sports love, the Cubs are a very close second. On the day of the Iowa State game, my friend Chris (a much bigger Cubs fan than even I am) and I left in the early afternoon to tailgate in Ames. Our first and probably only line of conversation was the Cubs as we reveled in the glory of the Cubs finally — *finally* — ending their World Series drought. Iowa State was 1-7 on the year. I *knew* Oklahoma was about to win by around 30 points, so I wasn't all that excited for the game.

In the tailgate lots that day, I talked on the phone to my now-wife, then-girlfriend Paige. I told her about my lack of excitement.

"It just feels like we're never going to be good at football," I said, as the Cyclones were in the midst of their fourth straight losing regular season. (What an idiot.)

"If the Cubs can do it, Iowa State can do it too. They just need a little time. It's only his first year," she said. (There's a reason I eventually married her.)

The game began to play out like I anticipated. Sooner quarterback Baker Mayfield led Oklahoma to a 14-3 first quarter lead. Then something unexpected happened. Iowa State answered with 14 straight points, including a 41-yard run by quarterback Joel Lanning on fourth-and-two to make the score 17-14.

Just as we were starting to feel like maybe this could be our night, Oklahoma did what Oklahoma does. First the Sooners completed a 65-yard touchdown pass, and then right before halftime drove 75 yards to take a 28-17 lead.

Iowa State hung around, cutting the lead to 31-24 with just over 13 minutes left. I was a cynical fan that night. I never truly believed Iowa State could or would win. But I also couldn't remember the last time the Cyclones had only been losing by a single touchdown to Oklahoma in the fourth quarter. Oklahoma effectively put the game away with a 12-play drive that took almost six minutes of time off the clock and ended with a field goal to make the final score 34-24. I recognized the positive growth of the Iowa State team that night, though I'm not sure whether I believed yet that it was sustainable.

Over the next two weeks, the Cyclones defeated Kansas and Texas Tech to carry a little bit of momentum into the offseason. But by the time the 2017 matchup with No. 3 Oklahoma arrived, that momentum felt a long way away. Iowa State was 2-2 and coming off a deflating loss to Texas at home. The Cubs were again in the playoffs, which only seems important because I remember we were watching Game 1 of their first round playoff series against Washington when I found out the news.

Iowa State's starting quarterback, Jacob Park, would not be playing.

"So is Joel Lanning going to start?" I asked Chris and my friend Charles, with whom I was watching the Cubs game. Lanning had played a number of games at quarterback for the Cyclones before being switched to linebacker in 2017, his senior year.

It felt like the season was about to unravel similarly to how the last four seasons had. I mentally put more of my energy into cheering for the Cubs, because, well, I was pretty sure the score for the next day's game in Norman was about to be of the 50-something to 14 variety.

As it turned out, Kyle Kempt, who I had never heard of, was the starting quarterback. The fifth-year senior had never started a game.

What better time than against Oklahoma, right?

Charles was staying at my apartment in Des Moines and we had planned to watch the Iowa State game together. A little while before it began, I got a call from my parents who were in Des Moines for the day. They were having car troubles. They had pulled into my apartment complex to assess the situation.

"Oh, you are watching the Iowa State game. We're so sorry to interrupt," my mom said.

I assured her it was OK. In my mind, the less I had to watch, the happier I would probably be.

As we problem solved on finding a mechanic, Charles decided to go see some family in town, and I received a number of text messages from friends about the game. I nervously thought about what I might be missing.

How lopsided is the score going to be?

I finally sat down to watch late in the second quarter. Much to my surprise … it was still a close game at 24-10. Iowa State had just forced a punt and got the ball back with less than a minute left. Kempt completed a 54-yard pass to Hakeem Butler, and Iowa State capped the half with a field goal to make the score 24-13.

The Cyclones still had a fighting chance.

The Cyclones began the second half with an 11-play drive that ended with another field goal to make it 24-16. Oklahoma took over and marched 70 yards in eight plays. *This is probably where it turns into a blowout*, I thought. Instead, on the ninth play of the drive, running back Trey Sermon fumbled on the six-yard line. And the fumble was recovered by … the quarterback-turned-linebacker Lanning. Iowa State had kept itself in the game.

Still, the Cyclones were backed up, and almost immediately faced a third-and-14 from their own two-yard line. I remember seeing the camera angle from the back of the endzone where Kempt was about to take the snap and thinking, *This is totally going to be a turnover or safety*. Instead, Kempt heaved it to Allen Lazard for a 35-yard gain. A few plays later, Kempt found Marchie Murdock for a 28-yard touchdown reception, and Lazard for a successful two-point conversion attempt.

With just a couple minutes left in the third quarter, the unthinkable was happening. Iowa State was tied with Oklahoma, 24-24.

The Sooners responded with a solid drive that ended with a missed field goal attempt.

No way.

Two plays later, receiver Trever Ryen turned a screen pass from Kempt into a 57-yard touchdown. *IOWA STATE IS WINNING IN THE FOURTH QUARTER!!*

I yelled, "YEEEEEES!" as I watched in my apartment by myself.

One of the most iconic moments of the game came on the next drive for Oklahoma. The Cyclones chased around Mayfield, still the OU quarterback and a Heisman Trophy front-runner, and Lanning caught him for a 10-yard sack. Lanning was earning his place as a Cyclone legend. Unfortunately, Oklahoma scored a few plays later to tie the game at 31-31.

On the next possession, Iowa State again drove down the field, this time aided by two runs by Lanning, who had come into the game during a short yardage situation to bulldoze ahead for yardage, helping him earn the nicknames "Joel-dozer" and "Lan-ram." On third-and-seven from the OU 25, Kempt threw to the senior Lazard in the endzone.

Lazard, a highly heralded recruit from the state of Iowa, had never experienced a winning season or anything close to it in a Cyclone uniform. He fought off two defenders for the catch and touchdown to give Iowa State the 38-31 lead with just 2:19 left.

Oklahoma picked up one more first down, but Iowa State forced two straight incompletions from Mayfield to take over possession of the ball and end the game for the Cyclones' first win over the Sooners since 1990.

I was shaking with nerves and excitement. I always imagined the day Iowa State would finally beat Oklahoma. I figured it would not be a 14-point comeback. I figured it would not be on the road. I figured it would not be with a quarterback making his first start. I figured it would not be a team that was .500 coming into the game.

Up until that day, I don't know if I really, truly believed Campbell's tenure in Ames was going to work out. I wanted to believe it. He seemed like a good coach. But I had also believed former head coach Paul Rhoads was going to be the person to lead Iowa State to previously unforeseen heights, and he was let go after three straight losing seasons. I was distrustful as a fan that Iowa State could be a perennial winning program. Nothing changed that more than winning in Norman in 2017.

Actually, nothing changed it more than what Campbell told his team after the game. In a postgame locker room video, he told them it was the start of something special, and asked them not to let this game be the high point of the season.

"This is the start of something special … the start of something really powerful and special. Only if you stay the course."

For as many big wins as Rhoads had in his tenure, his teams never seemed to be able to turn them into anything more than a one-time celebration. Campbell seemed to challenge his team to let the game be a springboard, "Only if you stay the course."

Iowa State did stay the course, winning its next three games and finishing the season 8-5 with a bowl win. It was the first of what is now five straight years that the Cyclones put themselves in contention for a Big 12 Championship Game appearance during the month of November. In the 2021 season, a few days after the Texas Tech loss, Campbell took heat from some fans and media members when he said winning the Big 12 wasn't his goal, but his goal was for the team to become the best version of itself. I'll get into that more later, but it reminded me that he has consistently used that type of rhetoric even after some of Iowa State's best moments. *Stay the course. Trust the process.*

In my mind, the 2018 game was going to be one of the most anticipated games in Cyclone football history. It was slated to be the third game of the season. I imagined a 2-0 Iowa State team coming off a win against Iowa hosting the Sooners at Jack Trice Stadium. Instead, Iowa State's first game got cancelled due to lightning (one of the most bizarre occurrences I had experienced at a football game), and Iowa State's first true game was a loss to Iowa. There wasn't the same electricity in the air as I hoped for, and No. 5 Oklahoma largely controlled the game. However, Iowa State hung around, tying the game at 10, pulling within 24-17 and later pulling within 31-24 and 34-27 before losing 37-27. It was the third straight game the Cyclones had looked like they belonged on the same field as the Sooners.

In 2019, Iowa State went into the game at Oklahoma still with a chance to make the Big 12 Championship Game. Oklahoma took control early, jumping out to a 28-7 lead. It felt like one of those 50-something to 14 games I had witnessed … except, I felt like Iowa State had played well enough to warrant it being a closer game than it was.

Oklahoma grabbed a 42-21 lead late in the third quarter. I was dejected. I hated the idea of a lopsided loss. It felt too much like the old days.

Iowa State scored on the first play of the fourth quarter to cut the deficit to 14. Things got interesting when the Cyclones forced a fumble in Oklahoma territory and drove all the way down to the three-yard line before turning the ball over on downs. With only half of the fourth quarter left, it felt like the game was over.

Until … Iowa State forced a punt and took only four plays to score and cut the lead to 42-35 with 3:35 left. They had a shot. Paige was already in bed in the other room, and I had to keep myself from yelling out loud when Lawrence White intercepted a Jalen Hurts pass in Oklahoma territory to give Iowa State the ball with excellent field position. Purdy found Charlie Kolar for a touchdown with 0:24 left. It was going to go to overtime … except, Campbell sent the offense out for a two-point conversion attempt. Iowa State was going for the win.

This would be an all-timer, I thought.

Purdy had Kolar open in the endzone, but instead threw to La'Michael Pettway. He was well-guarded and the ball was intercepted. I lost my mind watching the replay, as Pettway seemed to be interfered with, but no flag was thrown. The miracle comeback had fallen just short.

Still, Iowa State had continued to prove it could play with OU.

In 2020, I watched the game with Chris and my friend Joe. The world, as you may recall, was in a weird place at that time. We were in the midst of the pandemic, and even though the game was in Ames we watched from home. The presidential election was approaching, eliciting strong emotions in seemingly everyone. It felt so unimportant, and yet strangely healthy, to focus on a football game.

As had become the habit, Iowa State hung around long enough to make it a game. With just over a minute left in the third quarter, Purdy completed a pass to Xavier Hutchinson, who broke free for a 65-yard touchdown. I jumped around in Chris's living room.

"Time for 'Juicy Wiggle!'" I said.

Sure enough, I could hear it over the loudspeaker through the television as the 15,000-or-so fans able to be in Jack Trice Stadium danced.

Oklahoma put together a field goal drive to tie the game at 23, and then forced a fumble while sacking Purdy. The good field position set up the Sooners for a four-play touchdown drive to regain the lead, 30-23, with 8:17 left. It felt like the turnover was going to be the blow Iowa State couldn't recover from.

Instead, Kene Nwangwu broke free on the ensuing kickoff return, taking it 85 yards all the way to the Oklahoma 13. Iowa State scored a few plays later to tie the game at 30-30. I willed on the Cyclone defense through the television as Iowa State forced a three-and-out and took the ball back. Breece Hall ran up the middle for 36 yards, and immediately followed that up with a stutter-step-aided eight-yard touchdown run.

"That guy looks like a Heisman Trophy candidate!" I exclaimed.

Oklahoma had one more chance, and with just over a minute left Rattler heaved a pass toward the endzone on a play that started at the 34. Iowa State's Isheem Young *may* have gotten away with a small hold and put himself in position to make the interception to effectively end the game. No flag was thrown, and I didn't waste a second worrying about it. Iowa State 37, Oklahoma 30.

Incredibly, after decades of futility, Iowa State had won two of its last four games against Oklahoma. It was easily one of my top five days of an otherwise miserable year.

It was fitting that Iowa State had to go through Oklahoma to try to complete a Big 12 Championship run at the end of the season. It wasn't quite meant to be as the Cyclone comeback fell just short. It has become a compelling series between the two programs, one that I would love to see play out over the next 10 years or longer if only Oklahoma wasn't leaving for the SEC.

For the 2021 season, this was the only single game I would have predicted to be an Iowa State loss at the beginning of the season, and the only game Iowa State hasn't been favored in according to the oddsmakers. But I feel like Iowa State is fully capable of winning this game on the road. Oklahoma has had an up-and-down season (despite finding a way to win all of its games until going to Baylor and losing right before the Iowa State game). Iowa State is better than its 6-4 record.

I want this Iowa State team to get this signature moment. A win, while coming toward the end of a season that has not lived up to my hopes and dreams, would still be one I'd remember for years. It would probably belong on any top 10 wins list in Iowa State football history.

Iowa State started something special that day in 2017. This would be the punctuation mark on a remarkable run by this group of seniors, and just maybe the springboard to something special for the next group that will become great Cyclones hopefully starting in 2022.

CHAPTER TWENTY-FOUR

IOWA STATE VS. OKLAHOMA RECAP

CLOSE, BUT NO CIGAR

Nov. 23, 2021

"So, have you enjoyed the journey," my dad asked.

I had to pause. There were five minutes left in the second-to-last regular season game, and the last regular season road trip, so it was a fitting time to ask the question. Iowa State, however, had just given up a fourth quarter touchdown to go down 28-14 to Oklahoma. I wasn't enjoying the journey very much *at that moment*.

It had surprisingly been a somewhat controversial week after ISU coach Matt Campbell told reporters it wasn't his goal to win a Big 12 Championship. The Cyclones, the week prior, had given up almost all hope of that possibility in the loss at Texas Tech. As a fanbase, we seemed to collectively try to come to terms with the season that was, at the very least, not what we had hoped for. We wanted a Big 12 Championship.

If there was any question whether the Cyclones would be flat or not play their hardest at Oklahoma, that was quickly put to rest as Iowa State played inspired, if not always pretty, football. There was no doubt Iowa State really wanted to win.

And I really wanted them to win.

The reality I had been struggling with all week was that I wasn't going to be writing a book about a Big 12 Championship team. I chose to do what I'm doing this year in part because I thought this was going to be the best team in school history, the team to finally get over the hump and win a conference championship.

If I'm going to do it, this would be the year, I had thought.

So when it looked like the effort to pull off one last memorable upset at Oklahoma was about to fall short, I wasn't in the proper mood to reflect. My dad's question forced me to confront the reality that I was disappointed. It also forced me to again shift my perspective.

"Ahhhh. Yeah, I'm enjoying it. It's just … this has just been such a disappointing season," I said. I paused. "I'm glad I did it. Today has been a lot of fun. Ask me in a little while and I'll probably be feeling better."

It had been fun. My dad and my brother, Kent, a big Hawkeye fan, had made the trip to Norman with me. Kent had even agreed to miss an Iowa home game to be part of this experience. We had met up with my friend Jason, his wife and some friends. Our group had enjoyed our time together Friday night in Oklahoma City and at the tailgate with the Cyclone Club of Dallas/Fort Worth on Saturday morning. At the tailgate, we had made more friends and said hello to now-familiar faces that I had met along the way. It was a festive atmosphere.

But the game, like the season, wasn't quite living up to what I had wanted it to be, and the disappointment was seeping in.

Then, Iowa State did what this Iowa State team always seemed to do. Just when you counted them out, they pulled you right back in. The Cyclones scored a touchdown, forced a stop on defense and got the ball back with just a few minutes to set up a potential game-tying drive. It was so similar to how the Baylor, West Virginia and Texas Tech games had played out.

Just do it this time, I thought.

"This team doesn't win easy or lose easy," I told my dad.

Quarterback Brock Purdy found his favorite target, Charlie Kolar, over and over to push the ball down the field. The Cyclones converted one fourth down to keep the game alive but faced another fourth-and-10 from the 21-yard line with less than 30 seconds left. Purdy took the snap and, for a brief second, I thought it was going to be a big play. Tight end Chase Allen looked to be open.

The sequence that followed reminded me of the other painful moments we had experienced in the season. Like when Purdy's sure touchdown pass to Kolar was tipped and intercepted in the Baylor game before it could get to him. Or when Breece Hall's sure touchdown run at West Virginia was ruled a fumble. Or when somehow Texas Tech drilled a 62-yard field goal to win. Those all gave me such sick feelings. Feelings that the team was *so close* to having the season we as fans had dreamed about.

Purdy's pass to Allen was a touch too high and was intercepted. Another close, heartbreaking loss.

I was numb. The play had happened right in front of our seats. I saw Kolar sitting on the goal line, looking dejected. Like he didn't want to stand up. I saw Allen go and comfort him. Oklahoma took over possession, downed the ball, and the Sooners and their fans celebrated. I felt like I could feel the numbness, the sadness, emanating from the players as they walked off the field.

I had some tears well up in my eyes as well. The emotions of the season were hitting me. Again, I was forced to confront the reality that my dream season was sitting at 6-5. The chance for another signature win was gone.

I was disappointed, sure. More than that, I felt for the players. I felt for the parents of the players. Sports have this weird effect on fans. I didn't know any of the players personally. I had met just a few of the parents in passing along the way of going to all the road games. And yet I felt so connected to them. I felt so connected to fellow Iowa State fans who so badly wanted a successful season, and a win on Saturday at Oklahoma.

Sometimes we all put way too much meaning and emotion into a game. But then again, sometimes it is more than just a game.

Isn't that why I'm doing this in the first place?

—

In the age of social media, it can be impossible to predict what makes headlines and what gets everybody talking and tweeting.

I listened to Cyclone Fanatic's coverage of Campbell's Tuesday news conference on Tuesday evening. I wasn't at all surprised when a reporter started to ask a question about Campbell's goals for the season, including winning the Big 12 Championship, and Campbell interrupted the question.

"Not me," Campbell said. "That was never my goal. My goal has always been one thing, and that's to become the best version of ourselves we can be. You've never heard me say that word once, you've only heard me talk about becoming the best version of yourself you can be. My challenge for this year's team was to become the 'greatest together' team in the history of Iowa State football. And so far, all of our goals are still intact from a coach Campbell standpoint. Now, could our players have other goals and aspirations? Sure. Do I want them to have great goals and aspirations? Sure. But that's not coach Campbell's goal."

I had listened to nearly all of Campbell's Tuesday press conferences throughout the season, in addition to his interviews at the conference media day. I had heard Campbell speak a few times in more private settings. I had listened to a fair amount of his press conferences over his six-year tenure as head coach. The answer did not surprise me. In fact, any other answer would have surprised me. His delivery wasn't as eloquent as it could have been, but the substance of what he was saying was completely consistent with his past messages. Messages like "trust the process" and be "outcome aware," not outcome driven.

I thought it was interesting. I thought it was insightful to his thought process. I made a mental note that if I ever got a chance to talk with him, I wanted to dive into it further.

I did not expect people outside the Iowa State sphere to pick up on it and was surprised when I started seeing people on Twitter discussing it and debating about it. Somehow, Campbell's message got misconstrued to be interpreted as he didn't care about winning or somehow didn't *want* to win the conference title. I couldn't check Twitter on Wednesday without seeing the debate play out. It culminated in Fox and CBS sports commentator Brady Quinn saying on air, "I can't believe he actually said that out loud," and, "It's got to be bad for recruiting."

For what it's worth, current and former players came to Campbell's defense. If you've ever watched Campbell on the sidelines during a game, it's hard for me to believe he doesn't want to win. The point, as I read it, was that he wants his team to focus on doing the right things to be the best they can be. Do that, and more than likely the wins will come. More than likely the championships will come when the time is right. It would probably be fair to say at times the Cyclones had not been the best version of themselves, which led to the team being in position to lose close games to teams the odds said it should have beaten. I would even bet Campbell felt the same way. (Though I had never questioned their heart.)

I'm not a "hot take" type of person. I'll just say I was totally in Campbell's corner on this one. Anybody who had been paying close attention to Iowa

State football the past six years could tell that "the process" had worked and led Iowa State to heights previously unimaginable. Everyone, including national media members, loved Campbell's rhetoric when the team was the plucky underdog slowly working its way toward being a conference title contender, which is why every year he is speculated to take any number of other college or NFL coaching jobs.

I'll take my chances as a fan trusting the process.

His quotes and the ensuing controversy came at an interesting time for me in my journey. My strong hope, as a fan, was for Iowa State to win the Big 12 Championship. After the Texas Tech game, I had to come to grips not only as a fan but as an aspiring author that it was not going to happen. I had a couple people tweet at me in mocking fashion. I heard that a local sports talk radio show jokingly blamed me for Iowa State's disappointing season.

I had to have my own gut check: *Am I actually going to write a book about this season?*

The answer was always yes. It's not the book I thought it could be. Campbell's sentiments rung true in the sense that I knew I couldn't judge the success or failure of this book on the results of the season, in large part because I had no control over those results. I had to trust my own process, because I did this for the experience as much as the outcome.

Everything about the trip to Norman reiterated this.

Before the season, when I told my family I was going to go to every game and write a book about it, my dad and brother both wanted to go to a road game with me. My brother chose the game at Oklahoma because it could have been a big game and because OU's stadium is regarded as one of the better stadiums in the country. I was excited all season to experience this game with them, and despite my foul mood during the week, by Thursday I was giddy at the prospect of taking the road trip to Oklahoma.

We left Friday morning. We stopped at a rest area in southern Iowa, where we saw some Cyclone fans.

"Go State," one of them said to us.

We went through Kansas City right in time for lunch and stopped at Jack Stack Barbecue. I was used to having good luck at Jack Stack before Iowa State men's basketball Big 12 tournament games in KC, and it had also been good luck before Iowa State's game at Kansas State. I was pulling out all the stops to make it a good luck charm again. (To be fair, it was still the day *before* the game, so I can't really blame Jack Stack for the eventual loss.)

Throughout the drive, we talked about all things college football. Iowa State and Iowa, of course, but also the College Football Playoff system, other teams, national championship scenarios and the like. College football has always been a topic that we could talk about for hours.

We were staying in Oklahoma City, about a half hour from the stadium in Norman. We arrived a little after 5 p.m., and Jason and his crew arrived within five minutes of us. We checked in and grabbed spots at the hotel bar as those who didn't know each other introduced themselves. Jason made quick friends with Kent and my dad, telling stories of his interactions with Iowa State athletes and swapping stories with us about our trips to Lambeau Field (even though Jason cheers for the wrong team in the Packers vs. Vikings rivalry).

We went to dinner at a restaurant a few blocks away, Bricktown Brewery. Since it was a 45-minute wait, we grabbed spots at the bar. There were quite a few Cyclone fans in the restaurant, enough that Jason joked he should start a "Cyclone! Power!" chant. I briefly scrolled my phone and saw another Iowa State fan who I followed on Twitter was at the same place. A few minutes later, some people walked up to us at the bar.

"Aren't you the same people who we saw this morning at the rest stop?" one of them asked.

"Yes! That's awesome," I responded, dumbfounded.

I asked what their names were, only to learn that the same person I had seen post on Twitter just minutes ago was the person I was talking to. What a great, random connection.

After dinner, Kent, my dad, Jason, his friend and I had a nightcap at the bar. Jason and I swapped more stories about Iowa State football and past memories. I later joked to Kent that he got a crash course in being an Iowa State fan just by listening.

The next morning, we woke up early. The game was slated to begin at 11 a.m., so we wanted to be on the road to the tailgate by around 7. As I was still waking up, I checked my phone. Kent had left a message for me — "Gameday!" — despite being in the same room. Tradition is tradition.

The DFW tailgate was in the parking lot of the basketball arena. We parked and wheeled our coolers over to the tailgate. I found the club president who I had gotten to know over the course of the season and said hello. We set down our coolers and settled in.

A few minutes into the tailgate, a man I thought I might recognize walked right up to me.

"I know you, right?" he said.

"I think so … who are you?" I asked.

It turned out it was someone from my hometown, Pella, who had been a year behind me in high school. We had both played in the high school marching band. He was also an Iowa State graduate, and his job had taken him to live in Oklahoma. A couple of friends had come to visit and go to the game with him.

A little while later, another couple walked up to our group. I noticed they had a 12-pack of Old Aggie beer from New Belgium Brewing, which they quickly offered us. My wife, Paige, is originally from Fort Collins, the home of New Belgium. I immediately recognized the beer, which is named after Colorado State University's former mascot, the Aggies. I learned this couple lived in Fort Collins and had driven 12 hours to see Iowa State play in Oklahoma. I excitedly told them that my wife was from Fort Collins and we visit her parents there often.

Without this journey, these random encounters would not have happened.

I could have tailgated for six hours, but game time was approaching. There were shuttle buses near us, but the sun had come up and the weather was beginning to feel nicer. We decided to walk the mile-or-so to the stadium. As we walked, we began to blend in with the thousands of OU fans also making the walk. Everyone seemed in good spirits. It was a picture-perfect day for college football.

We weren't sure exactly how far we had to walk to get to the stadium, and just as it felt like we were never going to get there, we could see it in the distance. The stadium lights extended high into the sky. It looked like it was *just right there*, but it was still a 15-or-so-minute walk away.

Gaylord Family – Oklahoma Memorial Stadium opened in 1923. It is nicknamed the Palace on the Prairie, and I could see why. It looks like a massive building from the outside, and the brick façade gives it a historic feeling. When I was planning for the season, this was the stadium I was most looking forward to. When people talk about stadiums you need to visit as a college football fan, Memorial Stadium is usually on the list.

Once we were inside, it lived up to the hype. The stadium holds more than 80,000 people, but fits them in snuggly. For me, it felt comparable to Iowa's Kinnick Stadium, which I have been to many times, and Kansas State's Bill Snyder Family Stadium, which I had been to earlier in the 2021 season. It felt like the fans were right on top of the field and right up against the teams' sidelines. The difference is that the stadium itself was larger and seated more people. Both sidelines had an upper deck, giving it a massive, imposing feeling.

Our seats were on the sideline on the southeast side of the stadium, as close to the corner as you could be without actually being in the corner. We were 20 rows up, which felt much closer to the field than I had anticipated. I had purchased the tickets through the DFW Club, so fortunately Kent, my dad and I were in the midst of Iowa State fans.

Everyone was in a good mood. The Iowa State fans seemed like they were there to have a good time, and I reveled in the fact that I was in a historic stadium getting ready to watch my favorite team.

Today can be our day, I thought.

Iowa State got off to a great start. The Cyclones immediately converted a third-and-seven, aided by an Oklahoma penalty. They continued their march down the field until facing a third-and-18 from the OU 26. Purdy passed to Joe Scates along the sideline. The play was directly across the field from us coming toward the endzone we were staring at. I cheered as I thought Scates had come down with the catch before seeing the referee call the pass incomplete. Before Iowa State could line up to kick a field goal, the referees blew the whistle to go review the play.

On the stadium video boards, we could see what looked to be an ominous sign for Iowa State. It appeared Scates had come down with the catch and then fumbled the ball out of bounds through the endzone. We thought it was going to be a touchback and Oklahoma would take over possession, meaning Iowa State wouldn't even get to try a field goal. However, after further review, the call was a catch, and Iowa State would retain possession at the one-yard line. I couldn't believe the call went Iowa State's way. I wasn't apologizing to anyone as Hall punched it in for the touchdown and a 7-0 Iowa State lead.

"YEEAHHH!" I yelled with the other Iowa State fans around me. *What a start!*

It was short-lived. On Oklahoma's second offensive play, freshman quarterback Caleb Williams, who had become a household name within the sport after taking the starting spot midseason, went back to pass and then took off up the middle. Before I knew it he was in wide open space running toward the endzone. Nobody was going to catch him as he completed a 74-yard touchdown. It felt like the old days when teams like Oklahoma and Nebraska seemed to make those plays with ease against Iowa State. It was now 7-7.

Iowa State answered with a drive near midfield but was forced to punt. It worked out OK, as the Cyclones had taken more than five minutes off the clock before forcing Oklahoma to start the drive from its own 13-yard line. OU went three-and-out, and after a nice return by freshman Jaylin Noel the Cyclones started from their own 38. The teams traded punts again, and unfortunately this time the Cyclones were forced to start at their own 10. Iowa State picked up a first down, and then faced a fourth-and-one from its own 19-yard line.

In an unusual move for anyone, and especially Campbell, Iowa State lined up to go for the first down rather than punt. It appeared Campbell was going to pull out all the stops to win. The decision paid off as Hall powered forward for a two-yard run. Unfortunately, Iowa State was forced to punt a few plays later. Still, Iowa State had again taken five minutes off the clock and was controlling the game.

Oklahoma finally got things going but was forced to settle for a 25-yard field goal … which clanked off the goalpost.

"Ohhhhhh!" I yelled.

The Cyclone fans were again feeling good. Missed field goals by the opponent always feel extra positive.

With just more than five minutes left in the first half, we decided to use the restroom before facing long halftime lines. I wished I hadn't.

The line was already long outside the men's room. As we stood and waited, an Oklahoma fan struck up a conversation with us. He talked about how impressed he was with Iowa State's effort, and wondered how this team lost to Texas Tech. I told him I had wondered the same thing.

I turned to my dad. I was about to say, "You know, every time I go to the bathroom it seems like the other team scores." It had happened at Baylor and it had happened at Kansas State, and during the West Virginia game the Mountaineers had started a touchdown drive before I got back to my seat. Iowa State had the ball, so it was unlikely Oklahoma would score while we were in line. Still, I didn't want to jinx it. "You know," I said, and caught myself. "Never mind, I'm not going to say it."

We could hear the radio feed in the restroom, and I could hear Iowa State making positive plays to drive down the field.

Iowa State took the ball all the way to the 29 before disaster struck. Backup quarterback Hunter Dekkers came in for a trick play. He pitched it to Noel, and then ran a route to catch a return pass. The problem was, Dekkers initially had pitched the ball forward, meaning there were two forward passes in one play. It was a penalty and pushed Iowa State all the way back to a second-and-24 at the 43. It was a momentum killer.

As the play was ending, we were on the concourse and had found a television playing the video feed. We watched the replay as the radio announcers gave their interpretation. The color analyst was unforgiving, wondering aloud how the coaching staff didn't know the play was illegal. I wondered the same thing, though ultimately suspected it was an execution error rather than a play-call error.

No matter whose fault it was, it was costly. Two plays later on third-and-21, Purdy faced pressure. He got hit and sacked and lost the ball in the process. Oklahoma's Jalen Redmond picked up the ball and ran it all the way to the endzone. Oklahoma had taken the lead with just 0:09 left in the half. Iowa State was *that* close to going to the locker room tied. Instead, it was down 14-7 on a backbreaking play.

It's probably as mad as I had been all season.

It struck multiple nerves. It was a fluky play born of the type of errors a team trying to pull a big road upset just can't make. It was opposite of Campbell's "win in the margins" philosophy. It felt, again, like the old days of watching those types of plays happen regularly in these types of games. And, it confirmed the worst fears of my own stupid superstitious brain.

As my friend Chris texted, "Some years … just ain't your year."

Yep.

We walked back toward our seats as the half was ending. On the inner concourse, the Fox Big Noon Kickoff team was setting up its halftime stage right next to us. I tried to put my anger aside for a moment and appreciate that Iowa State was even good enough to play in a game that got this type of media coverage.

I seethed during halftime and tried to get myself into a better mental state before the second half began. I talked myself into believing Iowa State could come back from this. A fan a couple rows in front of us helped out.

"Let's go! That play was a fluke. We're going to win this!"

I was back on the bandwagon, even more so when Iowa State forced a three-and-out on Oklahoma's first drive and then downed a punt at the one-yard line. I saw the Iowa State fans in the endzone seats on the opposite end of the stadium stand. We were standing (as we had all game) and made noise to cheer on the ISU defense. On third down, Will McDonald forced a fumble in the endzone. Some days the ball doesn't bounce your way, and Oklahoma was able to recover the fumble and get out of the endzone. Still, Iowa State had forced another punt.

The Cyclones took the ball at their own 45, picked up a first down and faced a second-and-two at the Oklahoma 37. Iowa State failed to pick up a first down on the next two plays, and again elected to try a fourth down conversion. The Oklahoma defender timed the play perfectly, and Purdy's quarterback sneak went nowhere. Turnover on downs, and the momentum was back on OU's side.

It took the Sooners little time to capitalize on it. OU drove into Iowa State territory and faced a fourth-and-three of its own. Williams calmly rushed for four yards and a first down. Iowa State had no answer the remainder of the drive, and we watched in dejection as Purdy walked right by our section and headed to the locker room with an apparent injury. *Please don't let this be the last time he plays,* I thought. A few plays later, Caleb Williams found Mario Williams for a touchdown and 21-7 lead. Iowa State's hopes were teetering.

I thought the game was over when the backup quarterback, Dekkers, came in the next series, felt the pressure and heaved a ball up for grabs that was intercepted by Oklahoma's Delarrin Turner-Yell.

Iowa State's defense kept the game alive, turning around and forcing an interception by redshirt freshman Craig McDonald. We had reason to cheer for the first time in a while.

Dekkers came back out, and quickly faced a fourth-and-one, which he converted after recovering a fumble on the snap and finding his way forward for two yards. *Thank goodness.* The clock flipped to the fourth quarter, and Iowa State's offense was stalled. Another punt was seemingly on the way, killing the momentum gained by the interception. Punter Andrew Mevis took the snap, and I almost laughed out loud as he faked the punt and ran right up the middle with no OU defenders around him for 29 yards. I tried to remember the last time I had seen Campbell run a fake punt or field goal, and I couldn't.

A few plays later, Dekkers faced another fourth-and-six, and this time threw it up to Hall, who reached out and made a spectacular one-handed catch. The next play he found Allen, who bulldozed his way in for a 12-yard touchdown pass as we finally had reason to put our hands in the air and high-five for the first time since the first quarter.

Shortly after, Purdy ran back onto the field to loud cheers from the Iowa

State fans in our section. Iowa State's defense responded to the newfound momentum with a three-and-out, and the Cyclones were back in business. Unfortunately, with Purdy back under center, the Iowa State offensive possession went nowhere, and the Cyclones were forced to punt the ball back. Kennedy Brooks took the first play of the drive for 26 yards, and ISU committed a face-mask penalty to give Oklahoma another 15 yards all the way to the 27-yard line. The Sooner offense didn't look back, scoring on a seven-yard touchdown run by Eric Gray to push the lead back to 28-14. With just more than five minutes to go, I felt like I had seen this movie before. The game was over.

That's when my dad asked if I was enjoying the journey. I had so badly wanted this win, and it just wasn't going to happen.

I should have learned never to doubt this team. What happened next perfectly encapsulated why I chose *this team* to follow on this journey. It wasn't just because of what they accomplished. It's because of who they were.

Facing a third-and-six, Purdy got the offense rolling. He found Xavier Hutchinson for a 15-yard gain, and then Kolar for a 28-yard gain. (Kolar fumbled, and Tarique Milton luckily recovered the ball for Iowa State.) Two plays later, Purdy again found Kolar for 14 yards, and then targeted Hutchinson on a play that drew a pass interference flag. From the two-yard line, Purdy again threw to Kolar for the touchdown. It was now 28-21. With just under three minutes left, ISU had a chance and I started to believe the Cyclones could do it.

Iowa State kicked off and sent its defense on the field. I joined my fellow Iowa State fans in yelling for them. They responded by forcing a combined loss of six yards in the first two plays, and then forcing Williams out of bounds well short of the first down. Iowa State used its second timeout after the play. We chanted, "I-S-U! I-S-U!"

"Gosh, this team doesn't win easy or lose easy," I told my dad.

Iowa State got the ball back at the 14-yard line. If the Cyclones were going to do something epic, it would require a long drive. It mirrored the scenarios in the Baylor, West Virginia and Texas Tech games, but this time I just truly believed these guys were going to go down and score.

Purdy found Kolar for gains of 11 and 20 yards to get things rolling, before taking a crucial sack for a loss of nine. Iowa State was forced to call its final timeout. On second-and-19, Purdy's pass to Hall fell incomplete. Two plays to gain 19 yards. Purdy threw it to Kolar again for a gain of 13 to make it a manageable fourth-and-six, and Oklahoma called timeout to let my nerves intensify for a bit. With the crowd roaring and the game on the line, Purdy again found Kolar over the middle for a gain of 16 as I cheered. It felt like this could be the drive we remembered forever.

"I'm telling you, this team doesn't win easy or lose easy," I told my dad again.

Now in Oklahoma territory, Purdy again threw it to Kolar for a gain of 19 yards and another Cyclone first down. He ran up to the line and spiked the ball from the 21-yard line to stop the clock with 0:36 left.

"If they score, will they go for two?" My dad asked me. "Yeah, I'm almost sure they will." I wanted it so badly. I paused. "We need to score first."

Purdy threw back-to-back incomplete passes. It was fourth-and-10.

That's OK. This season deserves another crazy fourth down conversion.

I felt irrationally overconfident Iowa State was going to convert. Purdy took the snap. I saw where he was going with the ball. Allen was over the middle. He was open. It was going to be a first down.

The ball sailed just a little too high. Just a smidge too high. *Just* out of reach. Just *freaking* out of reach.

To add a little bit of insult to injury, an Oklahoma defender actually intercepted the pass. The OU fans let out a loud cheer as I said, "OH!" and put my hands on my head.

Just like in the Big 12 Championship Game against Oklahoma the year prior, Iowa State fell just short of the game-winning drive. Just like the Baylor, West Virginia and Texas Tech losses, a couple inches could have made the difference.

Williams came out and took a knee to run out the clock. I just stood and watched, unable to find the words as I watched the team jog off the field.

"Close, but no cigar," my dad said, which could ultimately have been the motto of the season.

I was distraught. Like the old cliché says, I wasn't mad, I was disappointed. Except, I wasn't disappointed in anything the team had done or not done. I was disappointed that their effort, their heart, their character, hadn't resulted in the big win like I so badly wanted it to, like so many Cyclone fans wanted it to. Like I'm sure they wanted it to.

I kept standing, making no move to exit the stadium. I looked around. Many other Cyclone fans in both our section and in the section behind the endzone had seemed to be doing the same thing. Everyone seemed numb. If, with five minutes left, the Cyclones had gone away quietly and lost by 14, we probably wouldn't have felt the same level of heartbreak. That's not who this team is, and I love them for it.

Maybe it's just a game, but it means more than that.

Behind me to my left, the Big Noon Kickoff crew was setting up for its postgame show in the stadium. OU fans had gathered around and were chanting "Boomer! Sooner!" and other chants. After a few minutes, we finally decided it was time to head out.

We ran into Jason on the way back to the car. The two of us dissected the game for a bit, including all the frustrating moments. At the end, we both came to the same conclusion. We loved the heart the team had shown.

We got back to the car and ate some snacks as Jason and his crew left. A little while later I saw a parent of one of the players walk by, looking dejected.

In his postgame comments, Kolar seemed to pour his heart out a bit in pointing out that even though Campbell and the team believe in following the process, the losses don't hurt any less.

But, "There's no frustration between each other, it's just we're competitors and we lost twice in a row on either the last play of the game or one of the last plays of the game. We never die easy, but we find some crazy ways to lose sometimes. As the season ends, just trying to find ways to lay the foundation for the young guys because this program has a bright future."

The quote made me love Kolar even more.

There's one more regular season game left. Thank God there's one more game left. One more game to cheer on this team.

Campbell talks about "the process." Earlier in the season, Athletics Director Jamie Pollard reminded fans to enjoy the journey and not worry about the destination. Iowa State fell to 6-5 and 4-4 in the Big 12 with the loss. In terms of results, it's a disappointment for a lot of people who have a lot more at stake than me. As a fan, and yes, as a fan writing a book, I wanted the journey to end with confetti. The moments along the way, both in enjoying watching my favorite team and immersing myself in the wider experience of being part of the Cyclone fanbase and everything it entails, in addition to creating lifelong memories with my family and friends, can't be diminished. I sincerely hope the moments and memories along the way, and the growth through "the process" won't be diminished for the players, or for the fans who want to fondly remember these players.

To answer my dad's question of "Have you enjoyed the journey?" I haven't enjoyed every minute of it, but I wouldn't trade a second of it.

CHAPTER TWENTY-FIVE

IOWA STATE VS. TCU PREVIEW

THANKS TO THE SENIORS

Nov. 24, 2021

Every year toward the end of the football season, I start to get a little melancholy and nostalgic.

The season goes so fast. Even as a fan, it can feel like such a grind. Typically, there are six or seven home games, which means six or seven Saturdays dedicated to little else besides tailgating and watching football. Even for the die-hard fans like me, it can get tiring. I still have to go to work Monday morning, not to mention do all the other responsible adult things like get groceries, cook dinner and pay bills.

And then the end of the season arrives, and it's just over until next September. I find myself wishing I had another month to watch college football, and particularly my favorite team. I find myself wishing I had more games to attend at Jack Trice Stadium.

That's never been truer than this year. The TCU game will be the 12th game I attend in 13 weeks. As I looked ahead to the schedule that included seven games in a row to end the season and back-to-back November road trips, it was daunting. I'm so glad I committed to it because I've had the time of my life.

And then there's the reality of what the final home game means: It's also the final time we get to see the team's seniors at Jack Trice Stadium. That piece of it is definitely more bittersweet this season.

We've watched guys like Brock Purdy, Mike Rose, Charlie Kolar, Chase Allen, Greg Eisworth and so many others grow up in front of our very eyes and lead Iowa State to some of the biggest wins and the best season in school history.

When men's basketball player Georges Niang graduated from Iowa State, and the following year when Monte Morris, Nazareth Mitrou-Long and Matt Thomas celebrated the end of their careers, I knew an era was over. It was an era that I'm sure people around my age will compare all other eras to, no matter how much success the program has in the future. Similarly, in the 2021 Major League Baseball season, the Chicago Cubs traded Anthony Rizzo, Kris Bryant and Javier Baez, the World Series heroes. That's the group Cubs fans like me will compare all future groups to.

The group of players we will celebrate before Iowa State's game against TCU on Saturday are Iowa State football's equivalent to the groups I've just mentioned. There will be more players we love. There will hopefully be more great teams. This group will always hold a special spot and has created a standard others must live up to.

All of that makes the TCU game even more of a must-win in my mind. This group deserves to have one more shining moment in front of home fans, and selfishly I want one more shining moment to cheer my head off for these guys.

In some ways, this game also feels like things have come full circle in my fandom. My first year of truly watching Cyclone football was 1997 — a miserable one-win season. The second year was 1998. Iowa State hosted TCU, which was at that time not yet in the Big 12, in the opening week of the season. I remember a decent amount of optimism that maybe this Cyclone team could begin to turn the corner toward relevance.

The Cyclones looked like they might get the season off to the right start. Quarterback Todd Bandhauer threw a 66-yard touchdown pass to Mike Brantley in the third quarter to give the Cyclones a 14-7 lead, and then completed a one-yard run toward the end of the quarter to make it 21-14 heading into the fourth. I was 12 years old, and full of opening day optimism. My young heart had one of its first heartbreaks from the Cyclones as TCU completed runs of 29 yards and 43 yards to take the lead, and capped it off with a 23-yard field goal to win 31-21. I remember how quickly the sentiment seemed to go from, "Maybe we can be good this year," to "Here we go again."

For what it's worth, we were a week off in our hopes for a better season. The next week, Iowa State broke a 15-game losing streak in the series against Iowa. It was a win that changed the trajectory of the program. Iowa State returned home the next week for a 38-0 win over Ball State, my first-ever game at Jack Trice Stadium. Iowa State ended up going 3-8 but had begun the ascent that would get the team to a 9-3 season in 2000.

These things are never black and white, but I can draw a pretty clear line in my mind. Iowa State was a fundamentally different program after that 1998 win against Iowa. The TCU game in 1998 was the last where I (and probably others) could feel no sense of hope for the future of the program. Following the TCU game, I had pretty much nothing positive to associate with Iowa State football (keeping in mind I just missed the Troy Davis years as a fan). Following the win over Iowa, I did.

The next time Iowa State ran into TCU, I was a freshman in the Cyclone Marching Band. The Cyclones were matched up with the Horned Frogs in the 2005 Houston Bowl. It was my first bowl trip. It was also, I believe, the first time I had stepped foot in an NFL stadium. What was then known as Reliant Stadium (now NRG Stadium) had me in awe. With three decks of seating, it felt like a palace. By that point of the season, I had gotten used to the fact that I got to march on the field at Jack Trice Stadium. This, however, felt different. I was pinching myself. *This is real. You are really doing this.*

The season had been somewhat disappointing with some close, gut-wrenching losses (sound familiar?). A bowl game win, in my mind, would have done a lot to make up for the disappointment. (I really hope I'm not foreshadowing as I write this.)

TCU jumped out to a 14-0 lead. In the stands, I decided to forget everything else, stop worrying and enjoy myself. I cheered on the defense, and cheered as Bret Meyer threw a 48-yard pass to Todd Blythe to cut it to 14-7 in the second quarter. Iowa State forced a safety to make the score 14-9, and took a 17-14 lead a few minutes later. The Iowa State portion of the crowd was loving every minute. Unfortunately, it didn't last. TCU regained the lead with an 84-yard touchdown pass. Iowa State tied the game at 24 late in the third quarter with another Meyer to Blythe connection, but TCU's field goal with less than six minutes left was the difference.

Oh well, I thought. *This is only the first bowl game I'll get to go to in the band.* I was wrong. Iowa State didn't make another bowl game until after I graduated.

In 2012, TCU joined the Big 12 and became a permanent fixture on Iowa

State's schedule. The Cyclones played their first conference game against the Horned Frogs in an October road game. TCU was ranked No. 15 in the country and was 4-0. Iowa State was 3-1 and coming off a loss to Texas Tech.

The way the game played out was one of the more random fun games I can remember. Iowa State took the lead on a 51-yard touchdown pass from Jared Barnett to Josh Lenz and eventually went up 10-0 and 16-7. TCU kept battling back, but couldn't quite take control. I cheered with dozens of others in a Des Moines bar as Lenz took the ball on a reverse and surprised everyone by throwing it to Ernst Brun for a touchdown to take a 30-20 lead. It was a classic trick play by coach Paul Rhoads. Iowa State sealed the win when David Irving intercepted a pass and ran 21 yards for a touchdown, followed by members of the Iowa State sideline mobbing him in celebration. Iowa State pulled off the 37-23 upset.

TCU had the upper hand the next four years, which was no surprise considering they were all losing seasons for the Cyclones. In 2017, a newly ranked No. 25 Iowa State team, experiencing its first season of success under Matt Campbell, hosted a 7-0 TCU team ranked No. 4 in the country. It was as electric of a crowd as I could remember in quite some time at Jack Trice Stadium. The Cyclones gave us plenty to cheer about as upstart quarterback Kyle Kempt, making his fourth start after taking over in the upset win at Oklahoma, completed a pair of first half touchdown passes to Matthew Eaton and Hakeem Butler to give the Cyclones a 14-0 halftime lead. The Iowa State defense was lights out, forcing five straight punts.

A fair amount of the crowd wasn't even back in their seats yet as TCU began the third quarter with a 94-yard punt return for a touchdown to cut the lead to 14-7.

"We've played so well," I said in exasperation. "How can you let that happen?"

A few possessions later, Kempt threw an interception at the Iowa State 43. TCU was in business and looked poised to tie the game. We came to our feet as the Horned Frogs faced a third-and-six from the seven-yard line. Quarterback Kenny Hill overthrew his intended receiver, and we roared as Brian Peavy picked off the ball and ran the other way. It looked like he was going to score, but he was tackled at the TCU 30 after a 70-yard gain. It was beginning to feel like our day the longer the team could just hold onto the lead.

A few possessions later, TCU was again in scoring range. On

second-and-goal from the three, we cheered as ISU defenders stacked up Hill for a loss, and almost couldn't believe our luck when he fumbled and Iowa State recovered. Sometimes I still go back to watch the replay and see the television cameras shaking.

Iowa State was unable to put the game away on offense, and TCU had one more chance taking over at its 46-yard line with less than two minutes to play. On second-and-10, Hill went back to pass, and Marcel Spears Jr. jumped the route to come up with the interception. Iowa State was going to win. We took selfies in the stands and cheered as we watched fans rush the field in celebration after the game. Not only was Iowa State football fun again, but these Cyclones were also really good.

After the game, in a locker room video that was shared publicly, Campbell told his team, "If you fall in love with the process, then eventually the process will love you back. But see here's what's crazy about that. You don't know when it's going to love you back. All you have to do is you've got to be prepared for your opportunity when it's ready to love you back."

I had bought into Campbell's coaching philosophies a few weeks prior when the Cyclones upset Oklahoma. When I heard the speech after the TCU game, I couldn't get enough of it. It turns out, I still can't.

The Cyclones lost a close game at TCU in 2018 before winning in 2019 and 2020. The TCU program is not the same one we thought we knew even at the beginning of this season, as it parted ways with its coach of the last 20 years, Gary Patterson. The Frogs responded with an upset win over Baylor before being dominated by Oklahoma State in a 63-17 loss. Last week, TCU hit a field goal in the final seconds to hold off an improving but still last place Kansas team. All this to say, despite Iowa State's recent struggles, it should win Friday.

Sometimes individual games take on meaning beyond the season, and sometimes the individual game itself takes a backseat to the larger meaning. The larger meaning for Friday's game is that we are celebrating the careers of a group of seniors we love. It will be an emotional day at Jack Trice Stadium. We want this win not because it really means anything in the standings, but because it means so much to all of us who have followed this program, and especially this group, to see the team get one more win at home.

In 1998, Iowa State football was irrelevant when it lost to TCU. In 2021, Iowa State is relevant largely because of the current seniors, and I really want a win over TCU.

CHAPTER TWENTY-SIX

IOWA STATE VS. TCU RECAP

THE PAST, THE PRESENT AND THE FUTURE

Nov. 30, 2021

"What do we want?!!" my friend Eric yelled into the Jack Trice Stadium night.

Nobody answered. I wasn't quite sure what we wanted. Iowa State was winning 41-14 in the fourth quarter against TCU. The outcome of the game was not in doubt. Everyone was in a good mood. The game had been pretty much everything we wanted it to be. The Cyclones were taking care of business. They were sending the most successful senior class in history out with a convincing win.

It was the kind of game in which a fan could afford to get greedy. We didn't just want the Cyclones to win. We wanted to enjoy the heck out of every senior playing their final home game.

So, what did we want, according to Eric?

"We want a Chase Allen touchdown!!"

I laughed. Others cheered. It made sense. Eric had been calling for this on the last Iowa State drive, which had instead ended in a Breece Hall touchdown. Allen was a popular senior tight end, sometimes overshadowed in ways by his star teammate Charlie Kolar, but still a key contributor and, by all accounts, a great teammate. The week before, quarterback Brock Purdy had just missed him for what would have been a key first down to keep the upset bid alive against Oklahoma. It just felt fitting that he would get a memorable senior moment.

Purdy threw it to Allen on the third play of the drive for a 15-yard gain. We cheered. Eric put his arms in the air.

"That's good enough for me," he said.

It wasn't good enough for Iowa State. As the Cyclones lined up for the next play, Chris pointed out to us that Allen was still in the game. We could see the play unfolding. Purdy went back to pass. We could see Allen running over the middle, open.

"He's open!" we all seemed to yell in unison.

Purdy delivered him the ball in stride and he streaked toward the south endzone, just a little way down from our seats in the southwest corner.

"YEAHHHHHHH!!!!!" we yelled. I was jumping up and down as Allen crossed the goal line for the touchdown.

Eric turned around and hugged Chris and me as I'm pretty sure all three of us were jumping around like little kids.

"I'm so happy!" Eric said, over and over, as though we couldn't tell.

"That's one of my favorite things that has ever happened at a game," I said, and I meant it.

It was the perfect way to seal a 48-14 win.

To begin the day, we had watched as 23 Cyclone seniors were honored and celebrated. Coach Matt Campbell had greeted them all as their names were announced, hugged them, in some cases appeared to give words of encouragement or wisdom or maybe just affection, and watched with tears in his eyes as they had their names announced to run onto the field to cheers.

All week, we had been reminded of the success of this senior class that had been unmatched in school history. Since 2017, when many of the seniors were just freshmen, Iowa State played in four straight bowl games and were in line for a fifth. They had led Iowa State to tie a school record in wins in 2020 and make its first ever Big 12 Championship Game, in addition to winning the most prestigious bowl game the program had ever won. 2021 was predicted to be the best season in school history because of these seniors. It didn't live up to the hype, but that didn't make me, or most fans, love them any less.

Reminiscing about the last five years also reminded us how far the program had come. Iowa State entered the day with a 6-5 record and a chance to finish the season with a winning conference record. Just a year before this group had started, and for most of my life, that would have been reason for celebration. This season, it was less than what we had hoped for.

But the past was the past, both in terms of what Iowa State was before 2017, and in terms of any disappointment we felt with the season. On this day, all we wanted to focus on was the present. These seniors deserved the best version of our fandom. They got it. The fans cheered loud all day and seemed to appreciate every last moment they had supporting this group at home. The team responded with an inspired effort. TCU never really stood a chance.

Almost immediately after the game, we were forced to confront the future. Not just the future of not seeing Purdy, Kolar, Allen and so many others play at Jack Trice Stadium in 2022 and beyond, but the future of whether we would see Campbell roaming the sidelines again as Iowa State's coach.

Campbell had, pretty much every year since 2017, been rumored for any number of jobs at other schools as well as professional teams. Most of the time, it had been easy to tune out the rumors. They never seemed to pan out into anything, and Campbell was typically quick to dismiss them. In the few days before the TCU game, rumors about Campbell being in the running for a job at the University of Southern California had picked up steam. And this time, for whatever reason, they seemed to have more credibility. Enough so that Campbell was forced to answer about it in his postgame news conference. Local reporters were writing about it and raising questions in a way that told me they believed this to be more credible than in the past.

It was likely we would know more in the next few days after the game, but at that moment it was maddening to have to wait and wonder.

Instead of dwelling on the past, or worrying about the future, I tried to remain in the present. I had just watched Iowa State dismantle a Big 12 opponent. I had gotten to cheer more times than I could count, high-fiving my dad and my good friends in the stands. Personally, I had completed a journey to attend every game in the regular season (while still looking forward to one more trip to whatever bowl game the team would go to). What would next season look like? That could wait. What regrets did I have about what results could have or should have happened in the season? I could reflect on that later.

After all, it was a great day to be a Cyclone.

—

Since we were staying with my family in Pella for Thanksgiving, I had talked my dad into coming with me to the last game of the season. I have a love/hate relationship with Black Friday games. On one hand, it takes away from time at home with family. On the other hand, it is typically the best college football weekend of the year (which proved true throughout the course of the weekend). Regardless, I had been to the first 11 games, and there was no way I was missing this one.

The game was scheduled for 3:30 p.m., so we decided to try to get to the parking lot a little after 1 to have a little bit to tailgate before heading in. Earlier in the week, Iowa State had announced it was unable to find enough people to staff the concession stands during the Thanksgiving weekend and would allow fans to bring their own food into the game. One of the many reasons I love following so many Cyclone fans on Twitter is because of the inside jokes that form when news like this is announced. Before I knew it, people were joking (or maybe not joking) about taking whole turkeys and pumpkin pies into the stadium.

As for my dad and I, we decided to pack ham sandwiches and pumpkin pie (just one slice in this case rather than a whole pie). We parked a little way away from the rest of our group that was already tailgating.

"Want to have a piece of pumpkin pie before we go over there?" my dad asked.

"Let's do it!"

After enjoying the pie and a few sips of our drinks, we wheeled our cooler a little way away to meet up with the rest of the group.

During the first tailgate of the season, I had offered my friend Tyler a Spotted Cow from New Glarus Brewing Company. He was so grateful that he vowed to pay me back. Which he did, two weeks later in Las Vegas, buying me a Coors Light in Allegiant Stadium for something like $12. I considered that even, but he insisted there was no way he could pay me back for a Spotted Cow with a Coors Light. It took him until the final game of the season, but ...

"Kyle, I brought you beer!"

It was a six-pack from a local Iowa brewery. I accepted it gratefully and offered him ... another Spotted Cow.

I caught up with my friends Chris, Charles, Dave, Derek and many others. I was wearing a number of layers and boots, but the sun was shining and it was surprisingly nice for a late November day. We were hoping TCU, a team from Texas, would think this weather to be freezing cold.

Around 2 p.m., I began to anxiously check my phone. The Senior Day ceremony was scheduled to begin at 3:05. I figured it would take a little while to get into the stadium, so my dad and I decided we were going to head to the gates at 2:30. As 2:30 arrived, I noticed the group was getting ready to play one more game, but I knew I had to go.

"Ready to head in?" I asked my dad.

I was glad we did. The line to get into the stadium was about as long as I could remember it being all season. I heard someone else mention they hoped we could get in by the team the senior celebration began. I had the sense that many people were of the same mindset.

Come on line, keep moving.

Finally, we were in with just a couple minutes to spare. We walked up the hill to the concourse toward our seats for one last time of the season. We walked through the tunnel to our seats just in time to see the parents and families of the seniors walk onto the field. Then the players lined up on the northwest end of the field. One by one, they had their names announced, hugged Campbell and jogged onto the field. I watched on the video board and couldn't help but tear up as I watched Campbell tear up. As guys like Rose, Greg Eisworth, Rory Walling, Allen, Kolar and finally Purdy were announced, I couldn't comprehend how this was it for them. And I couldn't kick that little bit of doubt. *What if this is it for Campbell?*

Our friends began to file in as the Cyclone Marching Band made its way to the field for one last pregame performance. A little while later, when the team ran onto the field at Jack Trice Stadium for the last time in 2021, I took a moment to soak it in. Each game, home and away, the team would gather in a circle and take a knee for a moment of silence. For years, I had appreciated this moment, but it took on an even different meaning when I discovered they did it at road games as well. It's hard to describe, but the fact that I was there in the stadium with them when I noticed it at Baylor made me feel more connected to the team. I had kicked myself for not getting a picture at each game. (I missed one of the first two home games and the UNLV road game, but had begun to take a picture every game starting in Big 12 play.) This time, I was ready for the photo. Despite announcing earlier in the week that the players would wear red jerseys, the team ran out in all black uniforms. This group of seniors had made the black uniforms synonymous with winning. It was only fitting they'd get to wear them for their final home game.

And just like that, they were ready for kickoff. I looked around at the crowd. The stadium wasn't full; it was the first time in the season I noticed empty seats. The majority were in the student section's upper deck as most students were still out of town on their Thanksgiving break. There were a few others scattered here and there. Yet it was drastically fuller than many of the November games I had been to, and another sign of how far the program, and fan excitement, had come. And the enthusiasm was just as high. In those moments, we didn't care that our Big 12 Championship hopes were gone, or that we had lost four heartbreaking conference games. We just wanted one more win for the seniors.

Iowa State took the ball first, and freshman Jaylin Noel immediately delivered the momentum to the Cyclones with a 39-yard return. Purdy threw to Xavier Hutchinson and Kolar for a combined 33 yards on the first two plays, before eventually settling for a field goal by Andrew Mevis to take a 3-0 lead. The teams traded punts before Hall broke off a 24-yard run to get Iowa State back in business to begin the second quarter. Iowa State faced a first-and-10 from the TCU 40. We noticed redshirt sophomore running back Jirehl Brock, not Hall, was in the game.

"The future is out there!" Chris said.

Seconds later, Brock was running up the middle of the field untouched for a 40-yard touchdown to make it 10-0!

"THE FUTURE!!!!!" Chris yelled in jubilation as we high-fived.

The present wasn't quite ready to be the past yet, though. Iowa State got the ball back after a 12-play TCU drive that ended with quarterback Max Duggan getting stuffed on fourth-and-one. A few plays later, it was Hall, from nearly the same spot on the field, bursting through for a 39-yard touchdown run. It was an emotional moment. Hall had just scored a touchdown in his 24th-straight game, which was a new NCAA record.

We had just witnessed history.

Hall went to the sidelines and gave his head coach a big hug, and then went behind the bench to find his mom. We all watched on the video board and cheered as he presented her with the game ball and gave her a hug. Only a junior, Hall was not honored with the seniors before the game. Most people, though, had little doubt he was playing his final game at Jack Trice Stadium before turning pro.

What a moment.

During the game, Hall would move into second place on Iowa State's all-time career rushing list, trailing only Troy Davis. I never saw Davis play beyond the highlights. I know a lot of people who went to games during that time period swear that he was the best football player they ever saw wear an Iowa State uniform, and I believe them. I can safely say at this point that Hall is the best I have ever seen.

The game was nearly an all-out celebration. As we stood and cheered for the defense on TCU's next possession, Duggan completed a third-and-seven pass to Blair Conwright for a 47-yard touchdown to make the score 17-7 right before halftime. Still, I had little doubt Iowa State was going to win.

As the players ran off the field for halftime, my dad and I got our ham sandwiches out of our pockets. I ate while the marching band played its halftime show. Each year at the last home game, seniors in the band get their names announced and line up in a mini-ISU formation. They step out of their shoes and march off the field in their socks one final time while playing the fight song, leaving their shoes on the field. And I can say from experience: It's cold! The 2021 seniors had a relatively warm November late afternoon to leave their shoes on the field. A few of us in the stands reminisced about our final game as seniors. Mine was the 2008 game against Missouri, and it was much colder.

Iowa State wasted little time continuing the party in the second half. Will McDonald sacked Duggan on a third-and-nine on TCU's first possession, and Darien Porter followed that up with a blocked punt. Purdy threw to Hall for a 22-yard touchdown to all but wrap the game up at 24-7.

"Get out your cellphone lights!" I yelled. Indeed, thousands of fans already had. We knew what was coming: "Juicy Wiggle."

I waved my cellphone left and right, up and down and every which way. I looked around at the tens of thousands of fans doing the same and tried to capture the mental snapshot. It would be nine months before I'd again get to experience this type of moment at Jack Trice Stadium. I was sure that by April I would be daydreaming about it.

The crowd was still pumped up as TCU began to move the ball but faced a fourth-and-one at the Iowa State 44. We came to our feet and yelled for the defense. The intensity was high enough that if I didn't know the score, I would have thought the game was tied. Duggan's fourth down pass was incomplete. Iowa State ran a methodical 10-play drive capped off by a field goal to make the score 27-7.

TCU tried to temporarily put doubt in the minds of the 50,000-plus happy fans when Duggan found Taye Barber for a 51-yard gain near the end of the third quarter. The drive was extinguished when Duggan's fourth-and-two pass was intercepted in the endzone by Eisworth, who got his senior moment. The next play, Hall took a handoff up the middle, reversed his direction and was off to the races. He had one man to beat, and Hutchinson did all he needed to in order to block that defender out of the way as Hall neared the goal line, right in front of our section. Hall calmly completed the run for an 80-yard touchdown. We cheered and high-fived and hugged. Iowa State was up 34-7. The game was definitely no longer in doubt, and we were now officially witnessing a special performance by a special player.

During the ensuing timeout, Iowa State players danced and swayed on the sideline to a song on the loudspeakers. The party was on. I almost didn't even care when Derius Davis returned the kickoff 78 yards and TCU scored four plays later to make it 34-14.

Iowa State immediately began to move the ball again. At some point during the drive is when Eric began to yell for the team to throw a touchdown pass to Allen. Instead, Purdy threw to Hutchinson for 32 yards, Hall ran for 35, then ran for a pair of four-yard gains to score another touchdown. *What a day.* Iowa State was up 41-14.

The Cyclones got the ball back a few minutes later, with time for Eric to yell, "What do we want?!" The answer, of course, being a touchdown for Allen. I'm *sure* Campbell and the team heard him as they drew up the play to get the senior his touchdown and give Iowa State a 48-14 lead.

Campbell's publicly stated goal for the team was for the players to become the best version of themselves. I'd like to think on Saturday, we saw the best version of the Cyclones.

I didn't want the game to end, but it did. The week prior, I had stood in the stadium long after the players left the field because I was so dejected for the team and fans (myself included) who so badly wanted to beat Oklahoma. After the TCU game, I didn't want to leave because, well, I just didn't want it to be over. The loudspeakers played "Sweet Caroline." The team lined up in front of the band and sang the fight song, and then eventually headed to the locker room. Everyone around us filed out, except for my dad, Chris and me.

"Isn't it crazy we have to wait until September to get this again," Chris said, basically reading my mind.

"Yeah," I answered. "I've struggled with how to describe this, but you look forward to the season for at least six months, and then it's over in three. It's just crazy."

I pointed out that if it was a baseball season, we'd only be halfway through the calendar season (baseball runs for six months). College football season comes and goes in the blink of an eye.

I surveyed the field. The sun had set on both the day and the regular season. After waiting for 21 months between the last game in 2019 and the first game in 2021, it was just over.

The last sporting event I went to before the pandemic shut down the world was a February 2020 men's basketball game between Iowa State and TCU at Hilton Coliseum. As I walked out that night, I remembered thinking, *When I walk out of Hilton for the last time, I wonder if I will know in the moment that it's the last time.* I'm sure on some level the uncertainty already caused by the virus had caused me to have that thought. As I began to walk out of Jack Trice Stadium following the TCU game in 2021, I couldn't help but have a similar thought. *Don't take this for granted.* I took a picture, walked toward the exit and turned around one more time to look at the field before exiting.

Luckily, we still had a bowl game to look forward to. We talked about bowl possibilities on the way out. Orlando, Memphis and Houston were all potential destinations. We would find out in a little over a week. I was grateful for one more chance to be able to watch the team, but also aware that the team could look differently even by that game. Some seniors, and also NFL-hopeful juniors like Hall, would likely opt out of playing to ensure they were healthy before the NFL draft. There likely wouldn't be another game with this group quite like the one we just witnessed.

The regular season didn't live up to the lofty standards I had, but still capped a record-setting era. At 7-5, the Cyclones had secured their fifth-straight winning season, a school record. More impressively, Iowa State secured its fifth-straight winning season in Big 12 play at 5-4, a school record by a long shot. According to the school's notes after the game, from 1996 — the first year of the Big 12 — through 2016, Iowa State had recorded a winning record in the conference just one time. From 2017 through 2021, Iowa State recorded five straight winning seasons. *Somebody pinch me.*

The pinch came quickly. The good vibes were short-lived. Immediately after the game, Campbell was asked about the USC rumors and said he hadn't talked with anyone associated with USC. He didn't say definitively that he wouldn't take the job.

I spent the next two days trying not to spend all my time reading the latest rumors, and I breathed a huge sigh of relief when USC hired Oklahoma coach Lincoln Riley instead of Campbell. There was plenty of speculation on what Campbell would or wouldn't have done. I don't know the truth behind any of it and most of us likely never will. All I knew was that, as of Sunday evening, I could rest easy.

Until Monday, when Notre Dame coach Brian Kelly took a job at LSU. It had long been rumored that Campbell would strongly consider the Notre Dame head coaching job if presented the opportunity. As of the time I wrote this chapter, I didn't know what the outcome would be (though signs were beginning to point to Notre Dame promoting a coach from within the program).

Not knowing what the future could hold made me apprehensive, but I knew a few things to be true. I wanted Campbell to remain the coach at Iowa State for a long, long time. I also had no control over it, and it wasn't my right to say what would be best for him or his family. We all have one life to live, and we better do all we can to live it with no regrets. Campbell had earned the right to chase whatever dreams he wanted to chase. I hoped those dreams would ultimately end up being at Iowa State, but knew they might not be.

I also knew this. Campbell had been a Cyclone for six football seasons. I had been a Cyclone for 25 football (and basketball) seasons. However many seasons I had left, I'd still be a Cyclone.

If I had learned (or re-learned) anything during my 12-game, 13-week journey, it was that the bond of being a Cyclone fan, or really a fan of any sports team, was deeper than one person. People like me look forward to games all year, develop networks of friends around the common interest, and in some cases travel the country to live out the passion. We care, a lot, whether the team wins or loses, but we show up the next time either way, toast each other in the parking lot and high-five after a big play.

That passion will live on. Whether Campbell leaves in a day, a year or 20 years, the most recent five-year stretch of unforgettable memories will live on. The joy we had in watching this group of players come together will live on. And we will always feel anticipation and excitement for the next group to wear the Cyclone uniform.

CHAPTER TWENTY-SEVEN

IOWA STATE VS. CLEMSON PREVIEW

IT MATTERS BECAUSE WE SAY IT MATTERS

Dec. 27, 2021

I almost didn't do it.

I almost decided not to go to the bowl game.

Bowl games bring unusual emotions in today's day and age. They can mean nothing or they can mean everything. They can matter or they can *not* matter. It all depends on your perspective.

The first time during my lifetime that Iowa State made a bowl game felt like a special occasion. I had only been a true fan for a few years when the Cyclones broke their bowl drought during the 2000 season. For Cyclone fans, I sensed that it was the light at the end of a long tunnel. For as much as winning a Big 12 Championship currently feels like it would be *the* defining achievement for this program, back then getting to a bowl game was seen as that type of achievement.

The Cyclones hadn't been to a bowl game since 1978 and had never won a bowl.

The 2000 season in many ways felt like a culmination of coach Dan McCarney's slow rebuild of the program from a laughingstock to a competitive team. I remember the feeling before the season: *Maybe this is the year we finally get back to a bowl game!* Iowa State was led by the likes of Sage Rosenfels, J.J. Moses, Reggie Hayward, Ennis Haywood and more, names that Cyclone fans have long remembered. They lived up to the hype. Iowa State began the season 4-0 before losing a hard-fought game against Nebraska, at the time the No. 2 team in the country and still considered a national powerhouse. Iowa State was 5-2 when Missouri came to Ames on a Saturday night. I watched from the stands; people hugged and high-fived as Iowa State put together a dominating 39-20 win to get its sixth win and become bowl eligible. The Cyclones finished an 8-3 regular season with wins at Colorado and at home against Kansas to earn an invite to the Insight.com bowl against a 7-4 Pittsburgh team.

From every account I have ever heard, somewhere around 25,000 to 35,000 Cyclone fans made the trip to Phoenix and drank the city dry. I watched on television and could tell the crowd was heavily in favor of Iowa State. The Cyclones jumped out to a 27-7 lead at halftime before Pitt cut the lead to 27-20. In what is still one of my favorite plays of my fandom, Jamaine Billups returned a punt 72 yards to put Iowa State up 34-20, and the Cyclones held on for a 37-29 win. There may be an alternate universe in which Pittsburgh completes a 20-point comeback to shock the Cyclones; in a sign of how I expect heartbreak as an Iowa State fan, sometimes I think about how sadly poetic it would have been to lose that bowl game. But Iowa State won, and we got to celebrate. I'm sure the party went on long into the night in Phoenix.

Most people would probably not consider an Insight.com Bowl win against a 7-4 team to be a major accomplishment, but for Iowa State fans that year, it meant everything. It mattered to us.

There are a couple ways you can look at a bowl game. One way is that it's an exhibition that happens a month after the season. It doesn't really mean anything. It's just one more game.

The opposite way to look at it is that it's a big game, the pinnacle of a hard-fought season, a reward for players and fans. It's the equivalent of making the playoffs in the NFL or the postseason tournament in college basketball.

The reality is likely somewhere in-between, and unique to each school and each season and each fanbase. In my opinion, bowl games as a whole likely meant more to college football in 2000 than they do in 2021. And the further back you go, the more they probably meant. There was no College Football Playoff, and there were at one time significantly fewer bowls, making each one feel more important. Now, the College Football Playoff has made the bowl games feel much more like exhibitions.

Adding to that, it has become more and more of a trend for players who are preparing for the NFL draft to sit out the game, a perfectly justifiable move given the potential for injury and millions of dollars on the line. It has become much more common for players to decide to transfer to different schools between the final regular season game and the bowl, meaning they will not play for the team in the bowl game. Bowl games happen in many cases after the postseason coaching carousel has been in full swing, meaning some teams are playing with new head coaches or coordinators, or both. Simply put, the makeup of many teams is fundamentally different between the final game of the regular schedule and a bowl game.

The ultimate meaningfulness of the game comes down to a combination of factors, including the destination, the matchup, the makeup of the team and even the general mood of the fanbase regarding the season.

For me and many fans, the period between the TCU game and the Cheez-It Bowl against Clemson was a rollercoaster.

When I wrote about the TCU game recap, there were rumors upon rumors coach Matt Campbell was on his way to a new team. First there were heavy rumors around the USC job. Then it was the Notre Dame job. Both were filled by people not named Matt Campbell. There were several other openings with rumors linking Campbell to those openings, but none of them came to fruition.

Meanwhile, photos were emerging from Campbell on the recruiting trail, helping ease fans' fear. It seemed to be business as usual for Campbell and the program. I mentally moved on to focus on the Cyclones' bowl matchup announcement.

Part of the fun of bowl games is that your team gets to play a matchup that fans don't get to see very often, and there is a certain anticipation in finding out where the team will play and who it will play against. Conventional wisdom said Iowa State had three likely outcomes: the Cheez-It Bowl in Orlando against an Atlantic Coast Conference team, the Autozone Liberty Bowl in Memphis against a Southeastern Conference (SEC) team, or the Texas Bowl in Houston vs. an SEC team. As with most aspects of the season, the options weren't exactly what we were hoping for before the first game kicked off. The Houston Bowl, which I had attended as a member of the Cyclone Marching Band in 2005, was scheduled to take place after the new year and after most people would return to work after the holiday season, making it the least desirable option to me. The Liberty Bowl, which I had attended in 2012 and 2017, was scheduled between the week of Christmas and New Year's, and Iowa State fans had a track record of traveling well to Memphis. This was a little higher on my list. The Cheez-It Bowl scheduled for Dec. 29 had hosted Iowa State in 2019 in a historic matchup against Notre Dame, a game that I and most other Cyclone fans would like to forget. There was buzz that Iowa State could match up with Clemson in that game, which excited me more than any other option.

By Dec. 5, the day bowl games were announced, I was eager to finally find out. It wasn't quite the anticipation of opening presents on Christmas morning, but I was curious all day and checking in on Twitter to read the latest speculation. Early in the afternoon, it became official: Iowa State would play Clemson on Dec. 29 in the Cheez-It Bowl in Orlando. It was the best-case scenario I could have imagined after a 7-5 season.

Clemson finished the regular season with a 9-3 record, but more importantly brought a pedigree that few other programs could have provided in a bowl game matchup. The Tigers had made it to the College Football Playoff each of the previous five seasons and had won two national championships in that time. 2021 was a down season record-wise, but Clemson still brought a brand name. My immediate reaction was the game would provide one more opportunity to get a big, memorable win for the current group of seniors and give the program momentum heading toward the 2022 season. I could sense a higher level of excitement among Cyclone fans than some other potential matchups could have produced.

The rest of the break between games was eventful enough that for a few weeks it was easy to forget the game was even happening. Several players, including some surprising names, announced they would transfer to other schools, which is a reality of modern-day college football. Some fans speculated there was turmoil in the program, or uncertainty caused by rumors of Campbell taking a new job. Others, including me, felt it was likely a factor of the current climate of college athletics: Transferring isn't personal; there could be any number of reasons a player wants to try a different place, and most of them aren't a negative reflection on the school the player is leaving.

A few days later, several players who could have chosen to move on from Iowa State announced they would return for 2022, including starting cornerback Anthony Johnson, sack king Will McDonald and star wide receiver Xavier Hutchinson. Right around this time, the Cyclones signed the best recruiting class in school history, placing it near the top of the conference in overall recruiting rankings. I felt confident the future was still plenty bright.

Finally, running back Breece Hall announced he was going to forego his senior season to play in the National Football League. Running backs are known for having a short shelf life, so to speak, in professional football due to the physical nature of the position. As a likely early pick in the NFL Draft, Hall's decision made total sense from my perspective. Make money while the opportunity is there. Unfortunately, but understandably, it meant Hall would not play in the Cheez-It Bowl, meaning we had seen him play for Iowa State for the final time.

Clemson had its own disruptions. Defensive Coordinator Brent Venables took the head coaching job at Oklahoma. Offensive Coordinator Tony Elliott left to take the head coaching job at Virginia. The game won't look or feel the same as it would have if the teams had played in the College Football Playoff, which seemed like a possibility at the beginning of the season.

For me personally, I was facing my own internal struggle. When the game was announced, I immediately started reaching out to friends. I couldn't find anyone else who wanted to go. Most people had holiday plans and didn't want to spend the money, and it was not quite a prestigious enough game to move the needle.

As I started pricing it out for myself, I was taken aback by the cost of plane tickets and hotels, and somewhat apprehensive about my lack of knowledge about the city. As I began to add up all the factors, I decided I was probably just going to miss this game.

The decision ate at me for weeks. I had gone to all 12 games during the season, and decided to begin this journey precisely for the reason that it would force me to go a bowl game in hopes that Iowa State would go back to a New Year's Six game or better. *Am I really doing this right if I don't go to the bowl game?* I tried to justify it to myself. *It's expensive, I don't have anyone to travel or stay with and I know nothing about the city. Besides, does the game really* mean *anything?* We had made plans to travel to Colorado for the holidays, and I thought maybe my wife and I could just go to an alumni game watch.

Yeah, this will be fine.

It wasn't fine.

I couldn't shake the feeling that I should make the trip. I continued to look at flights, and I continued to look at hotels, finally finding some semi-affordable options. On Dec. 19, just 11 days before the game, I brought it up again with my wife, Paige.

"Honey, I think you should go," she said.

I booked my airplane tickets and hotel that evening. Sometimes fandom makes you choose the more unreasonable option.

The reality is this game isn't as special of an occasion as the 2000 Insight.com Bowl. It isn't as special as the January 2021 Fiesta Bowl would have been if fans had been able to attend the game. But it still matters.

It matters for tangible reasons. The game counts toward the season record. They give a trophy to the winner. Two years ago, Iowa State had a chance to measure itself against a historic powerhouse in Notre Dame and fell significantly short. Clemson's program is one that defines excellence in college football. This game is another measuring stick for the program, which reportedly made quite a few changes in response to the end of the 2019 season.

It matters for a whole lot more reasons than that. Thousands, maybe tens of thousands, of Cyclone fans will make the trip to watch in person, and many thousands more will watch on television. We'll all share a common experience. We'll all remember it and talk about it for years to come. Some people may say it doesn't matter to them, but I guarantee they will be happy if the Cyclones win and upset if the Cyclones lose.

At a certain point, why do fans care about any of it? Why does any of it matter?

It matters because we say it matters. It matters because the players and coaches say it matters.

The 2000 Insight.com Bowl mattered. The four bowl wins and seven losses since that 2000 game have mattered. And this one matters.

CHAPTER TWENTY-EIGHT

IOWA STATE VS. CLEMSON RECAP

ONLY EIGHT MONTHS UNTIL FOOTBALL SEASON

Dec. 31, 2021

It was the end of the third quarter at Camping World Stadium in Orlando when we heard the first notes.

At halftime, the stadium announcer had encouraged fans to text their team's nickname to a five-digit phone number. Whichever team had more texts would get to hear their team's song between the third and fourth quarter. For Iowa State, it would be Redfoo's "Juicy Wiggle." For Clemson, it would be Survivor's "Eye of the Tiger." The winner was a mystery, until those first few notes came over the loudspeakers.

It was unmistakably the "Juicy Wiggle." The 15,000 to 20,000 Iowa State fans in attendance started dancing and clapping, many of them waving their cell phone lights. Despite the fact the Cyclones were losing 20-6, we still danced — more than 1,300 miles away from Ames.

A few minutes later, Iowa State scored to make it a 20-13 game. Brock Purdy found Charlie Kolar over the middle for a touchdown in the endzone right in front of me. I let out my biggest cheer of the night as I saw Kolar's fellow tight end Chase Allen run toward him and give the kind of fist pump that could knock someone out cold. After the extra point, the loudspeakers blared Timmy Trumpet's "Freaks." It had become a common song to be played at Jack Trice Stadium throughout the season, and fans tended to respond well to it. In Orlando, fans danced and clapped in excitement. The momentum had finally turned in Iowa State's favor, and we were going to enjoy every second of it. It's a series of moments that will be etched in my mind for years.

A little while later, Iowa State had one more chance to complete the comeback. Quarterback Brock Purdy scrambled for a first down only to have the ball knocked out of his hands for a fumble. The comeback hopes ended when Purdy dove backwards to recover the ball behind the first down marker. It was another tough loss, and it capped a season in which the Cyclones played five games with a chance to tie or take the lead on their final offensive possession. Only once — against Texas Tech — were the Cyclones able to tie the game, and that resulted in a three-point loss following a 62-yard field goal on the final play of the game. Iowa State finished the season 7-6, a disappointment for the fans who so passionately follow the team.

The Cheez-It Bowl was a microcosm of the entire season. High hopes. Exciting moments. Unexpected setbacks. A few plays that make you scratch your head. A never-give-up attitude. A few plays away from achieving special results.

They always kept it interesting. They always made me care. I'm not sure I could ask for much more.

When I think back on the Cheez-It Bowl loss, my first thoughts won't be about the loss. I'll think about watching Iowa State fans dance on a warm Florida evening. Those moments encapsulate the fun of fandom. Thousands of us made the trip. We soaked up the sun. We made new friends. We shared drinks and stories. We analyzed the team and the season and the future.

On its face, there's nothing that makes sense about being a fan to the level that so many of us are fans. There's nothing that makes sense about traveling across the country to watch what essentially amounts to an exhibition game, following a mediocre season.

After living it — heck, after figuratively living and dying with every play of the season — it makes all the sense in the world.

—

In the days leading up to the Cheez-It Bowl, I began to get worried about the possibility of the game being canceled. One after another, teams across the country backed out of their games because of positive COVID-19 tests and possible exposures. A new, more transmissible variant had emerged and case numbers were on the rise. Thousands of commercial flights were canceled around the Christmas holiday.

I mentally prepared myself for the possibility of my flight or the game being canceled. Such was life during a pandemic.

The game was on Wednesday, Dec. 29. On the morning of Dec. 28, my wife Paige drove me from her parents' house in Fort Collins, Colorado to the Denver International Airport to fly out. I thanked her again for being an incredibly supportive wife, and the conversation even turned to possible road trips during the next football season. She dropped me off, and I made my way through security and to my gate without a hitch. The flight was on time.

I was flying Southwest Airlines, meaning our seats were not assigned. As I was putting my carry-on suitcase into the overhead compartment, someone saw my Iowa State pullover and said, "Go Cyclones!"

"Yeah, go Cyclones!" I responded.

She offered me the seat right next to her, which was open, and we struck up a conversation. Her name was Amy, and she was traveling with her son, Jack, to Orlando to watch the game. They were meeting her father, who was traveling from Iowa. Amy told me she was an Iowa State graduate who now lived in Denver but still followed the team. I told her about my project of attending every game, which kicked off multiple conversations about the team, Big 12 stadiums, trends in college football and much more. The conversation in and of itself was worth the cost of the trip.

We landed, said our goodbyes and I ordered a ride to my hotel where I checked in and changed into shorts. When I had left Fort Collins in the morning, the weather was cold enough to wear a winter coat, stocking hat and gloves. I knew the forecast in Iowa a few days later called for multiple inches of snow and frigid below zero temperatures. Orlando was experiencing highs in the 80s. I figured I had better enjoy it while it lasted.

I headed to a different hotel to meet up with a friend, Gene. He had flown on the official travel charter through the university and Iowa State Alumni Association, and was staying at the same hotel as the Iowa State team. I met up with him in the hotel bar, which was already heavily populated by Cyclone fans.

After a drink, we went our separate ways. I walked to the convention center nearby where a Cyclones Unplugged event was taking place. I had missed the official Cheez-It Bowl pep rally due to the timing of my flight, but this served as its own pep rally of sorts. The Cyclone Marching Band played the fight song and several tunes. Iowa State radio announcer John Walters emceed a brief program. Coach Matt Campbell said a few words. He let the crowd know come game time, the team was going to make us proud to be Cyclone fans. (Spoiler alert: Despite the final score, they did make us proud.) Then, ISU Alumni Association President and CEO Jeff Johnson led the crowd in a few cheers, as is his custom. The thousands in attendance obliged.

I had been to a number of these types of events through the years, and they always get me in the Cyclone spirit. This one was no different. I finally felt like it was all real. There was going to be a bowl game and I was going to go to it.

The crowd began to disperse, and I figured I would head back to my hotel. As I was getting ready to walk out, I recognized Barry, the head of the Cyclone Club of Dallas/Fort Worth, walking in. I had met Barry at a few games throughout the season while tailgating with the DFW club.

I walked up to him and said hello. After talking for a minute, I asked, "Do you want a drink?"

He took me up on the offer. He was there with a few others who had traveled to the game, who were already in line for the bar. I recognized most of them from prior tailgates.

After a little while, they decided to go back to the bar at the team hotel, and kindly invited me to join them. We happened to walk into the lobby around the same time as several of the players were walking through.

"I always forget how big the players are," I said to one of my new friends.

We took seats in the open bar area. A little while later, I heard people at the bar begin to clap. I turned around to see Campbell walking through the lobby. He gave us a little wave as he continued his way to the elevator. If he had stopped to talk, I have no doubt a few fans would have offered him a drink.

I am grateful I ran into Barry and friends, because part of the fun of going to a bowl game is hanging out with other fans and reveling in the shared community.

Around 10 p.m., Gene was back, and I joined him in a patio area outside to enjoy fire pits and watch some other Big 12 games for a while. Finally, around 11:30 I headed back to my hotel, satisfied with the bowl experience so far.

On Wednesday morning, I woke up to the Florida sunshine and texted my brother.

"Gameday!"

I dressed in my red t-shirt with the Jack Trice stripes logo, shorts and my red walking Cy hat. One more gameday!

Rumors had begun to trickle out that senior linebacker Mike Rose, senior wide receiver Xavier Hutchinson and senior offensive lineman Collin Newell would not be playing due to injuries. Iowa State's chances of winning had taken a major hit.

My first stop was at a nearby bar and restaurant for a gathering hosted by the Cyclone Gridiron Club. I saw Barry at the bar and ordered a drink. The bar had an outdoor patio, and the windows to the patio were open, giving the entire place an airy feeling on a beautiful sunny day. I knew I was about to experience an Iowa winter beginning in just a few days; I reveled in the warmth while I could.

The event was a joint gathering of the Gridiron Club and the Letterwinners Club, which meant several former athletes were in attendance. One, a former basketball player who went to Iowa State around the same time I did, introduced himself to us. A few minutes later, I took a seat at a table with a few other former athletes. I listened as they reminisced about their time at school. I chimed in as we recalled old Ames restaurants and bars.

Around 2 p.m., I called a Lyft to head to the stadium, which was about a 20-minute drive away. I had made plans to go to a tailgate hosted by one of the message board posters on the popular news and fan site Cyclone Fanatic. Free will donation proceeds went to support a retired Iowa high school teacher who was battling cancer for the second time. It was a great cause, and I figured a good way to meet up with fellow Cyclones. I arrived and looked for the group, which was stationed on the southeast side of the stadium, about as close to the stadium as someone could possibly park. *This will work*, I thought.

The DFW crew was already there, along with a few fans who had traveled from Iowa. One of my new DFW friends offered me a beer (another reason why Cyclone fans are the best), and we enjoyed barbecue catered from a local restaurant — along with Cheez-Its, of course. I looked around; the tailgate lots had begun to fill up with Cyclone and Clemson Tiger fans. It was starting to truly feel like a gameday. I thought about the fact for years I had dreamt of traveling to a warm-weather location to watch an Iowa State bowl game. However, a lack of historical success meant there hadn't been many opportunities to do so, and when there was an opportunity it seemed like life always got in the way. Two years prior, when it was announced Iowa State would play in Orlando against Notre Dame, I very much wanted to attend but didn't make it happen. I pinched myself a little bit that I was about to watch the Cyclones in a Florida bowl game.

Speaking of that Notre Dame game, it hung over us a little bit like a cloud (even though there was hardly an actual cloud in the sky). Most people I was around seemed to have been at the game in 2019. The common refrain went something like this: "We were overmatched. I knew on the first play of the game it was going to be a long day."

With so many key contributors missing for Iowa State, and Clemson's recent history of success, I couldn't shake the worry that this game would play out the same way.

About 45 minutes before kickoff, I decided to head into the stadium. I wanted to take in every moment and, of course, watch the marching band. I entered on what was predominantly the Clemson side of the stadium. It was the first time I had been around Tiger fans en masse. I made my way to my seat in the second level behind the north endzone, on the Iowa State half of the stadium.

As the stadium began to fill up, it didn't quite get full, but it was still a good showing for both schools. The final attendance was announced at just over 39,000 fans. There were a handful of neutral observers, but for the most part everyone was a Cyclone or a Tiger, and it was almost impossible to tell which team brought more fans.

Unfortunately, a group of Clemson fans who appeared to be in their 20s took seats in the two rows behind me just to the right of where I was sitting. One was wearing what I believe was a half Clemson, half Jacksonville Jaguars Trevor Lawrence jersey. Lawrence was a national championship winner for the Tigers who was the first overall pick in the 2021 NFL Draft by Jacksonville.

I wonder if this group will figure out there are plenty of empty seats on the Clemson side, I thought. No such luck. I had no idea how bad it would be.

The Clemson band took the field first as the Tiger fans enthusiastically cheered. Then it was Iowa State's turn. Cyclone fans let out what I thought was an extra loud cheer, trying to exceed the enthusiasm of Clemson's fans. I stood and clapped to the fight song, swelling with pride.

Some people say there are too many bowl games, but if there weren't enough we'd be robbed of some of the truly bizarre, hilarious and just plain fun aspects that make the games unique. And that bizarre, hilarious and just plain fun detail of the Cheez-It Bowl was … Prince Cheddward. Here come some words I never thought I'd write. Prince Cheddward is a mascot whose head is a wheel of cheese with a crown on top, and whose body is dressed in royal garb. He descended from a rope high above the stadium onto the field. If that doesn't get someone ready for a game, I don't know what does.

The teams came onto the field, and I cheered with my fellow Cyclones as the team took a knee, all together, for one last time this season in the endzone right in front of me.

When I was in middle school and high school and went to significantly fewer games than I did as an adult, I would often watch as a broadcast began showing the fans in the stadium, cheering, waving at the camera, looking like they were having a good time. I imagined those moments to be a culmination of a day of fun: getting to the tailgate lots early, walking to the stadium with thousands of people, counting down the moments toward kickoff. It felt like an insider's club, one that you can imagine but not fully experience watching through the television. That was exactly how I felt in the moments right before kickoff, like I was part of a secret handshake of sorts with the tens of thousands of others who had made the trip. I was at the popular kids' table. Now the national television audience was joining us, many of them no doubt jealously wishing they were in the stadium, that they had taken in the 80-degree sunshiny day. I was there. *Pinch me.*

The game kicked off.

Clemson immediately faced a third-and-four as the Iowa State fans came to their feet, but quarterback D.J. Uiagalelei completed a pass to Will Swinney for 11 yards and a first down. The fan behind me, in the Lawrence jersey, yelled, "YES SIR! YES SIR!"

Oh no.

Clemson continued to move the ball, picking up two more third down conversions ("YES SIR! YES SIR!") in the process. Finally on third-and-goal from the 11-yard line, the Cyclones forced a stop and held the Tigers to a field goal to make it 3-0.

Iowa State went three-and-out and was forced to punt on its first possession. Things weren't looking great as Clemson converted another third down and then threw to Dacari Collins for a gain of 13 into Iowa State territory. This set off another round of "YES SIR!" (You get the point. Nearly every good play Clemson had resulted in my new acquaintance yelling those words as loud as he could. I don't think I'm being hyperbolic when I say he was the most annoying fan I've ever sat near.)

The Cyclones finally forced a fourth down, and Clemson punted to give Iowa State its second possession. On a crucial third-and-one, Jirehl Brock, starting in place of NFL-bound Breece Hall, pushed ahead for a three-yard gain. He then broke free for a 14-yard gain to end the first quarter. Iowa State finally had some momentum. (Right around this time, one of the Iowa State fans in front of me softly said "yes sir" to those in her group.)

As the second quarter began, Purdy threw a pass to Hutchinson. Throughout the day, Hutchinson's status had been in doubt due to a thumb injury, but he decided to give it a go and caught a 34-yard pass. Unfortunately, the injury forced him back to the sideline. Still, it illustrated his competitive spirit and showed me how much this team wanted to win.

Purdy found Kolar for 13 yards down to the Clemson 10-yard line. On third-and-goal, Purdy missed an open Allen for what would have been a touchdown. It was an opportunity squandered, and the Cyclones settled for a field goal to make the score 3-3. Regardless, I felt confident for the first time all day that this Iowa State team could hang with Clemson.

That confidence built when the Cyclones held Clemson to a three-and-out and picked up a pair of first downs highlighted by a 27-yard pass from Purdy to Jaylin Noel. The drive stalled, and the Cyclones sent Andrew Mevis in to attempt a 43-yard field goal. It looked good from where I was sitting, and I began to cheer … until the referees signaled "no good."

"YES SIR! YES SIR!" rang out behind me.

It felt like a turn of momentum, and it proved to be so. Clemson drove eight plays down to the Iowa State 34 and knocked in a 51-yard field goal of its own to go ahead 6-3. Iowa State was forced to punt after picking up one first down on its next drive, and Clemson began a march down the field right before halftime. It felt like a big moment; if Clemson scored a touchdown, it seemed it would be difficult for Iowa State to find a way back given how the game had played out so far. Luckily, it was Clemson's turn to miss a field goal from 36 yards out. The teams ran to the locker rooms, and I felt good about the Cyclones' chances in the second half.

A solid drive was just what Iowa State needed to begin the third quarter, and it looked promising when Jared Rus caught an eight-yard pass to give

Iowa State a first down. That was all the momentum Iowa State could muster before punting back to Clemson.

That's when the game got weird — seemingly a common theme in the 2021 season.

On third-and-four from the Clemson 38, Iowa State's Enyi Uwazurike broke through the line, broke through what appeared to be a holding penalty (not called), and had Clemson quarterback Uiagalelei in his grasp for a would-be sack. Uiagalelei somehow got rid of the ball, throwing it up for grabs. Iowa State's Myles Purchase was positioned perfectly in front of receiver Beaux Collins, and Greg Eisworth was right behind the receiver. Somehow, the ball fluttered toward the receiver, just out of the reach of both defenders into the hands of a jumping Collins, who came down with it. It was the first really big cheer I felt like I had heard from the Clemson side of the stadium all evening. The Tigers deservingly received a standing ovation. It was the kind of play I felt like I'd seen way too many times in my life as a Cyclone fan and way too many times in the 2021 season. Everything about the play said it should have been a sack or turnover, or a third down stop at the very least. Instead, it was first down Clemson with all the momentum.

"YES SIR! YES SIR!" the man behind me yelled.

"Some years just aren't your year," I said out loud to nobody in particular.

The Cyclone defense didn't give in. After giving up another first down ("YES SIR!"), the Cyclones forced a fourth-and-one from the 29. This time, instead of trying a field goal, Clemson lined up to go for it. Uiagalelei pushed forward, but …

He's short! Maybe.

It would come down to a measurement. *Please just be short.*

The referee extended the chain, and I groaned as the chain fell short of the length of the football, meaning it was a Clemson first down. (I watched the replay later and saw just how close it was. It was about as close as it could possibly be, and I'm not entirely convinced it should have been called a first down. Nor am I convinced it shouldn't have. It just would have been nice for that to go Iowa State's way.)

Some years just aren't your year, I thought to myself again. Iowa State had been agonizingly close to getting off the field without giving up any points on the possession. The inches had gone against them.

On first-and-10 from the 12, Will Shipley took a handoff and ran around the right side as the rest of the play pushed everything to the left. He calmly walked into the endzone. "YES SIR!" Clemson had taken a two-possession lead at 13-3.

Iowa State took the ensuing kickoff, and for a brief moment wrestled some momentum back as Noel was able to return the kickoff near midfield. Just as the play was ending, the referee in the endzone behind the play pulled his flag out and threw it. It was holding on Iowa State. It was a 50-50 call, in my opinion, but given the lack of holding call when Uwazurike was being held in similar fashion, it spiked my anger.

"Where was that call on the last possession!?" I yelled toward the field. The referee didn't seem to hear me. (This is another one that, when watching the replay, I felt could have gone either way, but it was a stretch when every 50-50 play went against Iowa State, making it even more frustrating.)

Instead of starting near midfield, Iowa State began the drive from its own 10-yard line. An Iowa State offensive lineman jumped early, moving Iowa State back five more yards. Campbell appeared to be furious on the sidelines, and I think I understand why. The Clemson marching band was still playing as Iowa State lined up. Given the band was right behind the endzone on the end where the players were positioned, I'd imagine it was pretty distracting. It could have resulted in a penalty against Clemson, but instead Iowa State was penalized. It was another bad break that went against the Cyclones.

Iowa State lined up again and was forced to call a timeout before running the play. Things seemed to be quickly unraveling. In the last few minutes, Iowa State had gone from a seeming third-down stop while down just 6-3, to now facing a drive starting at its own five-yard line down 13-3 against one of the best defenses in college football. In that span, I counted four 50-50 plays that went in Clemson's favor. (After the game, Campbell noted his belief that teams create their own luck in football. That may be true, but in my mind there's at least *some* external luck that *could* have gone differently that may have changed the complexion of the game.)

The Clemson crowd was loud, and the defense seemed to be licking its chops as Iowa State lined up for first-and-15 from its own five. Purdy calmly completed a pass to Darren Wilson Jr. for 10 yards. *Maybe this is where it turns.*

Every now and then, you see something in this sport that you can never remember seeing before and will never forget. In tailgates to come, we'll talk about the second-and-five play before sighing and taking a swig of whatever we're drinking. Purdy went back to pass, and the ball was tipped high into the air. It was coming right back to Purdy. Trying to make a play, he batted at the ball, I assume trying to spike it into the ground, end the threat of a turnover and live to see third down. Instead, he somehow batted it right into the hands of Clemson's Mario Goodrich, who ran it around the Iowa State players untouched into the endzone. Touchdown, Clemson.

I looked over at the Clemson side of the stadium. Their fans were (understandably) in a frenzy. Behind me, I heard "YES SIR! YES SIR!" I turned to see the man in the Trevor Lawrence jersey now had his jersey off and was shirtlessly waving it as he ran around the empty seats in the row behind him. At one point, his jersey hit me in the back. I couldn't help myself. I turned around and looked at him (he wasn't looking at me), and a young woman sitting next to him made eye contact with me. I gave her an annoyed look as if to say, "Is he serious?"

She returned a somewhat embarrassed smile.

It was now 20-3 Clemson. How quickly the tide had changed. I contemplated for a minute trying to find new seats, but I had come this far. I was going to ride it out.

It was beginning to feel like the Notre Dame game two years ago, like Iowa State was about to get blown out in embarrassing fashion.

I should have known this team better.

The Cyclones did, however, go three-and-out to begin the next possession, and punted the ball away to Clemson. On Clemson's first play, Will McDonald tipped a pass and Jake Hummel dove to make a timely interception. I jumped up and cheered for one of the first times all night.

With a chance to flip the script, Iowa State began its next drive. On the first play, Purdy had Noel wide open down the sideline. *It's going to be a touchdown*, I thought. Instead, Purdy overthrew the ball just a bit, and Noel had to jump to try to catch it. He landed a few inches out of bounds. No catch. Iowa State failed to move the ball a yard either of the next two plays and sent Mevis out for a 45-yard field goal attempt, which he hit to make it 20-6.

On Clemson's next possession, the Tigers faced a third-and-three and Craig McDonald knocked down a pass intended for a Clemson receiver. I knew it was incomplete before I saw it as I heard a jolt of noise come from the Iowa State fans who were closer to the field. We had just a little bit of a reason to believe the Cyclones could win.

After the punt, the third quarter came to a close. "Juicy Wiggle" played, and we danced. There was hope in the air.

For the first time since the second quarter, Iowa State put together a strong drive. Finally, a 50-50 play went Iowa State's way. Purdy threw a backwards pass to Noel, who lined up for a pass to Allen. The ball was tipped and intercepted, and then fumbled and recovered by Iowa State. The referees also called a roughing the passer penalty. After all that, Iowa State had a first down at the Clemson 28.

On third-and-nine, Purdy scrambled for a first down. A fan a few rows in front of me had apparently had enough of the "YES SIR!" guy.

"Yes sir!" he said in mocking fashion.

Purdy found Wilson for 10, and then on second-and-goal threw it to Allen in the back of the endzone for a touchdown.

"YES!!!" I yelled. (I did not say "sir.")

This team never wins easy or loses easy, I thought.

The momentum was back on Iowa State's side, and instinctively I knew the Cyclones were going to get the ball back with a chance to tie. It was how the script was supposed to go.

It became significantly more difficult when Shipley ran for nine yards on first down only to be dragged down by his horse collar, a 15-yard penalty. (As a completely irrelevant aside, I Google-searched how to correctly type "horse collar" and discovered there was a Wikipedia entry for the term "horse-collar tackle." The picture used to illustrate the play was of an Iowa State defender tackling an Oklahoma State player in 2009. Of all the teams in football, Iowa State is used as the example. I suppose we'll take recognition any way we can get it.)

The penalty moved Clemson all the way to the 49-yard line. The task had become more difficult, but the Iowa State defense forced a fourth down punt, which was downed at the three-yard line. Iowa State would need to go 97 yards to tie the game.

With their backs against the wall, Iowa State picked up a first down, but the drive moved backwards from there. The Cyclones were forced to punt from their own 11-yard line, and a 31-yard punt gave Clemson the ball at the 42. With 4:15 left, Iowa State had only one timeout and a first down would nearly end the game for Clemson.

The defense stepped up again, forcing a third-and-10. This time, Uwazurike did get a sack to force Clemson to punt. Iowa State took over again at its own 11 with 1:52 to play and a timeout.

I so badly wanted this team to have the perfect drive to tie the game, to give us a great moment to remember it by.

It wasn't meant to be. Iowa State picked up one first down, but then faced a fourth-and-two from its own 36 with only 0:42 left. Purdy went back to pass, and then scrambled. He had open grass in front of him, and picked up the first down. He began to move to his left and I got excited. There was room in front of him, room to pick up a much-needed chunk of yardage, to give Iowa State a legitimate chance to make a few plays to tie the game. Instead, Clemson's Goodrich evaded a block and popped the ball out of Purdy's hands. Purdy dove on it but landed behind the first down marker. It took me a few seconds to realize what had happened, but the play was a turnover on downs. The game was over.

"YES SIR! YES SIR! YES SIR! YES SIR!"

I stood silently. The Iowa State fans in front of me said goodbye and headed out. I briefly contemplated turning around and starting a conversation with the "YES SIR!" guy but thought better of it. I made my way to the exit.

It was not the same level of disappointment I had felt after other losses during the season. Maybe that is a sign that the bowl game mattered slightly less, or maybe it was because I had seen this type of game play out multiple times and was, in my heart, expecting this outcome. Knowing some of the key players for Iowa State were not playing, I was appreciative of the efforts of a number of young players and recognized the heart the team played with. Yeah, I was disappointed, but not devastated. The team had given me everything I could ask for.

I stopped back at the tailgate while waiting for a ride back to my hotel. We enjoyed some more food and dissected the game. A number of Clemson fans walked by and said, "Good game." None of them were wearing a half Clemson, half Jacksonville Trevor Lawrence jersey.

"Only eight months until football season," one person in our group remarked.

Over the next 24 hours, as I traveled home from Orlando, I read nearly everything there was to read about the game and thought about my emotions.

There was no looking forward to next week. No chance for the team to redeem itself. The final meaningful moment of the season was a negative one, sowing up another loss. Rival fans on Twitter pointed out that Iowa State's "best season ever" finished at 7-6.

I listened to the post-game press conference, during which Eisworth told members of the media "We earned our way here. That's what I told those guys in [the locker room]. And I'm proud of y'all. Be proud to wear the Iowa State logo. Because for a while, some people weren't that proud to wear the logo, and we've put ourselves in these situations, we're going to be here for a long time."

Campbell added, "Greg's right. There's a lot of people when I got here that were embarrassed to wear an Iowa State shirt, an Iowa State hat around, and now it's a sense of pride. Now we're comin'."

Two strains of thoughts from those comments nearly perfectly summarized my thoughts on the season and being an Iowa State fan.

For one, even though the season didn't live up to the lofty expectations, it was a moment in time. It was one season of six in the Campbell era, and there will be many more to come (hopefully with Campbell as coach). Six years ago, fans couldn't have imagined Iowa State would go to five straight bowl games, have five straight winning seasons in the Big 12, defeat every single team in the conference at least twice, play in a Big 12 Championship Game, get matched up against national brand names like Notre Dame, Oregon and Clemson in bowl games, and win a Fiesta Bowl. We would all have signed up for it.

To some, this season felt like the "most Iowa State thing ever." To finally have deservedly high expectations and come up well short, with bizarre plays going against the team and heartbreaking losses defining much of the season. But the only reason it felt that way is because we weren't used to having a team like this in the first place. This was the first time the team had ever been considered a true contender for the highest prizes in college football. There's a fear that this was it, this was our one chance, and now we'll go back to being the same old Iowa State. If you read this book five or 10 or 15 years from now, you'll know whether that's true or not. For me today, the future is bright. The program is going in the right direction and one 7-6 season won't change that.

The other strain of thought is around my fandom. Eisworth and Campbell were right; it hasn't always been easy or fun to be an Iowa State fan. We have often been an afterthought nationally and in our own state. That's no longer true. Even more than that, though, it has become more and more clear to me in my journey through the 2021 season that being an Iowa State fan is special.

In eight more months, I'll be back in Jack Trice Stadium to cheer on the 2022 team.

Yes sir. I can't wait.

CHAPTER TWENTY-NINE

POSTSEASON REFLECTION

Coming into the season, and for much of it, I wrestled with trying to nail down the reason I was doing this. I could justify it by saying that I've always wanted to pick a season and go to all the games, I've always wanted to write a book, I love writing about sports and I love the Cyclones. Those things are all true. But on Dec. 30, 2020, I wasn't thinking about writing a book. By Dec. 31, I had decided to do so. The primary reason was because I couldn't get rid of this thought: *Iowa State is going to have its best season ever in 2021. I can be the one to capture it in a way nobody else will.*

None of the rest of this would have happened without that hope. This was supposed to be a book about Iowa State winning the Big 12 Championship.

I knew I was taking a gamble. I knew there was a chance the season could turn out how it did. Yet I made the decision very early on that I was going to write, and publish, as the season went along. There would be no backing out if Iowa State didn't have a great season.

Part of my reasoning was that if this was going to be a special season, I wanted to soak in every single moment as much as I could. I wanted to document it in a way that would enhance the experience of other fans, and casual fans could relate to if they weren't sitting down to watch every minute of every game like I was.

Instead, I spent much of the season with the anxiety that if the team failed to live up to its expectations, my book might fail. There were a few times when I asked myself, "Am I really going to do this?"

There was a lesson to be learned. In truth, I should have learned the lesson five years prior. In the fall of 2016, the Chicago Cubs won the World Series. It's still fun to be able to say those words. Sometimes I'll joke with my wife: "Honey, do you remember the Chicago Cubs won the World Series in 2016? People forget that."

"Nobody forgets that," she answers, clearly annoyed.

The lesson in there, though, is that I spent my entire time as a fan up until that point wishing for that one thing to happen just once in my life. Then it happened. And it was fun. But it wasn't *more fun* than the 2015 season, in which the Cubs lost in the National League Championship Series to fall just short of the World Series. At some point I had to come to terms with the fact that seeing them win it all was just a little bit of a letdown. I had spent so much time hoping for the Cubs to win the World Series that I almost didn't enjoy the games leading up to it quite as much as I should have. Now I wish they could go on one more run so I could properly appreciate it.

I entered the 2021 Iowa State football season focused on the destination. I was imagining confetti flying in Dallas to celebrate the Big 12 Champion Cyclones. I was imagining a trip to the College Football Playoff. I was imagining the experience of the best season ever and writing a book that would capture it and be a must-have for Cyclone fans also celebrating the best season ever.

One of the worst days of the season was the loss at Baylor. That was the first time I truly questioned myself. (As you know by now, there would be a few more times like that.) But the best thing that happened during the season, for me, also happened in Waco. I heard Jamie Pollard, Director of Athletics at Iowa State, encourage fans to enjoy the journey and not focus on the destination. I made the decision that day that I had to enjoy the journey.

That was the lesson I was reminded of, over and over. Enjoy the journey.

I desperately wanted Iowa State to win the Big 12, both as a fan and as a writer. I still very much hope that someday soon Iowa State will have the season we all thought 2021 was going to be. I can't control that. I can control getting enjoyment out of every season, and every game. And if the thing I want to happen someday happens, I'll enjoy it more because I focused on the journey.

I briefly forgot about this lesson in the week following the Texas Tech game, when I again asked myself, "Am I really going to do this?" I almost felt embarrassed by it, embarrassed that I had put so much of my personal money and emotional stock into this team's success only to be let down. And then Campbell gave his press conference where he somewhat famously said winning the Big 12 wasn't his goal, but rather his goal was for the team to become the best version of itself. He took heat for that from rival fanbases, national media members and even some Iowa State fans.

For me, I felt like he was talking right to me.

The next weekend, I went to Oklahoma with my dad and brother, initially worried they would feel like it was a waste of a trip because Iowa State was no longer playing for a championship. It ended up being one of the most fun times I've had with either of them. I enjoyed sharing my passion with them in a way I had never done before. (Months later, my dad told me there was just something fun about the entire experience of the trip.)

When the bowl game approached, I had plenty of reasons I could have "opted out" (to use the same language we use when players decide to not play in the game). Yet, I knew I had to go. It was part of the journey that had to happen. Once I was there, I stopped worrying about everything else and had a tremendously fun time.

Chances are I will never do this again. I also learned there were times where I can and should choose other things (namely, family and friends) over going to the game. As much as I enjoyed the Baylor game, I skipped a friend's wedding to go to it. As much as I enjoyed the TCU game, I could have enjoyed a day at home while visiting family for Thanksgiving. As much as I enjoyed the bowl game, I could have enjoyed a few more days with my in-laws over the holidays. I appreciated my family and friends being overly supportive of this project, and this year all those decisions made sense precisely because of the project. I know there will be times in the future where I will evaluate things differently.

And still, I know there will be times when I decide *I just have to be there* and will go out of my way to make it happen.

This journey pushed me to do things that I never would have done otherwise. Going to a road game doesn't feel like as daunting of a task anymore, and I made friends through the DFW Club that I hope to meet up with at future games. My experiences in 2021 will help me enhance my experiences as a fan in years to come.

These lessons can be applied to many other areas of life, so much so that it almost sounds cliché to write it, but I will anyway. The advice that I'd leave anyone else (including myself) with is live life before it's over. Everything in life is temporary, and time flies.

Enjoy the journey or, as a wise man has said, trust the process.

Finally, one of the primary reasons I decided to document this journey was because I wanted to put positivity into the world in my own way. There are enough reasons to fight about any number of things, but what I've found is that nobody cares all that much about most of them on a college football Saturday. Cheering for our favorite team brings us together. The vast majority of interactions I had with Iowa State fans, and opposing fanbases, were overwhelmingly positive.

If you have made it this far, I sincerely hope you have found it to be a positive experience. I had the time of my life.

NOTES

To supplement my own knowledge and experiences, I used a number of sources to remember and ensure accurate game and player statistics from the 2021 season and prior seasons, and also to supplement my writing with quotes from coaches and players. Sources included game notes compiled by the Iowa State University Athletics Department, ESPN and Fox Sports, as well as articles, podcasts and videos published by CBS Sports, Cyclone Fanatic, the Des Moines Business Record, the Des Moines Register, ESPN, Fox Sports, the Iowa State Daily and Wide Right and Natty Light.

ABOUT THE AUTHOR

Kyle Oppenhuizen is a professional communicator and writer. The 2021 season was his 25th as an Iowa State fan. As a former Cyclone Marching Band member and longtime season ticket-holder, being a Cyclone is part of his identity. An Iowa State University graduate with a degree in journalism and mass communication, Oppenhuizen works professionally as Vice President of Communications for the Greater Des Moines Partnership and has worked as a journalist for the Des Moines Business Record, Iowa State Daily and other organizations. Oppenhuizen has been a Business Record Forty Under 40 honoree, the Des Moines Register's Juice Young Professional of the Year, and is a graduate of the Greater Des Moines Leadership Institute's Community Leadership Program. A Pella, Iowa native, Oppenhuizen and his wife, Paige, live in West Des Moines.